AVANCEZ

George E Feagans

The American Revolution

George Otto Trevelyan

THE

AMERICAN REVOLUTION

Volume III

THE

AMERICAN REVOLUTION

BY THE RIGHT HON.

SIR GEORGE OTTO TREVELYAN, BART.

AUTHOR OF "THE LIFE AND LETTERS OF LORD MACAULAY"
AND "THE EARLY HISTORY OF CHARLES JAMES FOX"

NEW EDITION

VOLUME III

LONGMANS, GREEN, AND CO.
FOURTH AVENUE & 30TH STREET, NEW YORK
LONDON, BOMBAY, CALCUTTA, AND MADRAS
1917

Norwood Press
J S. Cushing Co. — Berwick & Smith Co.
Norwood, Mass., U S A.

CONTENTS

OF VOLUME III

CHAPTER XXI

CHAPTER XXII

CHAPTER XXIII

CHAPTER XXIV

CHAPTER XXVII

APPENDICES

At the end of the volume

Map of the Northern part of New Jersey, and of New York and its Environs.

NOTE

The third volume of the " American Revolution " has been altered, and reprinted, as a consequence of the withdrawal of certain matter which, though not irrelevant, was somewhat in excess of the general scheme of the history. The four volumes of the " American Revolution," and the two volumes of "George the Third and Charles Fox," are now in their final shape and will never again be retouched by their author, nor (he sincerely hopes) by anyone else after he himself has passed away. Those six volumes, as read together, tell the whole story, in America and in Europe, from the imposition of the Customs Duties by the British Parliament in June 1767, down to the fall of Lord North's Ministry in March 1782 The story is complete ; it has been written with an honest desire to be fair and impartial ; it may be read with self-respect, and mutual respect, both by Englishmen and Americans ; and it throws a bright and striking light on the motives of the war in which all English-speaking peoples are henceforward fighting shoulder to shoulder The descendants of the farmers who turned out to defend their country at Lexington and Bunker Hill, and the descendants of the adversaries who did their best to defeat them in honourable and chivalrous battle, are shocked and revolted by the cruel and high-handed theory that the alleged resistance in arms to the invader of certain Belgian civilians justified the devastation, the plunder, the torture, and the enslavement of Belgium.

GEORGE OTTO TREVELYAN

Welcombe,
Stratford-on-Avon,
    May, 1917.

THE AMERICAN REVOLUTION

————◦◦◦————

CHAPTER XXI

FORT WASHINGTON. THROUGH THE JERSEYS. SUFFERINGS OF THE INHABITANTS

THE war was soon transported into the heart of New Jersey; for the British Commander-in-Chief had very speedily, and very successfully, completed the business that detained him on the east shore of the Hudson river Those arrangements which Washington had made, with the view of encountering all possible emergencies,[1] were workmanlike, and might even be pronounced faultless, save and except in one important particular. Public attention in the States had been keenly interested by a scheme of defence for the protection of the Hudson, — the great water highway of New York State. Four or five miles north of Haerlem in the island of Manhattan, at a point where the current was not more than a mile in breadth, a work called Fort Washington had been erected on a bluff that overhung the river. On the opposite bank stood Fort Lee; and up-stream, on the safe side of these strongholds, the American authorities, with energy much inferior to Arnold's, had collected and armed a small flotilla. For further security, athwart the river and between the forts, a barricade had been constructed of which all good patriots spoke with pride and confidence under the imposing title of the "sunken chevaux-de-frise;"

---

[1] Washington's disposition of his forces is shortly described on page 337 of the last volume.

although sceptics alleged that Washington's engineers had shirked the difficulty of extending it across that part of the channel where the current ran strongest On the sixth of October three British men-of-war came up the Hudson with a southerly wind, under a smart, and not altogether ineffective, fire from the batteries They sailed through, or over, or, (as was strongly suspected afterwards,) round, the chevaux-de-frise, without perceiving that any such obstacle existed; and, when they had reached the upper waters, they made very short work of the American naval preparations. They drove ashore, or captured, four or five ships and galleys; and they sank a sloop containing an ingenious machine for blowing up the British fleet. The inventor had designed his contrivance to act under water; and under water it went, and to this hour it there remains. The joyous and elastic national temperament, which has done so much towards carrying America through many a crisis, discerned in this untoward event nothing worse than a presage of future triumphs Congress desired General Washington, now that the British ships were entrapped above his forts, to take good care they never either got back again themselves, nor were reinforced from the main fleet which lay below But, in plain truth, both before and afterwards, Lord Howe's captains made no account whatever of the perils which beset them in their passage up and down the river An officer who did not mind a few holes in his sails, and a very few casualties in his crew, so far as the safety of his vessel was concerned might travel the Hudson as securely as the Humber, and much more securely than, without the aid of a good local pilot, he would have threaded the sand-banks of the Mersey.

The maintenance, or abandonment, of the two American stations on the Hudson river was therefore a problem to be determined in no sense by naval, but exclusively by military, considerations. Nathanael Greene was entrusted with the care of both the places, which were garrisoned by near five thousand men, of whom somewhat the larger part were at Fort Washington To keep that force cooped up on Manhattan Island, without any reasonable hope of escape in case of an attack which it was impossible successfully to resist, was an awful risk to run. Mount Washington, (as the general after whom it was named sometimes called it,) was not a fortress which, like Quebec, could only be captured by a regular siege, or reduced by famine. It was an open work, bordered on three sides by heights, and of small extent, which a few hours of shell-fire would render quite untenable It was, indeed, surrounded by an exterior position partially fortified, and so strong by nature that one of General Howe's officers asserted that all the world could not have taken it from ten thousand Englishmen.[1] But that outer circuit of defence had a front of more than six miles; Colonel Magaw, the American who was in charge on the spot, had barely the fourth of ten thousand men at his disposal, and that force, while utterly inadequate to the task imposed upon it, was much larger than Washington could afford to throw away in order to comply with the behests, and save the self-respect, of Congress.

The politicians, who sate at the Board of war in Philadelphia, had planned the operations of that summer with the declared object of holding New York City, and barring the mouth of the Hudson river against a British fleet, and the evacuation of Fort Washington would be, in their eyes, nothing short of an admission that their campaign had finally and totally failed Congress, bent on keeping the place, proclaimed their opinion by a vote which was equivalent to a peremptory injunction; and

---

[1] "About noon a young officer, smartly dressed and well mounted, rode up with his horse in a foam, and, pulling out his watch, observed that he had scarcely been an hour in coming from New York He was a genuine, smooth-faced, fresh-coloured Englishman, and from the elegance of his horse, and importance of his manner, I supposed him to be a person of family and consideration 'Becket,' (said he, looking around him,) 'this is a damned strong piece of ground Ten thousand of our men would defend it against the world'" *Memoirs of a Life chiefly passed in Pennsylvania;* chapter viii.

that injunction Greene, for his part, was keenly desirous
to obey.   He was in love with Fort Washington.   To
blockade it effectively, (according to his computation,)
would cost the hostile army a number of troops at least
double what would suffice for the American garrison;[1]
and if, instead of an investment, the English preferred
to try an assault by force, he bade them a hearty welcome.   For Howe was not the only general whose tactics were injuriously modified by a false analogy drawn
from the recollections of Bunker's Hill   Nathanael
Greene was still under an illusion that his countrymen,
behind a breastwork, could inflict cruel punishment on
an attacking force under all circumstances, and against
any odds.   His notion, (we are told,) was that, after
slaughtering a host of the enemy, the Americans might
methodically withdraw into the citadel of Fort Washington: and then, provided each had killed his man,
they might be snugly shipped across the Hudson, and
rejoin their main army with flying colours.[2]

   Such, and so sanguine, were General Greene's anticipations, but, after all, Greene did not command the
Continental army.   The occasion was one on which
Washington ought to have enforced·his own views
against his military subordinate, and his political
superiors; and concerning the nature of those views
there exists no doubt at all.   On the eighth of November the Commander-in-Chief wrote to Greene that, inasmuch as British vessels could not be prevented from
passing up the stream, and British troops possessed all
the surrounding country, no benefit could be expected
from the retention of the fortress on Manhattan Island
"I am therefore inclined to think," (he continued,)
"that it will not be prudent to hazard the men and
stores at Mount Washington, but, as you are on the
spot, I leave it to you to give such orders as to evacu-
ating Mount Washington as you may judge best, and
so far revoking the order given to Colonel Magaw to

[1] Greene to Washington, Fort Lee, November 9, 1776.
[2] *Pennsylvanian Memoirs*, chapter vii.

defend it to the last." Having despatched those lines, — which indicated a confidence in Greene that for once was misplaced, and a diffidence of himself, — Washington departed northwards on a visit to General Heath's quarters, and minutely examined the site for a new fortress near West Point. The orders which he left with Greene were, (to use his own epithet,) discretionary,[1] and the person upon whom the chief blame for those calamities, which promptly supervened, should rest has been a theme of frequent controversy. All that can certainly be said on the matter is that two very good generals contrived between them to commit a very signal blunder; and that Washington, as his rule was, insisted on assuming the responsibility for everything which went wrong under his auspices.

On the fifteenth of November Howe sent his Adjutant General to demand the surrender of Fort Washington, and reminded Colonel Magaw that, when an intrenchment had been carried by assault, it was difficult to prevent too free a use of the bayonet during the first moments of victory. Magaw returned an answer which Washington praised as a spirited refusal,[2] but the defiant tone of the reply was in excess of what the summons provoked, and most certainly beyond anything that the issue of the conflict justified. The American commandant interpreted the British general's humane and reasonable warning as a threat that the garrison would be massacred; and, with a glowing appeal to the justice of his cause, he proclaimed his intention of defending the post to the very last extremity. That extremity was not far off. At noon on the next day, under cover of a heavy cannonade which had begun in the early morning, the British army stormed in from every quarter except the west. To the south in the direction of Haerlem, Lord Percy, on a horse which soon was twice wounded, led his command into action, and

---

[1] George Washington to John Augustine Washington; Hackensac, November 19, 1776.

[2] Washington to the President of Congress, November 16, 1776.

came into collision with an advanced party of the Ameri
cans, so isolated and exposed that there was an interval
of two miles between them and their nearest supports.
Into this gap Howe despatched three regiments of infantry in boats across the Haerlem river. The Forty-
second Highlanders, who were the earliest on shore,
swarmed up a steep path under a deadly fire, which laid
low nearly a hundred men and officers ; beat off their
immediate adversaries ; and, scouring fleetly over hill and
dale, took Lord Percy's opponents in the rear, and secured then and there a considerable number of prisoners
One of those prisoners, who was a cool fellow, remarked
on a circumstance which he noticed even in that moment
of hurry and dismay. "Not less than ten guns were
discharged with their muzzles towards us, within the
distance of forty or fifty yards ; and some were let off
within twenty. Luckily for us, it was not our riflemen
to whom we were targets. I observed they took no
aim, and the moment of presenting and firing was the
same."[1]

The Royal soldiers, however wild might be their shooting, everywhere showed great alacrity in coming to close
quarters with the enemy. General Mathew and Lord
Cornwallis brought seven battalions over Haerlem creek
in flat-bottomed boats, made good their footing on the
eastern shore of Manhattan Island ; and pressed steadily inland, losing men, and capturing positions. To the
north of the fort the struggle was severe and bloody ;
for there the Provincials were in some strength, and on
ground exceptionally suited to their method of warfare
General Knyphausen and his Hessians advanced from
King's Bridge in two columns ; waded through a deep
marsh ; and climbed a precipitous rocky hill which rose
behind it. The acclivity was so steep in places that the
men had to pull themselves up by aid of the bushes
They were in heavy marching order ; and that, in the
case of German infantry, was heavy indeed. A grenadier went into action in a high cap, fronted with an im-

[1] *Pennsylvanian Memoirs ;* chapter viii.

mense brass plate, a very long-skirted coat; a canteen which held a gallon; and a sword of enormous size, that had never killed anything except the calf or pig of a Loyalist farmer. But beneath these absurd trappings there was, on this occasion, no lack of martial ardour. The generals themselves led the way, pulling down fences with their own hands; and the private men never turned back, but went forwards and upwards wherever they could find a chance. At length they stood victorious on the top, in sorely diminished number, for between the foot and the summit, more than three hundred of them had been killed or wounded.[1]

Their loss, (wrote one of their officers,) was far greater than that of the adversary, from the manner in which the rebels fought. They lay singly behind stone-walls, and boulders, and the trunks of trees which had been felled as obstacles, they shot at long range, and with certainty; and they ran away very fast as soon as they had discharged their weapons The Germans, on the other hand, could not shoot a third so far; and still less were they able to catch up their opponents when it came to running.[2] Nevertheless the Provincial skirmishers, with whatever agility they might retreat, very soon reached the further end of their course. By this time the Americans had been driven inwards, from far and near, over the whole circle of the battle Breathless and disheartened, they poured into the fort, and hud-

---

[1] According to one most competent and trustworthy observer, Knyphausen's people were even more heavily laden than with the ordinary burden of their regulation accoutrements. " Every private," wrote Colonel Enoch Markham, " carried a fascine before him in one hand, while he scaled with the other In some places only one man could get up at a time, who assisted the man in the rear with his vacant hand. The Hessians and Waldecks most deservedly received the highest praise for this action." Another English officer, (employing one of those not very recondite classical allusions which, even in the less learned professions, were a mannerism of that day,) said that Hannibal, in his passage over the Alps, could not have met with ground more formidable than what fell to the lot of the Germans to assail.

[2] Account by the Quartermaster of the Grenadier Battalion von Minnigerode

dled together behind ramparts which would become
nothing better than the walls of a slaughter-house as
soon as the British could bring up a single battery of
howitzers.   The affair in the commencement had resembled the escalade of the heights of Spicheren, and
it now assumed the complexion of a miniature Sedan.
Colonel Magaw, as his superior officer ought long ere
this to have anticipated, was forced to abandon all hope
of cutting a path through the serried array of excellent
troops by whom he was surrounded ; — even apart from
the consideration that the breadth and depth of the
Hudson river in any case lay between him and safety.

Nothing now remained for the Americans except an
immediate and unconditional surrender.   The garrison,
— to the number of nearer three, than two, thousand, —
marched out between the ranks of the regiments Rall
and von Lossberg ; laid down their arms ; and gave up
their white, and yellow, and light blue standards.   Already, on Long Island, the Germans had captured a
flag of bright scarlet damask, inscribed with the motto
" Liberty ; " a word which to all these high-born servants
of Grand Dukes, and Landgraves, and Prince Electors,
seemed wonderfully out of place upon military colours.
And the visible disdain with which now, at Fort Washington, the victors regarded the somewhat fantastic
banners of a brand-new republic, was remembered when,
after an interval of only six weeks, the same two Hessian regiments again took their share, — with the parts
reversed, — in a very similar ceremony.   Howe, handsomely enough, renamed the fortress after the German
commander, to whose soldiers it was generally admitted
that the honours of the day had fallen.   The ill fortune
which pursued our foreign auxiliaries, on all subsequent
occasions when they were called upon to act indepen-
dently, was so persistent and so notorious, that the charity of history has made the very utmost of their behaviour
at Fort Washington.   When the report of their exploit
reached Waldeck and Hesse Cassel, their respective
Sovereigns felt a thrill of conscious honesty at the

thought that their royal brother of England had already got some value for his money. But, however joyful might be the sensations excited in the lesser capitals of Western Germany by the news that Germans had defeated and captured Englishmen, pride and satisfaction were by no means universal in London. The glory acquired by Colonel Rall, (said Edmund Burke,) had no charms for him, nor had he learned to delight at finding a Fort Knyphausen in the heart of the British dominions.

Except for prisoners, the loss of the Americans was small. Colonel Markham, who went carefully over the ground when the action was concluded, saw very few of their dead bodies. The British never had the intention, — and in the heat of success did not feel the smallest inclination, — to end a gallant fight with a scene of butchery. A Pennsylvanian captain, who was taken early in the affair by the Forty-second Highlanders, published a lifelike account of what happened on the sixteenth of November, and the days thereupon ensuing It is an account which Englishmen may read with pleasure.[1] This was the first complete and crushing victory obtained by our troops since the commencement of a war which in their view was a rebellion. Military custom had long ago established humane, and often amicable, relations between conquerors and vanquished in the vicissitudes of a struggle conducted on both sides by regular European armies; but the notion that American insurgents possessed a title to friendly treatment,

---

[1] Valuable testimony to the authority of this narrative has recently been made public. In 1822 Colonel Cadwalader, who had been second in command under Magaw, was requested by Timothy Pickering, another veteran of the Revolution, to write down his reminiscences of Fort Washington The old man replied that, after forty-five years, his memory was dim. "I shall however," he said, "avail myself of a Statement, which I made in the year 1811, at the Request of a Friend of mine, formerly a Captain in the 3rd Pennsylvania Battalion which I commanded in the War of the Revolution, who was writing a book entitled, 'Memoirs of a Life chiefly passed in Pennsylvania within the last Sixty Years.'" Colonel Cadwalader's letter was printed by the Historical Society of Pennsylvania in July 1901.

and fraternal hospitality, was very novel, and had never
been statedly and officially recognised. On this point
our officers had no specific orders to guide them Each
man acted in obedience to the dictates of his individual
nature; and the result proved that there was plenty of
right feeling, and honourable self-control, within the
British ranks. The Pennsylvanian prisoners first came
into the custody of a decent looking sergeant. He protected them from a Hessian who cursed them in bad
English, and himself bestowed on them a friendly admonition in very broad Scotch. " Young men," he said,
" ye never should fight against your King." " The little
bustle," (the author writes,) " produced by our surrender
was scarcely over, when a British officer, apparently of
high rank, rode up at full gallop, exclaiming : ' What !
Taking prisoners ! Kill every man of them.' Although
by this time there was none of that appearance of ferocity in the guard which would induce much fear that
they would execute this command, I took off my hat
saying : ' Sir, I put myself under your protection.' His
manner was instantly softened. He met my salutation
with an inclination of his body ; and, after a civil question or two, as if to make amends for his sanguinary
mandate, he rode off towards the fort, to which he had
enquired his way."

That was the measure of British ferocity and im-
placability. As the captives were passed on from one
set of guardians to another, they sometimes got a surly
or an insolent word; and the subalterns of a smart
Light Infantry regiment were moved to irrepressible
mirth by the appearance and accent of an unrefined
and untidy militia officer. But for the most part the
prisoners met with reasonable civility, and very substantial kindness. Soldiers brought them a constant
supply of drinking-water, at great trouble to themselves. Officers shared with them a small and precarious ration during that period of destitution which
immediately succeeds a battle, and sent them out generous portions from the mess-tables when the tumbrels

had come up from the rear, and viands were again abundant The gentleman to whose charge they were finally entrusted was of a singularly amiable and chivalrous character Lieutenant Becket, (for that was his name,) was courteous himself ; and his example diffused an atmosphere of courtesy around him.[1] No one within his hearing addressed the prisoners as "rebels," and, if he had occasion to distinguish in conversation between the belligerents, he invariably made use of the expressions "your people," and "our people" When the Americans were formed up on the road to New York, between two lines of British infantry: "Come, gentlemen," he said; "we are all soldiers To the right face! March!" and he walked the first half mile on the flank of the column with the air of a good-humoured comrade. At the end of their journey, as they drew near the city, they were encountered by a mob of disreputable women from the cantonments, who were enthusiastic and turbulent partisans of the cause which, after their fashion, they served They crowded in upon the prisoners, calling out to know which of them was Washington, and assailing them with volleys of ribaldry ; until a disgusted, — and under the circumstances, a laudably plainspoken, — British colonel came to the rescue, and put the Amazons to rout.[2]

Lieutenant Becket informed his prisoners that he was forcibly struck with the poor condition of their

[1] "Mr. Becket applied to a gentleman on horseback, who had superintended the interment of the dead, to know whether he had met with the body of an officer in the uniform I wore, as I was anxious for the fate of a brother who was missing With much delicacy, addressing himself to me, he replied; 'No, Sir, we buried no one with linen fine enough to have been your brother' . . An officer, wrapped up in a camlet cloak, young, and of very pleasing address, who had been talking with Becket, came to me observing that the evening was very cool, and asked if such weather was usual with us at this season of the year He expressed his hope that I had been well treated. 'As well as possible,' I replied, 'by some , and as ill by others' 'I am extremely sorry for it·' he said ; 'but there are rascals in all services'" In the British regiments there were not many such , and those of no very deep dye

[2] *Pennsylvanian Memoirs*, chapter viii.

troops, the badness of their muskets, and the insuffi
ciency, in every respect, of their appointments, and
he remarked that a gentleman serving in their army
required more than an ordinary degree of fortitude to
take the field under such disadvantages   But everything
is a matter of comparison ; and the garrison at Fort
Washington bore less resemblance to a flock of indifferently armed and ill-clothed irregulars than any other
equally large section of the Provincial forces.   The
American Commander-in-Chief acknowledged that he
had lost his most carefully trained, and most expensively equipped, regiments ; a considerable proportion
of his artillery ; and some of the very best arms he
had   He witnessed the depressing scene from a high
bank at Fort Lee, on the opposite side of the Hudson
river,[1] with keen self-reproach ; although he knew in
his heart that the fault was not all his own   No plea
of having acted under superior orders was put forward
in the official report of the affair which he transmitted to the President of Congress : but a sense of
personal wrong is indicated, — not angrily, and very
sadly, — in a private letter to his brother.   He there
confessed that the hope of a successful termination to
the campaign had been alive in his mind until Fort
Washington fell.   General Howe, (he said,) but for that
unfortunate occurrence, would have had a poor tale to
tell, and might have found it difficult to reconcile the
people of England to the conquest of a few pitiful
islands, none of which had ever been really defensible
against a power whose fleet could at any moment
surround, and render them unapproachable   " I
solemnly protest," (Washington exclaimed,) " that a
pecuniary reward of twenty thousand pounds a year
would not induce me to undergo what I do , and after
all, perhaps, to lose my character ; as it is impossible,
under such a variety of distressing circumstances, to
conduct matters agreeably to public expectation, or even
to the expectation of those who employ me, as they

---

[1] General Heath's *Memoirs*, November 16, 1776.

will not make proper allowances for the difficulties their own errors have occasioned." [1]

Twenty thousand pounds a year would have made Washington just twice as rich as the then richest man in America; but such a prize would have small temptation to one who, (as he wrote in this very letter,) looked for no higher reward than to sit once more in the peaceable enjoyment of his own vine and fig tree, when the war should be over, and the country saved. That peaceful hour was now indefinitely postponed; and there was grave reason to doubt if it ever would arrive. The loss of Fort Washington, though not in itself a catastrophe, was one of those calamities which launched the weaker party on the downward road that almost inevitably leads to ruin, and, (to make the matter more serious,) that portion of the British army which headed the advance, was commanded by a general of a higher stamp than any whom the Americans had yet encountered.

Lord Cornwallis was an English aristocrat of the finest type. Over a vast space of time, and in many lands, he served the State in war, in politics, in diplomacy, and in high administration. Whether or not he was exceptionally clever was a question which he had never in his life considered; any more than he would have asked himself if he was brave and honest. Nor did his countrymen come to any very definite conclusion as to the pre-eminence and rarity of his abilities. It was enough for them that he was a man of immense and varied experience; careful and industrious, modest in success and equable in adversity; enlightened, tolerant, and humane; contemptuous of money, and indifferent to the outward badges of honour.[2] What a consular of

---

[1] Washington to the President of Congress; General Greene's Quarters, November 16, 1776. To John Augustine Washington; Hackensac, November 19, 1776.

[2] When, in the war against Tippoo Sahib, he took the field as Governor-General, Cornwallis found occasion to spend, from his own resources, near thirty thousand pounds in eighteen months; and yet he gave up his claim to not much less than fifty thousand pounds of prize money, which

old Rome, in Rome's greatest days, is traditionally supposed to have been, that Cornwallis actually was. Throughout the whole of his long career he presented, first to his own, and then to a younger, generation, a living and most attractive example of antique and single-minded patriotism. In the House of Lords he had consistently opposed all schemes for the taxation and coercion of the colonists; but, when they flew to arms, and he was called upon to fight against them, Cornwallis held that, as a soldier, he was not at liberty to disobey the order. If he had been Governor-General of New England during the years that Sir Guy Carleton was Governor of Canada, it is, humanly speaking, almost certain that there would have been no American rebellion. If, after hostilities broke out, he had been Commander-in-Chief instead of Sir William Howe and Sir Henry Clinton, it is quite certain that British strategy would have been far less halting and desultory. The energy and enterprise, which subsequently marked his two campaigns in the Carolinas, revived the dying credit of our national generalship; and military students may still draw valuable lessons from the counter-operations which were planned with solid ability, and conducted with manly pertinacity, by Cornwallis on the one side, and by Nathanael Greene on the other.

England's crowning misfortune in the American war will always be connected with the memory of Lord Cornwallis And yet, when Yorktown fell, the responsibility for its loss was attributed, and rightly attributed, not to the general who capitulated, but to the Com-

---

he left to be distributed among the troops.   There is a hearty letter from Cornwallis to his son on the subject of the Garter, which was bestowed on the Governor-General soon after his arrival at Calcutta. " I can assure you upon my honour," he wrote, " that I neither asked for it nor wished for it. The reasonable object of ambition to a man is to have his name transmitted to posterity for eminent services rendered to his country and mankind. Nobody asks or cares whether Hampden, Marlborough, Pelham, or Wolfe were Knights of the Garter " When, in obedience to the mandate of the King, Cornwallis opposed Fox's East India Bill, he insisted on resigning the Constableship of the Tower, so that no man might suspect him of having voted with the Court in order to keep an office.

mander-in-Chief at New York who had failed to support him, and to the First Lord of the Admiralty, whose scandalous mismanagement had resulted in the paralysis of our fleet at that moment of time when, and on the very spot where, the fortune of our empire was at stake. Sir Henry Clinton was recalled. In the House of Commons a very narrow majority indeed saved Lord Sandwich from a motion for inquiry into his adminis-tration of the Navy during the year 1781; and that motion, if successful, was to have been followed by an impeachment. But Parliament showed no inclination to bring Lord Cornwallis to account, all parties united in a strong desire as soon as possible to re-employ him,[1] and, after no long while, the Governor-Generalship of our East-ern possessions was forced upon his reluctant acceptance. There he played a famous part; and, (although some fea-tures of his internal policy have been gravely questioned,) his probity and public spirit communicated to the Govern-ment of India that high and pure tone which, to the abiding honour of the British name, it has ever since retained In 1798 he quelled the rebellion, and defeated a French invasion, in Ireland. With a courage all his own, and an authority which no man else could have exercised, he discountenanced, and greatly mitigated, the severities demanded and practised by the dominant party in that unhappy island As plenipotentiary in Paris he negotiated the Peace of Amiens; and at the last, an old broken man, in his country's need and in quiet sub-mission to her call, he sailed once more for India to die.

---

[1] Very striking testimony to the esteem in which Cornwallis was held, subsequently to his misfortune at Yorktown, comes from two exactly opposite quarters. Soon after he landed in England, while he was still a prisoner on parole, the approbation and confidence of George the Third were conveyed to him in a most generous letter, written throughout by the royal hand. A year later Charles Fox referred to Lord Cornwallis in the House of Commons, at a time when the two old friends had become politi-cal opponents. The name of such a man, (said the orator,) might make Parliament consent to the voting of very extensive powers in a Governor-General of India; but he was certain that nothing but the great character of that noble Lord could ever induce the Legislature to commit such power to one individual, at the distance of half the globe.

In November 1776 Lord Cornwallis was at the very top of his physical and mental powers. The Prince de Ligne, who knew war as intimately as he knew mankind, always maintained that a soldier was no longer at his best when the sap had ceased to mount. " I am aware," (said the uncompromising veteran,) " that the thirst for glory and the zeal for duty will, all through life, exalt men above themselves; but those admirable motives cannot replace that natural love of hazard, and fatigue, and adventures, which comes from the violent circulation of young and boiling blood. When I am told that an officer is a person of honour and loyalty, I reply that I am very glad to hear it, if only he has *le diable au corps* "[1] Cornwallis still preserved that indispensable, though oddly designated, qualification for active warfare at the time when he was commissioned by Howe to follow up the advantage which our army had obtained at Fort Washington. In after days he was accompanied on his Mysore expedition by certain allied Rajahs, in command, but in the hour of battle not always at the head, of their respective contingents. These potentates, — with a sense of injured dignity, sharpened by personal uneasiness at what they considered a very dangerous precedent for themselves, — complained that the Governor-General exposed himself under fire like a private grenadier. And during the invasion of the Jerseys, (when, instead of being a Viceroy, he was only a Major General on the Army List,[2] and two good years on the right side of forty,) Cornwallis was never far in rear of his advance guard, and that advance guard was seldom much behind the enemy With secrecy and celerity he passed six thousand British and German troops across the Hudson at points above King's Bridge.[3] On the twentieth of

---

[1] The section " Sur les jeunes gens ; " *Mélanges Historiques et Littéraires*, par le Prince de Ligne

[2] All through 1776 Cornwallis was " Lieutenant General in America." He became a Lieutenant General on the Army List in August 1777.

[3] The operations related in this chapter, and the two which follow, are clearly delineated in the map at the end of the volume.

November a party of sailors, whom Lord Howe had lent him, with infinite enjoyment dragged his heavy guns up half a mile of narrow stony road, and planted a battery on the top of a precipice which, within easy cannon-range, overlooked Fort Lee and the adjacent encampment. The surprise was all but complete. Cornwallis made a push to seize the passes over the Hackensac river, the occupation of which would have enabled him to shut up two thousand Provincials on a peninsula only fifteen miles long, and nowhere more than three miles wide ; at the further end of which the sole retreat was across a league of sea-water patrolled by the British frigates. It was the most that Greene and his colonels could do to withdraw their regiments, their ammunition, and a couple of twelve-pounders. They left behind them thirty-two pieces of artillery mounted on the ramparts of the fort; a thousand barrels of flour, that before long were grievously missed ; many tents, and much baggage; as well as a considerable amount of military reputation, and all that remained of the cheerfulness and confidence which had, up to a very recent period, inspired the Provincial forces.

These repeated blows descended upon a frame too ill-knit to resist their impact. The Revolutionary army was now in rapid course of disintegration and dissolution. Washington's nominal strength had fallen to less than six, and his real strength was not above four, thousand.[1] Near five thousand of his people had been made prisoners in the course of twelve weeks ; and the contagion of desertion, which had been epidemic in his cantonments, now raged after the manner of a plague. The ranks melted, it was said, like snow in summer ; but that was too genial and Arcadian a metaphor to use in connection with the dreary and

---

[1] These numbers were detailed in the text, and in the First Appendix, of *The Battles of Trenton and Princeton*, by William S. Stryker, Adjutant General of New Jersey, and President of the New Jersey Historical Society ; Boston and New York, 1898 A better book on the subject could not be compiled.

comfortless situation. For winter was setting in ; the frost was sharp, and the wind cruel, the troops were wretchedly provided with tents and blankets ; and Greene's soldiers, in the hurry of their escape from Fort Lee, had brought away with them nothing except their muskets. The militia, more homesick than ever, disappeared every night by scores and dozens. Those of them who scrupled to go off by stealth fondly reflected that they had only ten days more to serve, and proclaimed their intention of departing in mass so soon as their time was up. Even the regulars of the Continental line began to count, with ominous satisfaction, the dwindling residue of weeks during which they were bound by their contract to serve with the colours. A wreck of Washington's once numerous host lay in hopeless plight round and about the village of Hackensac ; cut off from any base of supply ; with no intrenching tools, and very few cannon. The Americans were certain to be beaten whenever the British came against them resolutely, and in full force ; and, if beaten, they would be hustled down southwards between the Hackensac and the Passaic rivers, and destroyed or taken to a man. Their general was keenly alive to the peril in which he stood ; and he already had learned enough of Cornwallis to know that it would not be the fault of that commander if so rare an opportunity was mishandled and wasted [1]

Washington accordingly crossed the Passaic by the bridge at Acquackanonck, and retreated to Newark, where he abode a week until a report reached him that Howe was taking measures for landing a detachment at South Amboy in order to catch the American army in the rear. On Thursday the twenty-eighth of November that army filed out of Newark, with the English close upon their heels ; [2] marched in two separate columns

[1] Washington's three letters of November 21, 1776, to Major General Lee, to the President of Congress, and to Governor Livingston of New Jersey.

[2] " Our force," wrote General Washington, " was by no means sufficient to make stand, with the least probability of success, against an enemy much superior in numbers, and whose advanced guards were entering the town by the time our rear got out." Letter of November 30, 1776.

along the roads which led through Springfield and Elizabeth Town; and took up their position at New Brunswick, behind the river Raritan. At this point the remnant of those ten thousand militiamen, who during the past summer had figured in the newspapers under the title of the Flying Camp, took wing in a flock, and migrated homewards. That contemporary historian, who said that the American army had ceased to exist,[1] did not greatly exaggerate as the case stood, and his description would have been absolutely and literally accurate if Cornwallis had been allowed to take his own course. So great, (to quote General Howe's official account,) was the confusion among Washington's troops that they must inevitably have been cut in pieces if they had not broken down a portion of Brunswick Bridge, and thereby disabled their pursuer from following them across the Raritan.[2]

It was a poor excuse for Howe to put forward, and most unfair to an alert and strenuous subordinate. On the first of December Lord Cornwallis marched twenty miles over exceedingly bad roads in a single day, and approached the Raritan, with a powerful force well in hand, before ever the rear guard of the enemy had passed the river. There he was overtaken by a message informing him that General Howe refused to sanction any further aggressive movements until he himself arrived at the front with reinforcements, and then a full week elapsed before the British Commander-in-Chief, accompanied by a single brigade, came into camp, and assumed the personal command of the army Howe's tactical arrangements, whenever and wherever his troops were sent into action, had hitherto uniformly been excellent, but this month of December ruined, once and for ever, his repute as a strategist. The true policy of the campaign was to keep the Americans per-

---

[1] "History of Europe" in the *Annual Register* for the year 1777; chapter 1.

[2] Letter from Sir William Howe to Lord George Germaine; New York, December 20, 1776.

petually on the run till their army was reduced to fragments , to take and hold their capital of Philadelphia ;
and to break up their civil administration, and their military organisation, beyond any possibility of repair or
resurrection.   All other schemes should have been postponed to the accomplishment of that supreme object ;
and every available man and horse should have been
launched on the chase of a decisive and overwhelming
victory.   The time had come for acting in the spirit of
the phrase which General Sheridan used at the crisis of
his battles : " Now let everything go in ! "   But this was
the precise moment which Howe selected to despatch
two divisions of infantry, in a fleet of seventy transports
escorted by eleven men-of-war, for the purpose of subduing Rhode Island ; — and only the actual island itself,
without extending their operations to the rest of the
province which bore that name.   It was a facile conquest; but the fruits were as insignificant as the undertaking had been ill-timed.   The American shipping
escaped up the bay to Providence ; and several thousand
Royal troops were thenceforward locked up in a sea-girt
slip of land no larger than the estate of many an English
Lord-Lieutenant.   Their head-quarters were at Newport; and, for any effect which they produced upon
the general result of the war, they might have been
as usefully, and much more agreeably, billeted in the
town of the same name in the Isle of Wight.

It was not till the seventh of December that Howe
resumed his onward march ; and Washington was already
far, or far enough, away.   While still at Brunswick, he
had issued orders to occupy the ferries above and below
Trenton ; to seize every boat on the Delaware, and its
tributary streams, over the space of many miles up and
down the river ; and to make sure that they were in
sound condition, and adequately provided with oars and
punting-poles.   Lord Stirling, with fourteen hundred
Southern infantry, — the flower of the army, though a
faded flower it was, — established himself strongly at
Princeton ; and, under cover of the slender force com-

manded by that vigilant officer, Washington very coolly
and deliberately carried through his arrangements for
abandoning the Jerseys, where he could no longer stay
without the certainty of utter and instant ruin. He
transported over the Delaware his military stores, which,
indeed, were no heavy burden, and his sick and disabled, whom, after that long and exhausting campaign, it
was not easy to distinguish from those of their comrades
who were still classed as hale and effective. On the
seventh and eighth of the month his fighting army crossed
the river. The shipping which the Americans had at their
disposal was in excess of their requirements. Washington had made a great point of securing certain barges,
from thirty to forty feet in length, which were known as
the Durham Boats, and which were ordinarily employed
for the conveyance of heavy goods and iron ore between
Philadelphia and the northern counties of New Jersey.[1]
So thin were his ranks that each of these vessels in some
cases afforded accommodation for an entire regiment.

Few or many, the Provincials were all safely landed in
Pennsylvania. Their rear guard had hardly disembarked
on the secure side of the river when their pleasing sen-
sation of, at least, a temporary intermission from danger
was enhanced by the almost simultaneous appearance
on the eastern bank of a baffled and outwitted enemy
Howe's vanguard came marching bravely down in full
expectation of being over the Delaware before nightfall.
The citizens of Trenton were deeply impressed by the
style in which a Hessian brigade entered their town,
played through the streets by a band of music superior to
anything that the whole of the armies commanded
by Washington and Gates could produce between them
But, extraordinary to relate, the English general had
been started on a campaign, in a region intersected at
frequent intervals by broad and deep streams, without
any of the appliances requisite for traversing an un-
bridged river. "How provoking it is," (exclaimed Colonel Enoch Markham,) "that our army, when it entered

[1] Washington to Colonel Hampton, December 1, 1776.

the Jerseys, was not provided with a single pontoon!
Unless the object was Philadelphia, entering the Jerseys
was absurd to the last degree.   If we had six flat-bottomed boats, we could cross the Delaware."   That was
the view of a practised soldier; and even civilians, who
had eyes in their heads, could not understand why the
ingenuity of British military engineers on the spot did
nothing to remedy the improvidence of the British War
Office.   A Loyalist gentleman, who had followed our
columns up to the Delaware, — and who expected, within
three days' time, to have been eating his dinner in
Philadelphia, where he would have found plenty of hosts
willing and proud to entertain him, — discovered for
himself that, at and near Trenton, there were forty-eight
thousand feet of boards in store, besides a great quantity
of strong wire.   A well-stocked timber-yard lay directly
at the back of the premises where the English head-
quarters had been established; and, if any additional
materials were needed, the town contained a hundred
wooden houses, and no less than four blacksmiths'
shops [1]   There was hardly a brigade in Washington's
army that would not have furnished artificers to construct the rafts, and ferrymen and boatmen to handle
them; but our soldiers were unskilled, and our commanders helpless, in front of an obstacle which they all
pronounced to be insurmountable.   On the morning of
the ninth of December Lord Cornwallis marched thirteen miles along the Delaware, as far towards the north
as Coryell's Ferry, in search of boats which had all been
carefully deposited either beyond, or beneath, the water.[2]

---

[1] Joseph Galloway's Evidence before the House of Commons, June 18,
1776. Jones's *History of New York;* Vol. I., chapter vi. The names of
the Trenton blacksmiths are given in Mr. Stryker's *Battles of Trenton and
Princeton.*

[2] "On Sunday morning we crossed the Delaware   About eleven o'clock
the enemy came marching down with all the pomp of war, in great expectation of getting boats; but of this we took proper care by destroying
every boat or shallop we could lay hands on.   They made forced marches
up and down the river in pursuit of boats; but in vain   The enemy are
at least twelve thousand strong, determined for Philadelphia."   Letter of
an officer from Trenton; *American Archives,* December 1776.

Stedman, the English historian of the war, remarked that General Howe appeared to have calculated with the greatest accuracy the exact time necessary for the enemy to make his escape; and Washington himself modestly attributed the entire credit of that escape to the "infatuation" of his opponent. The Delaware river, (he confessed,) and nothing else, had saved Philadelphia

The Americans needed all the consolation which they could derive from the very visible disappointment of their adversary; for seldom or never has any body of troops, that still held together as an organised and obedient army, been in much worse case than theirs. They had originally been equipped in headlong haste, out of the scanty resources, or on the fast vanishing credit, of an almost empty Treasury. By the time that Fort Washington was captured, three months of active warfare had already reduced most of their regiments to an aspect of beggary. Provincial officers, who were prisoners among the British tents, were painfully struck by a comparison between the private men of the two contending forces. While their own poor fellows, (they said,) were already ragged, and the best of them clad in flimsy threadbare clothes, with worse stockings and shoes, the Royal troops were tight and comfortable in their attire, and every man among them was provided with a thick nightcap to wear when asleep or off duty. Lord Dartmouth received, from one of his most regular correspondents, a letter remarking on the policy of Congress in having closed American ports against the introduction of Yorkshire woollens. If the rebels, (so this gentleman reported,) were obliged to keep the field during the winter, they would suffer much distress, if not destruction. He himself had seen advertisements in the newspapers asking for all the blankets that could be spared from people's beds throughout the country. This, however, would afford a very scanty and precarious resource for the army, since few civilians would find their patriotism warm enough to unclothe themselves without the prospect of being able to obtain a fresh supply from abroad during the whole of the winter; and a winter in that climate was severe indeed. Many of Washington's soldiers, (the writer added,) had no other covering than a rifleman's frock of canvas over their shirts, and were diseased, and over-run with vermin, to a degree that was positively revolting.[1] Such was the state of things on the seventh of November, when the retreat across the Jerseys had not yet commenced. Since that date four weeks of open bivouacs in sleet and hail-storms, — and long marches over roads to which, even before they had been broken up by military traffic, the least fastidious tourist from Western Europe would have scornfully denied the title of highways, — brought the remnant of Washington's followers into a state of destitution which in some instances hardly stopped short of nudity. The hunting-shirt of the frontier-men had been "the mortal aversion of every redcoat;"[2] but those dreaded marksmen now, by their miserable appearance, excited a movement of generous compassion in the breast of more than one English officer. Young militiamen, who had come on service in their farm clothes, were in a pitiable condition long before they reached Trenton Ferry; and the Continental regulars, who had begun the campaign in buff and blue, admitted, (with a touch of that American humour which defies misfortune,) that they would have been "all buff" had the retreat lasted a fortnight longer. There was nothing gay or showy except the regimental flags; and those were not of a conventional military pattern. The tattered footsore group, which was called a battalion, trailing wearily through rain and mud behind a banner gaudy with allegorical and emblematic devices, bore a closer external resemblance to some village benefit club in very poor circumstances than to a band of warriors who were on the eve of a world-famous exploit.[3]

---

[1] Ambrose Serle to Lord Dartmouth; November 7, 1776.

[2] *Pennsylvanian Memoirs*, chapter viii.

[3] The standard of the thirteenth regiment displayed a pine tree, and a field of Indian corn, on a ground of light buff. The supporters were

Inclement weather, and incessant toil and exposure, were all the more afflicting to soldiers who were worse than badly fed by their employers, and who had not the leisure or the permission to cater for themselves. The administrative departments had completely broken down; and, indeed, since their wholesale and repeated losses by capture of waggons and draught-horses, the Transport officers had not much left to administer. Carrying next to nothing along with them, the Provincials could procure very little from the country through which they travelled. Their force was small, and they had no men to spare from the duties of watching the enemy, and guarding the camp; the militia were so prone to desert that they could not safely be trusted at a distance from head-quarters; and, as long as Cornwallis managed the pursuit, the British skirmishers had been active, audacious, and importunate. For all these reasons the American commander did not venture to send out foragers in any great number over a considerable extent of country. At that season of the year the harvest of maize had long ago been cut and gathered; and Washington's soldiers could not, (like the troops of General Jackson in the War of the Secession,) eat their rations "off the stalk" in the corn-fields along their line of march   There is a casual mention of half a pint of whiskey having been served out daily to every American; but whether or not they received that allowance regularly, and whatever it may have done towards keeping them contented, they most certainly got very little solid or wholesome food to sustain them. They starved all the way from Hackensac to Newark, and from Newark to Brunswick, and, by the time they came in sight of the Delaware, those mothers and sisters, who had spun and dyed their garments, would with difficulty have recognised their pinched faces and discoloured rags [1]

"two officers in the uniform of the regiment; one of them wounded in the breast, the blood streaming from the wound. Under the Pine several children, one of the officers, pointing to them, with the motto, 'For Posterity I Bleed'" *American Archives*, September 1776.

[1] Mr. William Stillman tells in his autobiography how his maternal grandfather, a clergyman at Newport in Rhode Island, sent two sons into

The fate of the sick and the wounded was heart-rending. So far back as October there were five battalions, brigaded together above Haerlem, which had only one surgeon's mate among them.[1] The store of drugs and of bandages ran out early in the retreat, nor could the deficiencies of regimental chests be supplemented from the local resources of those petty towns which the army traversed[2] Many of the soldiers, who were too ill to walk, were left behind in the utter dearth of carriage; and most of these died for the want of care.[3] A very large proportion of the troops who retired across the Delaware were attacked by pneumonia, dysentery, and camp-fevers, and few, who once were prostrated, ever recovered and survived. During the coming quarter of a year three thousand deaths occurred in and about Philadelphia, where seventy funerals sometimes took place on the same day. Many of those militiamen, who left the ranks at one point or another of the retreat, carried away the seeds of disease in their frames. They died at their homes in great numbers, and spread typhus far and wide throughout the neighbourhoods where they resided[4] In December 1776 there existed a wellnigh universal impression that the military power of the Americans had been mortally stricken. A friendly hand likened the remains of their army to a tribe of wandering Arabs. "The Rebels," (a Tory journalist wrote,) "are mouldering away like a rope of sand. With the most impotent bravadoes they have not had

the Revolutionary army. As one of them "had no clothes fit for the camp, the sisters had a black and white sheep brought from the pasture and clipped, and within twenty-four hours had spun, woven, and made up a suit of mixed grey clothes for the brother to go to the war in." Such, and no better, was the outfit of many a poor lad who, within a month after he crossed the Delaware, was lying in the Philadelphia cemetery.

[1] The *American Archives* for October 1776

[2] According to a letter from Paul Wentworth, among the Auckland Manuscripts, "Rhubarb, Ippecacuana, and Globar Salts" then made up almost the whole furniture of an apothecary's shop in the rural districts of the most civilised and thriving colonies.

[3] Colonel Enoch Markham, December 14, 1776.

[4] Ambrose Serle to Lord Dartmouth, March 20, 1777.

the spirit to make anything like a stand in a single encounter. Mr. Washington, with about two thousand poor wretches who can get no subsistence except by following him, has fled into Pennsylvania."[1]

Howe's easy and triumphant advance, and the hardships of Washington's retreat, were in no small part due to the apathy and indifference of New Jersey. The middle colonies did not share the revolutionary enthusiasm of New England, and their inhabitants, who always had been a peace-loving folk, were not inflamed by the mutual pugnacity, and even ferocity, which made Whig and Tory fight each other to the death in Georgia and the Carolinas. The citizens of the Jerseys, (as an English officer described them in September 1776,) were a very good sort of people; very industrious, and with no great stomach towards the war. Their country, before it was desolated by the invasion, had been termed the garden of America[2] They themselves possessed those milder virtues which belong to the small proprietor in a prosperous rural district, together with his modest ambition of ranking as a tranquil and obscure supporter of the winning side; and, in their estimation, that side was no longer the American. General Greene declared that, if New England had been the seat of hostilities, the Provincials would not have been under the necessity of retreating more than six or seven leagues; but the fright and disaffection were so great in the Jerseys that Washington, in his rearward march of over a hundred miles, was never joined by more than a hundred men.[3] On the thirtieth of November a proclamation was put forth, signed by the British General, and by his brother, Lord Howe, — a family name which inspired respect, and something of affection, among Americans who were not stiff and determined partisans of the Revolution. A free pardon, and

---

[1] *New York Mercury;* December 23, 1776.
[2] *Travels through the Interior Parts of America*, Vol. II., Letter 58.
[3] Letter from General Greene, December 21, 1776.

the assured enjoyment of liberty and property, were promised to all who within sixty days would subscribe a declaration of loyalty to his Majesty; and the offer included even those who had borne arms against the Crown. During the best part of a fortnight, adhesions came in at the rate of three or four hundred in the twenty-four hours. Colonel Enoch Markham, who was stationed at Perth Amboy on the mouth of the Raritan river, had infinite trouble from dawn to bed-time, swearing in the neighbours, and signing their certificates. That gallant old soldier, — who, like the true brother of an English Archbishop, had faith in the permanent efficacy on the human conscience of oaths of Allegiance and Supremacy, — drew up an additional attestation of his own, which he imposed upon active and notorious rebels before consenting to accept their submission. The farmers of New Jersey, however, did not look very critically into the exact wording of an engagement which secured their persons from imprisonment, and professed to guarantee their homes against pillage. Unless the wheel of fortune made a speedy and most unlikely turn, it seemed as if there would be a very small minority of non-jurors left throughout the entire province. "The conduct of the Jerseys," (so Washington told his brother,) "has been most infamous. Instead of turning out to defend their country, and affording aid to our army, they are making submissions as fast as they can. If the Jerseys had given us any support, we might have made a stand at Hackensac, and after that at Brunswick; but the few militia, that were in arms, disbanded themselves and left the poor remains of our army to make the best we could of it"[1]

[1] Letter to John Augustine Washington; Camp near the Falls of Trenton, December 1776.

In the course of that same week General Macdougal reported to Washington from Morristown that the New Jersey Militia there had fallen to two hundred. "When I anticipate," he said, "the bad consequences that will result to the common cause from the submission of this State, it renders me almost unfit for any business The Northern expedition of last year cost me my eldest son, and the capture of the other."

Whether or not the people of New Jersey deserved that exceedingly strong adjective which the angry and despondent Washington applied to their conduct, most undoubtedly the course which they had chosen to pursue entailed upon their province severe and instant penalties. The Royal army included in its composition an element of violence and rapacity, which five long months of impunity had fostered and emboldened. Our foreign auxiliaries brought with them to America certain ideas and habits alien to the creed and customs of a British army. Their officers had the military aristocrat's contempt for civilians, and especially for peasants; and, when the peasant was a rebel as well, they regarded him as a being with no rights, no feelings which deserved consideration, no claim to decent treatment, and no property that he could call his own when once a well-born captain or lieutenant, who served the Elector of Hanover, had done him the honour of stepping across his threshold. Even the most well conducted of the soldiers could not be expected to maintain a higher standard of honesty and humanity than was recognised by those to whom they looked for an example. During the whole of the voyage from their distant home the Germans, — officers and privates, better or worse, alike, — had consoled the tedium and discomfort of their life at sea by picturing America as a Promised Land, whose inhabitants had forfeited all title to its possession by wicked ingratitude towards their rightful sovereign. When they entered New York Bay, and looked around them, the aspect of the inheritance, which they proposed to occupy, exceeded their brightest and most sanguine anticipations. They were much struck, (we are told,) by the appearance of wealth and plenty which they found on Staten Island; by the commodious houses, embowered in gardens and orchards, and by the light waggons, painted red, and drawn at a brisk trot by pairs of small, neat horses. They bade each other remark that a colonist, who was nothing more than a farmer or a dairyman, lived in as

good style as a German country gentleman   They declared it to be inexplicable that people should revolt
against a Government under which they enjoyed so
many blessings;[1] but, though such perversity was not
capable of explanation, it was none the less highly convenient for a gallant adventurer who wanted to settle
down in affluence and security when once his campaigns
were over.   " Abuse of the rebels," (said a Loyalist in
Government employment,) " and the hope of plunder,
— for I hear that all the Hessian common soldiers have
a notion of making their fortunes, — have stimulated
them to such a degree as by no means inclines them to
show tenderness and mercy.   They are very expert in
foraging, and have made good use of their time.   The
company and example of the British troops have
hitherto prevented all excessive cruelties."[2]

That was written early in September; and, some two
months afterwards, the Hessians crossed the Hudson.
To do their impartiality justice, they left behind them
on the east of the river very little moveable property,
belonging to the Tories of New York province, which
it repaid them to take ; and now, without delay, disguise,
or pity, they fell beak and claw upon New Jersey.
Their behaviour in that unlucky colony aroused a chorus
of indignation in all the thirteen States, the echo of
which has ever since gone rolling down on the stream
of history and popular tradition.   The outcry of anger
and disapprobation was swelled by the voices of Englishmen and colonial Loyalists, whose shame and compunction at the military licence practised by their own allies
found vent in protests more strongly worded than anything which had been dictated by the resentment of
American Whigs.   Before Cornwallis had penetrated as
far south as Newark, the Deputy Adjutant General of
the British army confessed that his Lordship would not
be able to restrain the troops from plundering the country, now that their excess in that respect had already

[1] Chapter v. of *The Hessians,* by Edward J. Lowell.
[2] Ambrose Serle to Lord Dartmouth ; September 5, 1776.

been carried to an unjustifiable extent.[1]   In warmer and less official, but not more honest and honourable, language Judge Jones declared that the war was levelled not so much at rebellion, as at his Majesty's loyal subjects within the lines ; against all persons wherever the army moved ; against erudition, religion, and literature in general.   Public libraries, (said the indignant Tory,) were robbed, colleges ruined, and churches of all denominations burned and destroyed.

In those passionate words there was emphasis, but no exaggeration.   On the seventh of December Howe's army took possession of Princeton, a seat of learning and culture which was the pride of the central colonies. The female camp-followers, who in the friendly city of New York sold the choicest books in three great public libraries for the price of a glass of gin or a morsel of finery, had learned to regard the collections preserved in an academic building as their special and familiar prey ; and their own view of the matter was shared by those less decently-behaved soldiers who were their bullies and their admirers.   Between them they soon gutted the library, the museum, and the lecture-rooms ; carried off or destroyed every volume upon the shelves ; and broke up all the philosophical and mathematical instruments for the sake of the brass fittings.   Among other scientific treasures there perished a "celebrated orrery, made by Rittenhouse, said to be the best and finest in the world."[2]   A more pathetic calamity, to the mind of a classical scholar, was the profanation and pillage of the residence occupied by the distinguished President of the College.   He had called his dwelling Tusculum, and had endeavoured, — as far as might be done at that distance from Italian antiquarian shops, and Birmingham and Leipsic printing-houses, — to render it worthy of the name by the character and value of the decorations and contents.   What took place at Princeton

---

[1] Journal of Major Stephen Kemble , November 24, 1776.

[2] "History of Europe" in the *Annual Register* for 1777.   Jones's *History of New York*, Vol. I., chapter vii.

was repeated in every cluster of houses situated on or
near the roads along which the Royal army advanced.
A single representative passage may be quoted from
one among an infinite number of contemporary letters
which all gave the same monotonous recital of anarchy,
oppression, and misery. "The fine settlements of
Maidenhead and Hopewell have been broken up. The
houses are stripped of every article of furniture; and
what is not portable is entirely destroyed. The stock
of cattle and sheep are drove off, every article of clothing and house-linen seized and carried away. Scarce a
soldier but what has a horse loaded with plunder.
Hundreds of families are reduced to poverty and ruin,
and left at this inclement season to wander through the
woods without clothing."[1]

When December was half through, the campaign, —
so far as the course of events was under Howe's con-
trol, — came to an end. The Royal army was distributed
among farms and hamlets up and down New Jersey, to
remain under cover of a roof, and to live at rack and
manger, until the spring should arrive. The condition
of the local population, so far from mending, grew more
intolerable than ever. The colonists eagerly and wist-
fully put forward their claim to that immunity from
rapine and confiscation, which had been promised them
when they made their submission and took the oath of
loyalty. But a German fusilier could no more read a
protection-paper drawn up in English than if it had
been a Baskerville Virgil from the wreck of President

---

[1] Letter in the *American Archives :* December 12, 1776 According
to a trustworthy spectator, the process of collecting booty had by this time
been developed into a systematic business. " I saw the soldiers plundering the houses, — the women of the village trembling and weeping, or flying with their children. A scene of promiscuous pillage was in full
operation. Here a soldier was seen issuing from a house armed with a
frying-pan and gridiron, and hastening to deposit them with the stove
over which his help-mate kept watch. The women who had followed the
army assisted their husbands in bringing the furniture from the houses, or
stood sentinels to guard the pile of kitchen utensils, or other articles,
already secured and claimed by right of war." Dunlap's *History of the
American Theatre.*

Witherspoon's study in Tusculum ; and he most certainly would not go out of his way to find a British officer who might explain to him the contents of the document. Wherever Hessians were billeted, they at once made free with money and valuables ; they inventoried, and began to pack up, the furniture ; and they detected hidden deposits of domestic stores and precious metals with an instinct which to their unhappy hosts seemed nothing short of infernal. Under the odious recruiting system that then prevailed in Central Europe, most German regiments comprised a dangerously large infusion of the refuse of the street and the sweepings of the jail. There were ruffians and vagabonds in the ranks whose presence as guests was a torment and a terror to quiet colonial households. America rang with the story of incidents that were maddening to a proud, a strict, and a self-respecting people ; whose home was their shrine ; whose wives were their counsellors and true helpmates ; and whose children were tenderly cherished, and carefully instructed in religion and at least the elements of learning, under a system of education which, rude and imperfect as compared with modern requirements, was superior to anything then existing in the rural districts of most European kingdoms. Sir Henry Clinton, who followed Howe as Commander-in-Chief in America, and who succeeded to the inheritance of all his blunders and negligences, regarded the wrath and distrust engendered by the lamentable occurrences in New Jersey as the most hopeless feature in the impossible situation which was left for him to encounter. "Unless," he wrote, "we would refrain from plunder, we had no business to take up winter-quarters in a district we wish to preserve loyal. The Hessians introduced it."

That was a point which has never been disputed Writers of all parties and of both nations, and eye-witnesses of every profession and calling, — whether they wore a red coat, or buff and blue, or the drab of a Quaker, or the sombre garb of a clergyman, — united

in maintaining that our foreign stipendiaries were the
earliest, and incomparably the most flagrant, offenders
against the dictates of honesty and compassion. This
grave allegation, so far from being refuted, has not
even been combated. No counter-case was so much as
attempted to be made out on behalf of the German
soldiery; and the explanation of that silence is very
simple. When a German prince had sent troops to
America, it was to him that the world looked as the
natural guardian and vindicator of the military honour
of his own subjects; but he, and his courtiers and ministers, did not conceive that military honour had been
in any way tarnished by anything which our auxiliaries
had done in New Jersey. Indeed a Hessian or Wal-
decker, who was lucky enough to find himself the temporary autocrat of a wealthy American homestead,
would have been regarded by his friends at home, and
especially by his presumptive heirs, as wanting in common-sense and family feeling if he had neglected to
make the very utmost of his facilities. Robert Morris
wrote to France that, according to information which
reached him, the British troops were restrained from
pillage; but that the Hessians and other foreigners
looked upon plunder as the right of war, and indiscriminately robbed all civilians with whom they came in
contact. Such is the testimony placed on record by a
leading statesman of the Revolution; and the same
charge was urged, with far greater severity of denunciation, by Englishmen who had a stronger grievance
against their German allies than any which could be
alleged even by an American [1]

For the conduct of those allies not only discredited
and weakened the British cause, but it inflicted upon
our nation a still deeper injury by impairing the moral
tone, and relaxing the discipline, of the British army.[2]

---

[1] Robert Morris to the American Commissioners in France; December 21, 1776.

[2] "It was scarcely possible that the devastation and disorders, practised
by the Hessians, should not operate in some degree by their example upon

Before very long, in the ranks of that army, the inevitable contagion of remunerative and unpunished licence generated a constantly increasing number of marauders. And yet those Englishmen, who followed the bad example of their German comrades, imitated them but tamely, and with half a heart. A Pennsylvanian Whig, — whose mind was perfectly impartial as between the nationalities which composed the Royal army, and who had disagreeably advantageous opportunities for watching their respective methods of proceeding, — observed that the Hessians were conspicuous by their cruelty and avidity, but that a mixture of generosity, and a tinge of commiseration, were noticeable features in the most lawless of the British soldiers.[1] One of our officers, who had been made prisoner with Burgoyne, in the course of his captivity slept at the mansion of a Jersey planter, who, Loyalist as he was, had suffered like others during the invasion and occupation of his native province in December 1776. The English depredators, (so this gentleman told his guest,) only pilfered chickens and pigs; but the Hessians went into houses, broke open wardrobes and drawers, and took away silver plate, clothes, and any object, — small or large, light or heavy, — which would tempt a pawnbroker. He related that he saw some Germans enter a house which had been abandoned by the owner, in which had been left an eight-day clock, and a few tables and chairs. He shortly afterwards observed one of the soldiers come out of the house with the works of the clock, the pendulum, and all the leaden weights. This very considerable load, "in addition to his knapsack and accoutrements, the fellow had near twenty miles to carry to New York,

the British troops It would have been difficult to have punished enormities on the one side, which were practised without reserve or apprehension on the other. Every successful deviation from order and discipline in war is certainly and speedily followed by others still greater." "History of Europe" in the *Annual Register* for 1777; chapter 1.

[1] The Common-place Book of William Rawle, (the elder,) dated October 12, 1781, an extract from which has been published by the Historical Society of Pennsylvania.

where the most he could possibly get for it would be three or four dollars."[1]   A common musketeer had nowhere to pack his acquisitions except on his own shoulders, unless he could steal a horse; but there was no limit to the rapacity of his Colonel, who would not find the German Quartermasters inexorable if he had occasion to ask for the loan of one of King George's baggage-waggons.   The Hessian brigades, (according to a British writer of the day,) at length became so encumbered with spoil, and so anxious for its preservation, that it grew to be a great impediment to their military operations.[2]

Our warlike annals provide a memorable example of the policy which a great general, who was likewise a true statesman, would have pursued under circumstances so fraught with scandal and the gravest public danger. Towards the close of the year 1813 Lord Wellington crossed the Bidassoa, and assailed Napoleon within his own borders.   A very large part of the force, on which he relied for the successful prosecution of that final enterprise which was to crown and consummate the long series of his splendid exertions, consisted of Spanish troops who, under his sedulous care, had at length attained to a respectable point of martial efficacy. Unfortunately those troops, now that their turn had come, not unnaturally thought themselves justified in exacting a payment on account of that terrible score which had been run up by the French during their protracted occupation of the Peninsula.   As soon as the Spaniards were on Gallic soil they began to plunder; and the certain consequences forthwith ensued.   Peasants were scared away; supplies no longer flowed into the provision-markets of the English army; and Wellington foresaw that, unless he could prevent rapine, he must forego the hope, (which was very dear to him,) of being regarded by a large part of the French popu-

---

[1] *Travels through the Interior Parts of America;* London, 1791; Vol. III., Letter 58.

[2] "History of Europe;" *Annual Register* for 1777.

lation as their deliverer from a grinding military tyranny. The course which he followed is described by Sir William Napier in the language of manly approbation. " He put to death all the Spanish marauders whom he could take in the act, and then, with many reproaches, and despite the discontent of their generals, forced the whole to withdraw into their own country. Morillo's division alone remained with the army. These decisive proceedings, marking the lofty character of the man, proved not less politic than resolute. The French people immediately returned, and, finding the strictest discipline preserved, and all things paid for, adopted an amicable intercourse with the invader." Wellington's action was beyond all question wise and expedient; but in taking that action he was mainly guided by the primal and spontaneous impulses of a high-spirited gentleman, which before everything else he was In a letter addressed to some of the Spanish generals he commented on the wickedness of a system of spoliation. There was much, (so he went on to write,) which he could say against such a system from a political point of view; but it was unnecessary, because, careless whether he commanded a large or a small army, he was resolved that it should obey him, and should not pillage.

In the autumn of 1812 Wellington had been seriously, — and, as some of his generals thought, unduly and even unjustly, — dissatisfied by the symptoms of laxity and insubordination which he detected among his troops during the retreat from Burgos. He sent to England for a lawyer of established character, and great ability and industry, to fill the post of Judge Advocate in the Peninsular army. He admitted this gentleman to his friendship and familiarity, with the result, and doubtless with the intention, of securing the respect and confidence of military men for an official whose functions, however necessary, were apt to be unpopular and invidious; and, amid all his vast and urgent occupations, before confirming or remitting a sentence, he read through the evidence which had been given at the Courts-

martial.[1]   Timely severity, exercised with discerning
judgement and minute attention by a leader who once a
month was winning a brilliant victory, soon restored discipline to a perfection which satisfied even Lord Wellington.
By the time the British crossed the Pyrenees, a single
friendly, though very decided, word of admonition from
his lips was a sufficient check upon any tendency to
excesses and disorder.[2]   Officers and soldiers alike had
caught the spirit of their chief.   A captain in the
Ninety-fifth Rifle Regiment, which formed part of the
famous Light division, was accompanied into France
by his wife, — a Spanish girl of family, whom he had
rescued from the sack of Badajos.   He was afterwards
known as Sir Harry Smith of Ferozeshah and Aliwal;
and she gave her name to a very celebrated town in
South Africa.   In one French village the young couple
were hospitably entertained by a widow, who brought

[1] *Private Journals of Francis Seymour Larpent, Deputy Assistant
Judge Advocate General to the Army in Spain*, London, 1853
   "Lord Wellington," wrote Larpent, "told me that I kept him up reading Courts-martial until twelve o'clock at night, or one in the morning,
and this every night." "His papers," (the Judge Advocate says elsewhere,) "had increased upon him in his five days' absence ; and, when
I went in with a great bundle to add to them, he put his hands before his
eyes and said, 'Put them on that table, and do not say anything about
them now.'" The first of these entries is dated halfway between the battle
of the Nivelle, and the battle of St Pierre.   On the second occasion Wellington had been away from head-quarters, conducting some very critical
manoeuvres with Soult for an opponent.   It is difficult to imagine General
Howe spending his nights in such employment during an interval in the
military operations.
   [2] After the first affair which took place in France, the prisoners were
sent to the rear in the charge of a young lieutenant, who met the Commander-in-Chief during the march back to camp.   "Halloa, sir," said
Wellington ; "where did you get those fellows ?" "In France," replied
the subaltern, "Colonel Colborne's brigade took them." "How the
devil do you know it was France ?" "Because I saw a lot of our fellows
coming into the column with pigs and poultry, which we had not on the
Spanish side." Wellington soon contrived to see General Colborne, and
told him that, although his brigade had even more than usually distinguished themselves, they must respect the property of the country.   Colborne said the most he could in defence of his men ; which amounted
to something.   "Aye! Aye!" said his Lordship.   "Stop it in future,
Colborne." And stopped it was. *Memoirs of Lieutenant-General Sir
Harry Smith*, Vol. I., chapter xiv.

forth in their honour a choice basin of Sèvres porce-
lain. At their next stopping-place this object of art
appeared on their breakfast table; and their soldier-
servant, when questioned, admitted that he had thought
it too pretty to be left behind them. The lady at once
ordered out her horse and groom; rode thirty miles
through a hostile country swarming with stragglers;
and came back late at night after having restored the
piece of china to the rightful owner. "The story,"
said her husband, "got wind; and the next day every
officer in the Division loaded her with praise."

If Wellington could have commanded in America in
the year 1776, it may confidently be asserted that, within
ten days after Fort Washington fell, he would have
been across the Delaware, which was not more of a
river than the Douro,[1] and some very high-placed officers would already have been on their way back to
Germany in disgrace, beneath the hatches of a return
transport. A political opponent, generously attempting to defend Howe from the charge of indifference to
crime and outrage, pleaded that he could not venture
to hazard the success of the war, so far from England,
and in such precarious and critical circumstances, by
quarreling with auxiliaries who were nearly as numerous
as his own forces.[2] But the distance from home, and
the important issues dependent on the campaign, were
so many additional reasons why the Commander-in-Chief
should insist upon being the absolute master in his own
household. Howe was so deferential towards his foreign
lieutenants, and so heedless of his personal obligations,
that he took no effective measures for the protection
even of those Loyalists to whom his honour, and that of
his brother, had been pledged. The local population,
without distinction of party, or regard for political services and merits, was delivered over to the greed and

[1] The Douro at Oporto was something more than three hundred yards,
and the Delaware at Trenton something less than a thousand feet, from
bank to bank.
[2] "History of Europe" in the *Annual Register*, 1777.

insolence of the Hessians. "Neither age nor sex, Whig or Tory, is spared. Indiscriminate ruin attends every person they met with Children, old men, and women, left without a blanket to cover them ; doors and windows broke to pieces, the houses uninhabitable, and the people without provisions. As a proof of their regard and favour to their friends and wellwishers, they yesterday burned the elegant house of Daniel Cox Esquire, of Trenton Ferry, who has been their constant advocate, and the supporter of Toryism in that part of the country."[1] Ever since the days of Tilly and Wallenstein, — and more recently, when Frederic was over-running Saxony, and when his own dominions were being ravaged by the Cossacks, — robbery and devastation had been familiar inflictions to the inhabitants of Germany. But this very short taste of the Thirty Years' War was a dose altogether too strong for an English-speaking people. Theirs was a race which did not breed willing and passive victims, but men who fought in defence of home and family more readily and fiercely even than for cause and country From that time forward, whenever a State was menaced with invasion, the memories of those winter months which the Hessians spent in New Jersey seldom failed to rally the manhood of the whole country-side to the standards of the Revolution.

[1] Letter in the *American Archives* of December 1776. Mr. Daniel Cox retired to New York, where he helped to found the Board of Loyalist Refugees, which consisted of representatives from the different provinces in America. He was placed in the Chair, " to deprive him of the opportunity of speaking, as he has the gift of saying little in many words " His property in New Jersey and Pennsylvania was confiscated after the war, and he died in England. *Sabine's American Loyalists.*

CHAPTER XXII

CHARLES LEE.   THE REVOLUTION AT BAY

THE Americans, for the moment, had the Delaware as a protection against the invader; but their general knew that for himself and his army it was not a reprieve, but at the most a respite.   Washington reported to his Government that the British intended for Philadelphia. All military men, (he wrote,) were agreed that the line of a river could not be made good for any length of time against a superior force; and the troops that he commanded were far less numerous than those which were opposed to him.   His little handful was daily decreasing by sickness; and the loss of Philadelphia, — an event which would be "severely felt by the common cause, and would wound the heart of every virtuous American," — could only be averted by the prompt, willing, and unsparing exertions of the people.   He had counted upon those exertions; and he confessed himself cruelly disappointed.   The inhabitants of New Jersey, either from fear or disaffection, had with few exceptions refused to take the field against the invader, and even on those who came forward very little dependence was to be placed   Experience, (so he definitely stated,) had brought home to his mind that to rely upon the militia was a perilous, and might ere long prove to be a fatal, delusion [1]

Even so, however, Washington ought not to have been at the end of his resources; for there lay within easy reach of him a powerful body of Continental regulars upon whose services he had every title to reckon.

---

[1] Washington's letters of December 12, 1776, to the President of Congress, and to Governor Trumbull of Connecticut.

When, early in November, he transported a portion of his troops into New Jersey, he left General Lee on the east of the river, in charge of a force fully equal to that which marched under his own immediate command. He drew up for that officer's guidance a paper of instructions in which the closing, and the governing, sentence was to the effect that, if the Jerseys were invaded by the main part of the British army, Lee was to come to the rescue with all possible despatch. Within the next ten days the pair of forts, which were called after the two American generals, had successively been captured; nothing short of a concentration of his whole available power could enable Washington even to attempt to hold his own against Cornwallis; and he requested Lee at once to cross the Hudson, bringing all his Continental regiments with him. Four days afterwards, in the secure belief that his order was in course of being obeyed, Washington wrote another most important letter which was intended to meet Lee on his way southwards. But time flew; there were no signs of the approaching reinforcement, nor any satisfactory assurance that Lee had so much as broken up his camp on the Westchester peninsula; and the Commander-in-Chief could no longer refrain from sending a message which expressed anxiety, and indicated a rising anger. "My former letters," Washington wrote, "were so full and explicit as to the necessity of your marching as early as possible that it is unnecessary to add more on that head. I confess I expected you would have been sooner in motion." [1]

It might have been thought that such an appeal, indited by such a hand, at a crisis when the very existence of the nation was so gravely imperilled, would have overcome the irresolution of the most unstable and the most perverse among mankind. But Charles Lee, who in his own estimation was made in no common

[1] Instructions to Major-General Lee, November 10, 1776. Washington to Lee, Hackensac, November 10; Newark, November 23, and again November 27. Washington to the President of Congress, November 23

mould, considered himself absolved from all ordinary rules, and even from those laws which constitute the code of military and civic honour.   His head, which never could have been a wise one, had been turned by early successes, and was at present kept in a state of effervescence by a great deal of extravagant, and in some cases rather interested, flattery.   He was an Englishman of good family; a member of the class which in the eighteenth century almost monopolised the opportunities for advancement and distinction Lee was an Ensign at sixteen, and he became a Colonel at thirty.[1]   In Portugal, under Burgoyne, he performed a brilliant feat of arms which won for him the favour and intimacy of his general, and, after the Peace of Paris in 1763, he retired on half-pay, and spent the next few years in the pursuit of bustle and notoriety in whatever quarter of the world events were stirring.   Constitutionally unable to stay long in one place, or to remain for many months together in the same mind, Lee rambled over Europe, following that which, (according to his own account,) was the career of a paladin, but which, in the view taken by his matter-of-fact contemporaries, very closely resembled the life of an adventurer.   He accepted service as a Major General of King Stanislaus, and fought in aid of the Russians, and against the Turks and the Confederates, in those confused and aimless hostilities which ushered in the first partition of Poland   He is said to have been concerned in a series of desperate, and even mortal, duels.   But what he writes about himself is not so told as to conciliate

---

[1] According to his official biography, Lee obtained a commission in the army as a child of eleven ; but an unsupported statement, drawn from that work, is not sufficient authority.   Lee's mother was a Bunbury of Suffolk, daughter of the third baronet.   The sixth baronet married Lady Sarah Lennox.   " You ask me," wrote Lady Sarah in the summer of 1775, " what I say to my cousin Lee.   Why, I say it is the element for *boiling water*, and, as I dare say he persuades himself he is acting right, I don't pity him for falling in a cause he thinks glorious, as I fear he will erelong I shall be very sorry for him ; for he has many good and great qualities to make up for his turbulent spirit and vanity, which, to be sure, are his weak side.   But everybody has their faults."

belief; and fate allotted him exactly the biographer whom he deserved. The narrative compiled by the editor of his papers and correspondence is inaccurate, insincere, and vague to nebulosity.[1] There is a strange contrast beween the reputation which enveloped Charles Lee during what may be called the mythical and legendary period of his history, and the figure that he presented after his actions began to be watched, and his words noted, by the hard-headed observers who surrounded him in America.

From the earliest days of the Stamp Act Lee declared himself against George Grenville's policy. In 1767 he wrote from Warsaw to a nobleman of his acquaintance, condemning what he described as the abomination of disfranchising three millions of people of all the rights of men, for the gratification of the revenge "of a blundering knavish Secretary of State, and a scoundrel Attorney General."[2] When war was imminent, Lee had an opinion on the merits of the controversy which, for him, was genuine and long-lived, and he likewise was a disappointed man, with a grievance against his own Government A pertinacious, and anything but a fastidious, place-hunter, he had of late years got nothing except a grant of twenty thousand acres in Florida; to which shadowy benefit he would have vastly preferred a patent place bringing in a hundred solid guineas at the end of every quarter. He had purchased, on borrowed money, a small landed property in the colony of Virginia; but he was not a colonist; nor was he any relation, (as every American takes care to assure himself,) of Light Horse Harry Lee, the right arm of General Greene in the Carolinas, — or of that magnificent soldier who, forty years ago, led the Confederate

---

[1] *Memoirs of the Life of the late Charles Lee, Esquire,* Lieutenant-Colonel of the Forty-fourth Regiment, Colonel in the Portuguese service, Major-General and Aide-de-Camp to the King of Poland, and Second in Command in the Service of the United States of America during the Revolution. Dublin, 1792.

[2] General Lee to Lord Thanet; May 4, 1767.

army in the War of the Secession to many victories, and some glorious defeats.

When in 1775 Charles Lee declared himself for the Revolution, it was a strong step for a British officer to take, and he did not under-estimate the value of the support which he bestowed upon the party of his adoption. Lee never concealed his belief that he brought a large contribution of social prestige, and military talent, to the assistance of people who were lamentably devoid of both. He set a very high price on his personal sacrifices and his professional accomplishments. While better men, in that season of public distress and denudation, were spending largely of their own, and accepting nothing from the Federal Treasury, Lee exacted thirty thousand dollars as compensation for the loss of his estate in England, (which was no rich or unencumbered possession,) and for the surrender of the half-pay which he drew as a commissioned officer in the Royal army. He expected that, so soon as he declared himself an adherent of the Revolution, he would be hailed as Commander-in-Chief by acclamation; but the gratitude of Congress, although excessive, stopped short of fatuity. Lee was included in the earliest list of Major Generals; a compliment which he accepted with the studied indifference of one who five years previously had received that title from the hands of a European monarch.

Lee's disdain of American soldiership was as unbounded as his appreciation of his own genius and capacity. He had composed a treatise on a theme which always has had a peculiar attraction for bad generals with facile pens, — the nature and importance of the military *coup d'œil*. That was a gift of which, when subjected to a singularly decisive test at the battle of Monmouth Court House, he proved to be as utterly destitute as any theorist that ever wore a sword; but he none the less sneered at his colleagues behind their backs, and lectured them to their faces, about the arts of strategy and fortification, with a profuse assortment of technical verbiage, and in a tone of insufferable superiority. Every month that passed, his arrogance and pedantry grew more and more distasteful to men who were making themselves into good officers by applying to the business of war the sound sense, and honest purpose, which had already brought them prosperity in the civil affairs of life. It was not to be expected that a merchant or a farmer, who had reluctantly put on a uniform because his country was in danger, should relish being informed that one of his comrades, whose antecedents had been exactly the same as his, was an ignorant bumpkin "who did not know a sandbag from a *chevaux-de-frise,*" and such criticism would be even less acceptable when it related to his own deficiencies, and was addressed directly to himself. Lee had been in chief command at Charleston when Sir Peter Parker was so roughly handled in June 1776. The repulse of the British squadron was mainly due to Colonel Moultrie, who knew the land and water of old; who was acquainted with the character and capabilities of the local troops; and who, a Carolinian himself, extracted from a Carolinian garrison the best fighting which they had to give. It was Moultrie who assisted in building, and displayed rare skill and resolution in defending, that fort on Sullivan's Island which still bears his name. Lee's part in the affair was to mar, and meddle, and scold; until his gallant and blunt subordinate contrived to make him understand that a competent and zealous officer, when the enemy is within gun-shot, does not relish being catechised like a cadet in a military academy who has fallen behindhand in his course of studies.[1]

---

[1] " Does your engineer understand what is the necessary degree of *talus* for the traverse in the fort? If I recommend the construction of an advanced *flèche* on the right flank, will he comprehend it? For heaven's sake, Sir, as you are in an important post, exert yourself. When you issue orders, suffer them not to be trifled with. I expect that you enforce the execution of whatever is necessary for the honor and safety of your garrison." After pages of this ludicrously misplaced objurgation, Lee suddenly remembered that there were limits to the docility of a Southern gentleman, and apologised to Moultrie for his prolixity and didactic manner. He would have done better to tear up his letter; but he was of those who cannot endure to waste a literary composition.

Lee did not confine his strictures to American generals. At a moment when, overtaken by the consequences of his faults, he had ample food for reflection on his own account, he found leisure to compile an elaborate essay on the imperfections of Sir William Howe.[1] As an executive soldier, (he said,) Howe was all fire and activity, brave and cool as Julius Cæsar. But he was seldom left to himself. Never had poor mortal, thrust into high station, been surrounded by such fools and scoundrels. "M'Kensey, Balfour, Galloway, were his counsellors; they urged him to all acts of harshness. They were his scribes. All the damned stuff which was issued to the astonished world was theirs. I believe he scarcely ever read the letters he signed." That, at all events, was a charge to which Lee himself was not amenable. He and the officers of his staff were a happy family together. Although very few military people were exactly to his fancy, he never was dissatisfied with his aides-de-camp,[2] and they, on their side, had easy times under a chief who, (if literary style is any guide,) must undoubtedly have penned or drafted every line of his own correspondence. For Lee's official despatches, and his private letters, are all in the same characteristic, and, (most fortunately,) inimitable manner. His accents, always strident, touched their shrillest note wherever he saw reason to apprehend that Congress would recognise the deserts of another as above his own. "Great God!

---

[1] Lee's *Character of General Howe*, written in June 1778. The author was then under arrest, and awaiting a Court-martial.

[2] Lee gave General Gates a glowing account of the behaviour of his own Staff during the bombardment of Charleston. "Old Jenifer and little Nourse strutted like crows in a gutter. The fire was, I assure you, very hot. This affair is only the prelude to a more serious one, the event of which the great God of battles only knows. I mean the great and universal God, not the partial God of the Jews."

Lee's religious views kept turning up in very odd places. "I desire most earnestly," (so ran a provision in his Will,) "that I may not be buried in any church or church-yard, or within a mile of any Presbyterian or Anabaptist meeting-house; for, since I have resided in this country, I have kept so much bad company when living, that I do not chuse to continue it when dead."

Is it come to this?   Have I not once already waived my
military claims in deference to the whim and partiality
of some of your members?   Did I not consent to serve
under an old churchwarden, of whom you had conceived
a most extravagant and ridiculous opinion?   Your eyes
were at length opened, and Deacon Ward returned to
his proper occupation, and would you now a second
time load me with a similar disgrace?"

That passage was a fair specimen of the intemperance
and impertinence with which Charles Lee discussed
questions of military promotion.   He did not regard the
native American officers as his equals.   He scoffed and
railed at the sober and religious among their number;
he was seldom a guest at the rather coarse and boisterous festivities in which others of them were well satisfied
to indulge; and he was accused of not being ready to
show, under his own roof or tent, sufficiently frequent
examples of a more refined hospitality.[1]   With some justice, but extraordinary indiscretion, he protested against
the tendency of Americans to bedeck themselves with
titles of office.   He bade his companions remark how
much more true dignity there was in the simplicity of
address which prevailed among the ancient Romans; —
how majestically Decimus Brutus imperator, and Caius
Marcellus consul, sounded as compared to His Excellency Major-General Noodle.[2]   Lee himself pointedly
affected the English mode of dispensing with the desig-

---

[1] Captain Graydon, the author of the *Pennsylvanian Memoirs*, was present at a barbecue; an entertainment which consisted in a hog roasted
whole, with Madeira wine in proportion. Most principal officers of the
army were there; but not Washington, nor any of his staff. "Neither,"
(wrote Graydon,) "was General Lee of the company. He had been invited; but had drily replied, that 'he did not like barbecues.' In fact,
they are seldom a very Attic entertainment   The party was joyous, and
pretty full of liquor, and I had the chagrin to observe that the drummer
and fifer who made music for them, and were deserters from the enemy,
were sneering at some of the gentlemen, who did not entirely preserve the
dignity of their station, and were by much too liberal in the reciprocal use
of the term 'General.'"

[2] Charles Lee to his Excellency Patrick Henry, jun., Governor of Vir
ginia, July 29, 1776.

nations of military rank in familiar conversation, and
habitually spoke of "Mr. Wolfe," "Mr. Howe," and
" my Lord Cornwallis " He fondly hankered after the
lost popularity which he had once enjoyed in the Royal
army.   He reluctantly began to perceive, (a conviction
which, strange to say, was only gradually borne in upon
him,) that, when he crossed over into the American camp,
he had irretrievably forfeited the goodwill of gentlemen
who still bore his Majesty's commission.   He had made
his choice, and he could not have it both ways; but he
never could prevail upon himself to acquiesce frankly in
that inexorable fact.   While acting the part of an enemy
to Great Britain, he more or less consciously played to
the British public ; and his eagerness to renew friendly
relations with British officers at length conducted him
up to, and over, the brink of actual treason to America.[1]
If he had had Arnold's sinister courage, and his power
of concentrated, sustained, and passionate resentment,
he would probably have taken a step similar to that
which resulted in Arnold's ruin.   Lee was saved by his
poorer, rather than by his finer, qualities from the destiny
which otherwise might have befallen him   The catastrophe that terminated his career was humiliating and
crushing ; but he was spared from the less tolerable fate
of a detected traitor, who had escaped to live out the
fag-end of his life in exile.   A fine writer has remarked
that into the story of Arnold there enters the element
of awe and pity which is an essential part of real tragedy;
but that the story of Lee, from the first act to the last,
is little more than a vulgar melodrama.[2]

[1] Fiske's *American Revolution ;* chapters vii. and x.   Tyler's *Literary
History,* note at the end of chapter xviii.   Wharton's *Diplomatic Correspondence,* Vol. II., pages 68 to 70, in the note ; and also section xi.
of the introduction to the work.

[2] *The American Revolution,* by John Fiske, chapter xiv.   In August
1778 Lee was tried for disobeying orders in not attacking the enemy at
Monmouth Court House, and for making " an unnecessary, disorderly, and
shameful retreat "   He was found guilty and sentenced to be suspended
from his command.   That was the last which was heard of him as a soldier.
" It would have been impossible," (Mr. Fiske writes,) " for a man of strong
military instincts to have relaxed his clutch upon an enemy in the field, as

That was the man on whom, during three critical weeks, the safety of America depended.   At no period of his career did he act, or write, more entirely in character.   On the twenty-first of November Washington directed General Heath to occupy the passes on the road to Albany with the whole of his division, and called upon Lee at once to rejoin the main army with all his Continental battalions.   It was an order that brooked no delay, and admitted no doubt whatsoever as to the meaning; but Lee preferred to construe it in a sense which favoured the views of his own personal ambition. He informed one of his correspondents that he had been summoned southwards across the Hudson, but that he regarded the message as dictated by "absolute insanity;" and he desired Heath to detach two thousand of his troops, and send them, with a Brigadier General, to the assistance of Washington.   Heath courteously represented that it was impossible for him to neglect the Commander-in-Chief's specific instructions, a copy of which he enclosed for Lee's inspection , and Lee thereupon, piqued and baffled, fell to arguing the point in harsh and overbearing terms.   " I perceive, Sir," he wrote, "that you have formed an opinion to yourself that, should General Washington remove to the Straits of Magellan, the instructions he left with you on a particular occasion have invested you with a command independent of any other superiors.   I, of course, command on this side the water.   For the future, I must and will be obeyed."   In thus addressing Heath he mistook his man.   Eighteen months previously that brave and modest veteran had willingly handed over the chief command to Washington, in the persuasion that it was more honourable to obey, than to out-rank, a greater soldier than himself ; and the answers which he now sent to Lee's bullying requisitions were by no

Lee did at the battle of Monmouth. If Arnold had been there that day, with his head never so full of treason, an irresistible impulse would doubtless have led him to attack the enemy tooth and nail ; and the treason would have waited till the morrow."

means wanting in the natural eloquence which springs from good sense and right feeling. And so, having come off second-best on paper, Lee determined to try what could be effected by the magic of his bodily presence. On the thirtieth of November, — a full week after the date on which he ought by rights to have reported himself at Washington's head-quarters, — he appeared at Peekskill; announced to General Heath his intention of carrying off two New England regiments; and commanded that they should be got ready for the march. Heath peremptorily forbade his Deputy Adjutant General to take any action in the matter; and then, turning towards Lee, he expressed himself in language that there was no mistaking. "Sir," he said, "if you issue orders here which will break those positive ones which I have received, I pray you to do it completely yourself, and not draw me, or any of my family, in as partners in the guilt." Those old-fashioned words went straight to the mark. Lee stepped into the piazza, and observed to an officer that General Heath was in the right; and early next morning he withdrew his demand for the two regiments, and betook himself back to his own camp at White Plains.[1]

From that camp, save and except for the purpose of inciting a colleague to disobedience, Charles Lee had no present intention of stirring. In a letter to the American Adjutant General he adduced certain strategical arguments in defence of his refusal to move southwards; although, as he candidly admitted, the weight of those arguments was perhaps overbalanced

---

[1] Heath's conduct received complete approbation in a letter written from Newark, on the twenty-fifth of November, by Colonel Harrison, aide-de-camp and secretary of Washington. "In respect to the troops intended to come to this quarter, his Excellency never meant that they should be from your division. He has wrote General Lee since so fully and explicitly that any misapprehensions he may have been under at first must be now done away. He will most probably have reached Peek's Kill before now with his division, and be pushing to join us." If such was the expectation which prevailed among the Head-quarters Staff, they had still something to learn on the subject of General Lee.

E 2

by the consideration that his own presence with the main army would do something to supplement Washington's inefficiency. "To confess the truth," he wrote, "I really think our Chief will do better with me than without me." Lee had no substantial excuse for his inaction. If he had punctually and expeditiously advanced along the route which Washington had minutely indicated to him,[1] he would have encountered no difficulty whatsoever. The distance between White Plains and Newark was almost exactly the same as that which was covered in twenty-six hours by General Craufurd and the Light Division, when they marched to the support of Sir Arthur Wellesley at Talavera. But the obstacles which prevented Lee from going whither duty called him were moral, and not material, — within him, and not in front of him. To his immense satisfaction he found himself invested with a separate command ; and he was fully determined that that command should be independent, until in the order of events it became supreme. Washington, and half his forces, had already been defeated ; and America would best be served by keeping from him the other half of an army which he was totally incapable of directing. That was Lee's diagnosis of the military situation; and he was at small pains to conceal his opinions and projects. He openly asserted, — even before hearers whom such expressions affected with contemptuous disgust, — that General Washington was not fit to order about a sergeant's guard, and that the Continental Troops, under such leadership, could not hope to withstand the British Grenadiers and Light Infantry. The day, according to Lee's anticipations, was close at hand when Washington's incompetency would be universally acknowledged ; and on that day he himself was prepared to step forward and save the country   National gratitude would then be the reward of that prescient general who, at the risk of his own reputation, had preserved a body of fine troops, intact and in good heart, from the rout

[1] Washington to Lee ; Newark, November 24, 1776.

and demoralisation which must inevitably overtake the rest of the American forces. A similar thought, justly or unjustly, was believed to have governed Bazaine's course of policy in the Franco-German war of 1870, and all France united to stigmatise that Marshal as a traitor. In November 1776 Lee already recognised, with serene complacency, the light in which his own conduct was liable to be regarded. "There are times," he wrote, "when we must commit treason against the laws of the State ; and the present crisis demands this brave, virtuous, kind of treason."[1]

In the meanwhile he could not deny himself the luxury of addressing the civil authorities throughout the States as if he was Commander-in-Chief already. He inundated America with his imperious advice, and his unsparing and most offensive criticism. He wrote to the authorities of Massachusetts recommending that the stores should be evacuated from the magazines at Boston, as the city was in danger of an attack by the enemy's fleet. He informed them that the officers of their provincial regiments were lacking in spirit, integrity, and public virtue; and that, if the men ran away in action, it was on account of the example set them by their superiors. He warned the Governor of Rhode Island that no confidence could be placed in New England generals The highest trusts, (he complained,) were committed to those least qualified to exercise them ; although it was an axiom in warfare that "theory joined to practice, or a heaven-born genius," constituted the only title for a command in the field.

[1] It is instructive to compare Lee's military action in December 1776 with a letter which, not long before, he had taken upon himself to send to Congress. "For Heaven's sake rouse yourselves ! For Heaven's sake let ten thousand men be immediately stationed somewhere about Trenton ! In my opinion the whole depends upon it " That was written early in October, when the armies were manœuvring on the other side of the Hudson, and when there was not a British regiment within eighty miles of Trenton. Two months afterwards, — when Trenton and Philadelphia itself were in imminent risk of capture, — the author of this exhortation contrived, as far as in him lay, that no reinforcements whatever should reach the seat of danger.

He flatly refused to obey an order which had come to
him through the agency of Nathanael Greene, — whose
sash he was not fit to tie.   Most astonishing of all was
the correspondence which he exchanged with Washington's own Adjutant General.   Colonel Reed wrote to
assure Lee that the safety of the army, and the liberties
of America, rested upon him, and upon him alone.
"You have decision," the Colonel said; "a quality often
wanted in minds otherwise valuable.   Oh, General!
An indecisive mind is one of the greatest misfortunes
which can befall an army.   How often have I lamented
it this campaign!"   Lee, in reply, accepted the tribute,
and concurred in deploring that fatal indecision which
in war was a much greater disqualification than stu-
pidity, or even want of personal courage.   Lee's answer,
which externally had been made up in the form of a
public despatch, was opened, in official course, by the
aide-de-camp on duty, and placed beneath the eyes of
the Commander-in-Chief.   Washington had a strong
regard for his Adjutant General, and set much value
upon his abilities.   A civilian of mature age, Reed had
surrendered a most influential position at home, and, at
the earnest request of the Commander-in-Chief, had accepted service in the Staff.   The confidences which,
in a weak moment, he had bestowed upon Charles Lee,
were suggested by intense anxiety for the distresses and
perils of the cause, and were expressed with the freedom habitual to a politician of long, and high, standing
who had not schooled himself to military reticence and
self-repression.   Of this Washington was well aware;
and he found no difficulty in ignoring, and forgiving, a
transient flash of unfriendliness towards himself which
was not accompanied by disloyalty to the Republic [1]

[1] It must be remembered, on Reed's behalf, that he was frank and bold
in direct remonstrance against what he regarded as timid and dilatory
strategy.   On the twenty-second of December, 1776, he sent Washington
an appeal couched in vigorous, and even passionate, language.   "Our
affairs," he wrote, "are hastening fast to ruin if we do not retrieve them
by some happy event.   Delay with us is now equal to a total defeat   . .
Pardon the freedom I have used.   The love of my country; a wife and

Washington cared little what gossip might be circu lated about his indecision of character, if only he could have got hold of those two brigades of Continental infantry which still were idling at White Plains. On the first of December, in an urgent despatch, the Commander-in-Chief certified General Lee that, from information not to be doubted, the enemy were making for Philadelphia. "The force I have with me," he declared, "is infinitely inferior in numbers, and such as cannot give, or promise, the least successful opposition. I must entreat you to hasten your march as much as possible, or your arrival may be too late to answer any valuable purpose." That message, which breathed a perceptible flavour of an impending Court-martial, brought its recipient to a semblance of compliance. In the course of the next two days he crossed the Hudson, and began to loiter and dawdle down-country in the direction of Trenton; marking the very short stages of his southward progress by epistles which were each of them more absurd and improper than the last.

A week after Lee started on his expedition, (and by that time he had travelled barely five-and-thirty miles,) he informed General Heath, who was anything but a sympathetic confidant, that he was in hopes of reconquering the province of New Jersey, which before his arrival had been at the mercy of the enemy. He was just then full of exhilaration over an unexpected stroke of business which he had done for his own profit and glory. Sir Guy Carleton's retreat to Canada had removed all hostile pressure from the northern quarter. So soon as Washington's entreaty for assistance was

---

four children in the enemy's hands; the respect and attachment I have to you; the ruin and poverty that must attend me, and thousands of others, will plead my excuse for so much freedom." That was an unusual style for a communication addressed by a staff-officer to the general under whom he served; but Washington made full allowance for the emotional nature of a man that he liked, and never ceased to trust There exists a generous testimony to the merits of the Adjutant General, written by his chief a few weeks subsequent to the date of Colonel Reed's own unbe coming correspondence with General Lee *Washington to the President of Congress;* Morristown, January 22, 1776.

conveyed to Albany, General Schuyler responded without
an hour's hesitation, and put in motion such regiments
as he could spare, if regiments they might be called.
The strongest of them had been reduced by hardship
and disease below the size of a couple of companies;
but the soldiers who survived were all the more intent
on being in time to help their countrymen. Enfeebled
in health, and ill supplied with food, in a single week
they accomplished a hundred and thirty miles; until
they reached a neighbourhood where Lee contrived to
lay hands on four out of their seven battalions. He
attached them to his own command, and ordered them
to take their place in his column of march, where they
were thenceforward as completely out of the game as
if they had been intercepted and captured by Lord
Cornwallis. It was a cruel injury to Washington,
whose vexation was aggravated by the triumphant tone
of the despatch in which the unwelcome tidings were
imparted. This addition to his own army, (so Lee
reported with an excruciating air of self-satisfaction,)
enabled him to dispose of five thousand good troops,
full of fight, and glowing with patriotism. He very
soon threw aside the last pretence of subordination.
On the eighth of December he plainly notified to the Committee of Congress that it was no longer his intention
to unite forces with Washington; and the same post
carried the same information to the Commander-in-Chief
himself. "If," (so that letter ran,) "I was not taught
to think that your army was considerably reinforced, I
should immediately join you; but I am assured you are
very strong, and I imagine we can make a better impression by hanging on their rear." On the morning of
that very day Washington, with an attenuated band of
famished and exhausted followers, was making his
escape across the river Delaware in quest of a temporary and precarious refuge from destruction.

Deserted and flouted by his principal lieutenant,
and robbed of half his army, Washington was racked

by solicitude of which no outward traces appeared in his placid features, and his composed and dignified bearing. Brave and patriotic men, who were themselves in the forefront of danger and responsibility, rightly conjectured, from their own sensations, the care and sorrow which underlay that calm exterior. " My heart bleeds for poor Washington. I wish to God that it were possible to lead the fifteen hundred hardy veterans you left with me to your assistance, but for one day. But as that is out of my power I can only wish you success, and assure you that the post you left to my charge shall be maintained." Those words were in a letter addressed to General Gates by Anthony Wayne, the fiery warrior to whose guardianship the great national outpost of Ticonderoga had been committed Washington himself, in his despatches of December 1776, refrained to a noticeable degree from the touches of sadness, and personal vexation, which he sometimes allowed to be observed in him under less trying emergencies. Those despatches were of a multifarious nature, voluminous in bulk, and scrupulously specific in detail; but with never a syllable more than the elucidation of the subject demanded. They contained as little as possible which could discourage colleagues and subordinates who needed all the equanimity and hopefulness that they were able to command Where Washington had occasion to impress upon a correspondent the necessity for instant, and intense, exertion he would sketch the situation in a sentence or two, very sparingly interspersed with adjectives; and that situation was sufficiently formidable without any word-painting [1] During one short moment, in the course of those terrible weeks, he

---

[1] "It is a matter of concern to me that, in my last, I directed you to take back any of the militia designed for the support of the army under my command, and have to request that you will hasten them on with all possible expedition, as I see no other chance of saving Philadelphia, and preventing a fatal blow to America, in the loss of a city from whence so many of our resources are drawn" Washington to Major-General Spencer, December 22, 1776.

unpacked his heart to his younger and favourite
brother, who never allowed a secret entrusted to him
by George Washington to get abroad, whether that
secret referred to facts or to feelings "You can
form," (the General wrote,) "no idea of the perplexity of
my situation. No man, I believe, ever had a greater
choice of difficulties, and less means to extricate himself from them However, under a full persuasion of
the justice of our cause, I cannot entertain an idea that
it will finally sink, though it may remain for some time
under a cloud." [1]

That self-control which the Commander-in-Chief
practised as a duty, and which well became him, was
not to be looked for in writers of the revolutionary
party who held no official position that bound them to
dissimulate their anxiety, and to weigh their phrases.
The agony of the crisis lent to their archaic, and somewhat artificial, rhetoric a note of very genuine power
and passion. The most telling appeals in the pages of
the public journals were addressed to those of their
readers who lived in closest proximity to the scene of
action. What apology, (it was asked,) could Pennsylvanians make to their brethren in Virginia, and South
Carolina, and Massachusetts Bay, who themselves had
repelled the invader from their coasts, if he was
enabled, through local apathy and cowardice, to get
possession of the vitals of the Continent? "Such an
event would render the name of a Pennsylvanian as
infamous as that of an ancient Cappadocian Let
the words of the prophet sound perpetually in our
ears: 'Cursed is he that doeth the work of the
Lord deceitfully, and keepeth back his sword from
blood '" "Should you now," (so ran another passage,) "by a miserable lassitude suffer your exulting
enemy to cry Victory, what must be your miserable
lot? You will be a hissing among the nations, and the
despised of the world. 'He is an American : he dared

---

[1] Letter to John Augustine Washington , Camp, near the Falls of Trenton, December 18, 1776.

not be free,' will be a proverb translated into every language." [1]

These incitements and admonitions were not superfluous; for the fears which pervaded Philadelphia were fast assuming the dimensions of a panic. The Whigs were crestfallen and desponding, and profoundly distrustful of the neighbours among whom they lived. Those numerous and very influential citizens, who had opposed the Declaration of Independence, saw that an opportunity had now arrived for assailing the Revolution with such weapons as, in each respective case, their conscience permitted them to wield The Quakers, with the courage which is never wanting to them, conspired in the face of daylight. Their Meeting for Sufferings, under date of Twelfth Month Twentieth 1776, called upon all the members of their Society to withstand the arbitrary injunctions of men who assumed to themselves the power of compelling others to take part in war, and who imposed tests not warranted by the precepts of Christ, or by the laws of that happy political constitution under which the Friends had long enjoyed tranquillity and peace Other Loyalists, — whose bellicose intentions were not a more serious menace to the American cause than the meek, but invincible, ill-will of the Quakers, — made active preparations to rise in arms as soon as the British should come within striking distance of the Pennsylvanian capital. These people had skated up and down the Delaware, as boys and men, almost every winter of their lives; and they confidently anticipated that the first hard frost would bring Cornwallis and his infantry dry-footed across the river. The condition of the streets was so alarming that General Israel Putnam, whom Washington had placed over the city as military Governor, gave orders that any of the inhabitants who appeared abroad after ten o'clock at night should be arrested and detained. Putnam's ostensible mission was to

[1] Hampden to the Associators of Pennsylvania; Epaminondas to the people of Pennsylvania; November, and December, 1776.

fortify the approaches to the suburbs with a line of earthworks; but the real motive of his appointment was a hope that his vigour and popularity might do something to restore public confidence, — a confidence which there is reason to believe that the old general himself was very far from sharing.[1]   A report had been diligently put about that, rather than surrender Philadelphia to the British, the Continental troops would destroy the town   Washington judged it necessary publicly to refute the story; and, by his direction, Putnam announced that he should consider an attempt to burn the city as a crime of the blackest dye, and would punish capitally, without ceremony, any incendiary who had "the hardiness and cruelty" to engage in such an enterprise.[2]

Scared by the alarm of fire, and by the more imminent probability of a visitation from the Hessians, families of all ranks loaded waggons with their furniture, and fled forth into the comparative security of the rural districts.   Apprehension, and even despair, affected some who ought to have been proof against the contagion; and more especially certain politicians who, ever since Philadelphia was in danger of attack, had been inditing heroic letters, and making very gallant speeches. A great deal had been said and written about those Conscript Fathers who sate in their porches awaiting the irruption of the Gauls; and about the sale of the plot of land on which Hannibal was encamped outside the walls of Rome, — that celebrated auction to which, in the course of the last two thousand years, approving reference has so often been made by people who, had they been alive at the time, would have been the very last to come forward as bidders.   On the tenth of December, Congress solemnly resolved to defend the

---

[1] Ambrose Serle, in a letter to Lord Dartmouth of December 3, 1776, reported some remarks which Putnam, while lodging in the house of a rich New Jersey Loyalist, was said to have made concerning the hopeless situation of the Revolutionary army.

[2] Order of December 13, 1776.

Federal Capital with all the force that could be mustered, and fell valiantly to the work of assembling and organising a garrison. On the eleventh of the month, they invited the several States to appoint, each for itself, a day of fasting and humiliation. During the same sitting they carried a Resolution denouncing as "false and malicious" a rumour that they were about to disperse, or adjourn, from Philadelphia; and they requested the Commander-in-Chief to publish their denial of the calumny in a General Order to his army. Washington declined to adopt their suggestion in a letter marked by admirable good sense, which he certainly did not find cause to regret having written.[1] After another interval of just twenty-four hours, the very few Members of Congress who still were attending to their duties voted an adjournment, and next day transferred themselves southward to Baltimore; leaving Robert Morris, and two others of their number, to act for them in Pennsylvania. Their departure accentuated the terror in the city, and was very ill taken by the army "For God's sake," (asked an indignant Colonel,) "why did you remove from Philadelphia? You have given an invitation to the enemy, and have discovered a timidity that dispirits our friends. A good face among men in power keeps up the spirits of the people, and one cheerful countenance may do wonders. I have run off with complaints, and am led to make them by the damned gloomy countenances seen wherever I go, except among the soldiers."[2]

On the other side in politics soldiers, and civilians as

---

[1] Washington respectfully, but very clearly, explained to the President of Congress why the Members should not have made their staying or going, the subject of a Resolution "Their remaining in, or leaving, Philadelphia must be governed by circumstances and events. If their departure should become necessary, it will be right. On the other hand, if there should not be a necessity for it, they will remain, and their continuance will show the report to be the production of calumny and falsehood" Washington to the President of Congress; Trenton Falls, December 12, 1776

[2] Colonel Cadwalader to Robert Morris, December 15, 1776.

well, wore beaming faces, and were liberal in their
exultation over the prospect of a triumph which now
seemed fairly within their grasp   There had been one
short period of the campaign when the Loyalists were
nervous and uneasy; but, in the main, they had all
along made sure of victory. "The whole say and
desire of the army," (wrote a Queen's Ranger in September,) "is to have the rebels stand their ground; and
the jig will be at an end."   As time went forward, and
the Americans were decidedly worsted, partisans of the
Crown began to speak as if serious fighting was over, and
the hour of retribution had already sounded.   Every
door in New York, behind which there was a family in
sympathy with rebellion, had long ago been marked
with a broad R; and the Tories of the city promised
that an example should soon be made of the inmates.
On the second of December an English field-officer
wrote home that Mr. Washington had been seen retreating with two brigades to Trenton, which he talked of
defending; but that the revolutionists were in such a
panic that no part of New Jersey could hold them, and
it would require very little pressure to make them evacu-
ate Philadelphia   "The Congress," this gentleman
added, "consists now of only seven members; and they
are in such consternation that they know not what to
do.   The two Adamses are in New England, Franklin
has gone to France; Lynch has lost his senses; Rutt-
ledge has gone home disgusted; so that the fools have
lost the assistance of the knaves.   However, should
they embrace the enclosed proclamation, they may yet
escape the halter."   In England it was very generally
believed that the flame of colonial resistance was flicker-
ing out, and might at any moment sink into ashes
Even Horace Walpole, who always read his news in a
light the most unfavourable to the policy of the Cabinet,
allowed that the Americans must submit to such terms
as they could obtain unless France, without reserve or
hesitation, interposed for their benefit.[1]   Edmund Burke

---

[1] Walpole to Mann, December 20, 1776.

knew the Stock Exchange, not altogether from the out-side , and he was already watching for the moment when the collapse of the American cause should be signified to the London world by an upward leap in the price of Consols which would fill the pockets of speculators favoured with private information from Downing Street. Government, (he said,) would no doubt make the fortunes of all their creatures by imparting to them the earliest intelligence.[1]

The sky was very black, and hope had almost died out from the hearts of Americans, when of a sudden the light broke forth in a most unlikely quarter of their gloomy horizon A people observant of anniversaries, — the best of whom retained the old belief that their national welfare and security did not depend on their own exertions, but were in the keeping of a higher power, — might well have marked the thirteenth of December with a white stone in their calendar; for that day was signalised by two events which, to a New Englander of four generations back, must have presented every appearance of special providences. Then, for the first time, General Howe disclosed to those about him his intention of suspending further military operations until the spring came. He distributed the greater part of his army into winter quarters throughout the northern counties of New Jersey, he covered his front with a line of detachments which, during the next fortnight, was admiringly described by military critics as a strong and impenetrable "chain of posts;" and he himself withdrew to New York City, taking Lord Cornwallis with him. Intelligent Loyalists, even such as were not professional soldiers, then and there-after were unanimous in accounting that fatal resolution as the death-blow of their party. American Whigs, — when they came to understand the full consequences of the step which Howe had taken, — were not disposed censoriously to examine his motives for a course of action which was so exactly to their own mind; but

[1] Edmund Burke to Richard Champion ; January 1777

Tory refugees, in the bitterness of penury and exile, disseminated the story, (which to them, at any rate, was no legend,) that the British general was in a hurry to exchange the hardships of the open field for a life of sloth and gross self-indulgence beneath the roof of an urban mansion.[1]

Howe might love ease and pleasure; but he was no selfish voluptuary, and he liked to see others comfortable and happy around him. The return of the Headquarters Staff to New York was followed by ten days of universal jollity, — the harbingers, as everybody anticipated, of a cheerful and plenteous winter. All the town markets were regularly and largely supplied, and cantonments in the provincial districts overflowed with rural luxuries. Good beef, veal, and mutton might be bought at threepence to fourpence a pound, bread was as cheap as in London; and there were apples and peaches for the asking, with cabbages and potatoes in abundance. Our officers amused themselves with pastimes, innocent, questionable, or estimable. Balls were given; faro-tables were set up; and a play was rehearsed at the theatre, which was to be performed for the benefit of families left destitute by soldiers who had fallen in the war Bright expectations centred themselves round the banquets which were in preparation to celebrate Sir William Howe's approaching investiture as Knight Commander of the Bath; for that rank had been conferred upon him as a reward for his victory on Long Island. Cornwallis, always very indifferent to the titles and honours which were conferred upon himself, did not wish to spend more evenings than he could help in wetting his Commander-in-Chief's red ribbon. Since apparently no fighting was at hand for some months to come, he obtained leave to sail for England; not, like Burgoyne, to push his fortunes, but in order to visit his children and his wife. That poor lady could not endure the separation from

[1] Judge Jones's *History of New York;* Vol. I, chapter viii., pages 171 and 176

her noble and kind companion, and was perpetually tortured by anxiety for the safety of a life of which her husband was so little chary in battle Two years afterwards Lady Cornwallis died, if ever woman did, of a broken heart.[1]

Washington who, according to his unvaried practice, had " a number of small parties out to make discoveries," [2] very soon perceived that the stress of the campaign was relaxed, and that he might count upon a breathing-space which would enable him to collect his means, to mature his plans, and to refurbish his energies. He felt as the captain of a dismantled vessel, driven by the tempest towards a lee-shore, would feel if the wind veered straight round when he was within a few score fathoms of the rocks Nor was he yet at the end of his mercies ; for the thirteenth of December had another gift in store for him. Lee was still meandering, at his own pace, through the northern townships of New Jersey. The record of his march stands by itself in the annals of modern warfare After receiving the order to move, he remained stationary for ten days at White Plains ; during the next week he travelled less than six miles a day ; and then his rate of progress came down to an average of three miles for every twenty-four hours Tradition avers that General Jomini, the famous writer on Strategy, first introduced himself to the notice of

---

[1] Cornwallis contrived to see his wife in England during the earlier months of 1778, and then returned to America with Lord Carlisle, who was bound thither as a Special Commissioner, and who thus wrote to George Selwyn from Portsmouth : "Poor Lord Cornwallis is going to experience something like what I have felt; for he has brought with him his wife and children, and we embark to-morrow if the wind serves. My heart bleeds for them."

When the ship weighed anchor, Lady Cornwallis returned to her life of solitude Grief played upon her health, and brought on the illness which killed her Cornwallis was fetched home in time to be with her at the last, and she begged of him that a thorn tree should be planted above the vault where she was buried, as nearly as possible over her heart, and that no stone should be engraved to her memory. Both wishes were carried out *Correspondence of Marquis Cornwallis;* chapter i

[2] Washington to the Council of Safety of Pennsylvania ; Head-quarters, Bucks County, December 15, 1776

Napoleon by naming the precise date when the Emperor would reach a certain point in the map on his way to Jena   But Jomini himself, even if he had Von Moltke to assist him, might well have shrunk from the problem of calculating the moment at which Charles Lee would ultimately have rejoined Washington.   The solution of that problem can never be known; for an untoward accident abruptly terminated the leisurely journey.   On the twelfth of December Lee left his troops at Vealtown with General Sullivan, who had shown such alacrity in hurrying forward those reinforcements which Schuyler had despatched from Albany, and which Lee had arrested and detained   Lee himself, — probably with the notion that his absence from the column might afford an excuse for an another day's halt upon the road, — slept that night in a tavern at Baskingridge, under the protection of a small escort, and separated by the distance of more than a league from the bulk of his command.   There he lay in bed till eight o'clock on the following morning, when he was aroused for an interview with Major Wilkinson, aide-de-camp of Horatio Gates, who had brought him a message from that officer.   Lee passed two hours with Wilkinson, vapouring and growling, and cavilling at the shortcomings of all his fellow-generals.   He was in low spirits; for he had recently lost his three best horses; most assuredly not by over-work.[1]   At ten he breakfasted, and then, as if the day was still young, he sate down to compose an ornate reply to Gates.   "The ingenious manœuvre," he wrote, "of Fort Washington has unhinged the goodly fabric we had been building. There never was so damned a stroke.[2]   *Entre nous*, a certain great man is damnably deficient. . . .   It is said

---

[1] General Lee's advertisement, offering a reward for the recovery of his horses, is given in the *American Archives* for December 1776   They were a black, a bay, and a sorrel, — none of them over fifteen hands high.

[2] Lee had told Colonel Cadwalader that, when he learned the fall of Fort Washington, he was so excited that he tore the hair out of his head.   Lambert Cadwalader to Timothy Pickering ;   May 1822.

the Whigs are determined to set fire to Philadelphia.
If they strike this decisive stroke, the day will be our
own; but, unless it is done, all chance of liberty in any
part of the globe is for ever vanished." The letter
was not yet folded when Wilkinson, who was looking
from the window, cried out, "Here are the British
cavalry."

It so happened that Colonel Harcourt had ridden
forth from Lord Cornwallis's head-quarters in the neighbourhood of the Delaware, in order to ascertain for
himself what Lee and Sullivan were about. The colonel was never too fine a gentleman to do his own scouting; and he now got his reward; for a Baskingridge
Loyalist brought him information of the unique chance
which awaited him at the tavern on the cross-roads.[1]
Harcourt was attended by thirty troopers of the Sixteenth Light Dragoons. It was the same regiment that
had followed Lee in his dashing raid across the Tagus
on the fifth of October, 1762, — the only unequivocal
day of honour in his diversified career The party was
very strongly officered, for they had with them their
Colonel, and one of their Cornets; while Banastre Tarleton, — then a subaltern in the First Dragoon Guards,
and afterwards famous as the cavalry-leader whose
deeds of valour and of cruelty alternately illuminated
and darkened the later history of the war, — accompanied them as a volunteer. When Harcourt and
Tarleton heard the news, they were on fire at the prospect of fun and glory. The young fellows turned their
horses' heads for Baskingridge, and arrived there an
hour before noon, early enough to find Lee still in his
dressing-gown. The house was surrounded, and the
glass began to fly as bullets rained in at the windows.
The assailants were so skilfully disposed, and made
such a din with their carbines, that they produced upon
the enemy's nerves an effect of being more than double

---

[1] Colonel Harcourt's presence at Baskingridge is very clearly explained
in Sir William Howe's despatch to Lord George Germaine of the twentieth
of December 1776

their actual numbers.[1] Lee's escort ran away; and he
himself had no choice except to surrender. His behaviour, according to rumour, displayed neither manliness nor dignity; but it is not easy to be taken prisoner
heroically Howe, in his report of the affair, recommended Colonel Harcourt to his Majesty's gracious
attention for his infinite address and gallantry; and the
compliment was just. Within four minutes after the
attack began, Lee, — in the garb of a half-dressed slip-
shod civilian, and mounted on Major Wilkinson's
charger, which had been left tethered outside the tavern,
— was careering southward amid the little troop of
British horsemen, and, during those four minutes, the
dragoons had contrived to let off more than a hundred
cartridges. There was need for haste. Harcourt had
near thirty miles to travel along causeways much less
evenly laid than the coach road between Nuneham and
Oxford, and the Whigs, in the townships through
which he passed on his way to Baskingridge, had risen
in arms behind him. During the return journey, his
Cornet was shot dead from the saddle by the gun of a
Jersey farmer;[2] but Harcourt allowed nothing to divert
or to delay him until he had securely lodged his man
within the British lines at Pennington.

General Lee's capture was everywhere regarded as
an event of first-rate magnitude, and excited an emotion
by no means confined to our own islands, for in several
European capitals he was personally and familiarly
known to military men for whom Washington was only
a name. The tidings created extraordinary elation in
England, and more particularly throughout those counties which bordered on the Thames valley, where the
Harcourt interest was strong, and the Colonel himself

---

[1] Washington, in his official account of the occurrence, spoke of the English Light Horsemen as seventy strong.

[2] During more than a century afterwards local tradition pointed to a
spot by the roadside where this young officer was said to have been hastily
buried. In 1891 the grave was opened, and regimental buttons of the
Sixteenth Light Dragoons were found amid the mould.

had always been a special favourite.[1] Lee's showy qualities, and his dramatic history, had caught the imagination of the writing world; and, when he was announced to be under lock and key, there were joy and triumph in London as though a battle had been won. The metropolitan newspapers, — in a phrase which to Lee's own taste must have seemed exceedingly fine, — congratulated Sir William Howe on having taken the Palladium of America. One journal related how the prudent advice of our distinguished prisoner had saved the Continental army from being cut to pieces on the Westchester peninsula. Another, when fortune had at length smiled upon the Americans, discovered that it was General Lee who had reconnoitred the Hessian position at Trenton in the disguise of a peasant, and had devised the plan of attack which an ignorant world attributed to Washington. In America itself, Charles Lee had already been detected and judged by a discriminating few,[2] but the great mass of his fellow-countrymen still believed in him as implicitly as ever. His mishap, coming on the top of their other disasters, bewildered and disheartened them; and they insisted, with an importunity which the governing authorities were compelled to heed, that as early as possible, and at any cost, he should be redeemed from captivity, and placed once more in exalted command Their anxiety on his behalf was sharpened by a report that he was to be court-martialled as a deserter from the British army, because the resignation of his position as a half-pay officer had not yet been officially accepted by the War

---

[1] "This is to give notice that Thursday night will be held as a day of rejoicin in commemoration of the takin of General Lee, when there will be a sermint preached, and other public demonstrations of joy; after which there will be a nox roasted whole, and every mark of festivity and bell-ringing imaginable, with a ball and cock-fighting at night in the Assembly-room at the Black Lyone" Notice by James Clinch, Parish Clerk and Cryer of Tring in Buckinghamshire, February 13, 1777.

[2] "There is something so eccentric in the man's temper, and such a vacancy of principle, that it is impossible for all his talents, which have been much enlarged upon, to support a reputation." Ambrose Serle to Lord Dartmouth, August 1776

Office in London.   He was said to have been placed in
close confinement, and deprived of all materials for
writing; which in his case would most certainly have
been the refinement of cruelty.   Whatever might be
Washington's inward reflections, they were draped beneath a decent veil of conventional, and apparently
quite sincere, regret.   In a private letter to his brother
he mentioned Lee's incarceration as an additional misfortune for the public cause, — the more vexatious as
it was by the General's own folly and imprudence, and
without a view to effect any good, that he had fallen
into hostile hands.[1]

Washington before long, to his grievous loss, got
Charles Lee back once again; but he was quit of him
for the time being, and of that precious time not a
shred was wasted.   The next fortnight was a season of
immense activity in the American lines.   A spark of
hope soon appeared in cheerful minds; and in more
sombre dispositions there was a fixed intention of dying,
if death must be faced, elsewhere than on the gallows,
or amid the horrors and rigours of the New York jails.
The Commander-in-Chief now at last enjoyed an assurance, — the utmost boon which a strong man claims
from destiny, — that, however bad the situation might
have become, it henceforward depended upon himself
alone to make the best of it; for Congress, when ad-
journing to Baltimore, had resolved that "General
Washington be possessed of full power to order and
direct all things relative to the department and to the
operations of war."   That access of authority in the
right quarter was welcomed by the American army.
Washington, in his relations with others, had always
evinced the unselfishness of a good comrade, and the
self-abnegation of a true leader; — those qualities which
cannot fail to secure the willing obedience of all honest
and earnest men.   "I knew," wrote Sherman to Grant,
"that, wherever I was, if I got into a tight place you
would help me out of it alive."   That was a compliment

---

[1] Washington to John Augustine Washington; December 18, 1776.

which Washington seldom, or never, failed to deserve. Eight or nine months previously, at the opening of a formidable campaign on the result of which his fame and career were staked, he had despatched ten regiments, of his very best, to the assistance of General Sullivan, then in jeopardy on the northern frontier; and now his own turn had come to appeal for aid from all his colleagues who were not so immediately and urgently threatened as himself. Sullivan had faults, but his warm Irish nature contained no particle of disloyalty or ingratitude. On learning what had happened at Baskingridge tavern, he took prompt and resolute hold of the command which had so suddenly fallen vacant. Having assembled Lee's division upon parade, he rode jauntily along the front of the lines in order to show the troops that they still had a competent leader to direct them; and, with his own voice, he gave them the word to start on their journey to the place where they were sorely wanted. He made a sweeping circuit to the westward, which took him well outside all risk of contact with the British outposts; but he marched four times as quickly as the measure of speed with which his predecessor had of late been contented. On the fifteenth of December Sullivan crossed the Delaware at Easton, a point forty miles above Trenton, and on the twentieth, in a heavy snowstorm, he handed over his troops to the Commander-in-Chief, and reported them as fit and keen for duty, although "much out of sorts, and much in want of everything."[1]

A few days after Sullivan had passed through Easton,

---

[1] On the seventeenth of December Doctor Shippen wrote to Richard Henry Lee, from Bethlehem in Pennsylvania, a letter which is preserved in the *American Archives.* "I have not heard of any clothes and old wine. I fear the varlets have them as secure as poor General Lee. Oh! What a sneaking way of being kidnapped! I cannot bear to think of it I saw all his troops, about four thousand, this morning, marching from Easton in good spirits, and much pleased with their general."

David How, the diarist of Bunker's Hill and Boston siege, was in Lee's army, and his humble narrative indicates the vastly increased energy which Sullivan infused into the movements of that force.

he was followed across the Delaware by four other battalions which General Schuyler had detached from the garrison of Ticonderoga as soon as Sir Guy Carleton's back was fairly turned. Anthony Wayne, sickening for a fight, had eagerly volunteered to conduct these reinforcements in person. Schuyler, however, could not spare him from his post; and this second contingent of the Northern army was brought into the camp on the Delaware by Benedict Arnold. Washington, before November ended, had directed General Mifflin to visit the capital of Pennsylvania, and raise what force he could from that province. It was an admirable selection, inasmuch as Mifflin had a singular gift for arousing enthusiasm, and the sense of obligation, in the hearts and consciences of other men. He was very successful with the city militia, who turned out in a most spirited manner, and rallied round the drooping standard of their country fifteen hundred strong.[1] Mifflin received that reward which is the most acceptable to a zealous man who has done a good stroke of public work. He was at once given something more to accomplish; and having secured so large a muster from the town, he was ordered off again, then and there, to try his hand on the rural districts. Nor was Arnold detained on the banks of the Delaware; for Washington was too good an economist of motive power in war to keep at his own elbow, in subordinate employment, a soldier of such commanding vigour and dauntless initiative. The coast population of Connecticut and Rhode Island lived under the perpetual menace of Governor Tryon's vindictive forays. Arnold was sent there with

"Dec. 15. This morning, at Day Brake, we set off, and at 10 o'Clock at Night we got to Philips Borough, then crossed Dullerway River and went to East Town in Pennsylvania.

"16. We have ben geting our Baggage a Cross, and geting waggons for the March this day.

"17 This morning we set out And marched 12 miles to Bethlem and staid in the woods there."

[1] Washington to Governor Trumbull; Trenton Falls, December 12, 1776.

a roving commission to protect the eastern sea-board from incendiarism and rapine; and, in the successful prosecution of that service, he soon had two horses shot under him, and only saved his own life by his coolness and dexterity in a personal encounter.[1]

Washington had no occasion to withdraw men of ability from distant quarters and important duties; for his cantonments swarmed with excellent officers. He could not desire more alert and enterprising generals than Greene and Stirling, or braver colonels than Stark of New Hampshire, and Haslet of Delaware. Two special departments of the army were destined to exercise a decisive influence on the events of the next few weeks; and in both of those departments Washington was eminently well provided. His field batteries were in charge of Colonel Knox, who in the previous winter had brought the great train of heavy ordnance from Lake Champlain to the American trenches outside Boston. Knox was chief of the artillery all the while that hostilities lasted; and his practical acquaintance with the use of cannon in siege-work, and in battle, greatly enhanced his efficiency as an administrator. The personal authority which he exerted over his own branch of the service was henceforward firmly established by the skill and dash with which his guns were manœuvred during the operations now impending.[2] The other implement of war which Washington had in perfection may be described as his pontoon-corps; although it was designated on the roll of the American army as the Fourteenth Continental Foot. It was composed of the

---

[1] After the action was over, some thrifty New England farmers took the skin off one of the animals, and found in it no less than nine bullet-holes. Arnold killed with his pistol a soldier who offered to bayonet him as he lay entangled in his stirrups on the ground.

[2] Washington described Knox as a very valuable officer, of great military reading, sound judgment, and clear conceptions; who, combating almost innumerable difficulties, had placed the national artillery upon a footing that did him honour. Those were the terms in which the Commander-in-Chief answered a proposal, emanating from the politicians, to supersede Knox by a Frenchman. Washington to the President of Congress, May 31, 1777, to Richard Henry Lee, June 1, 1777.

men who, during the blockade of Boston, had swept crops and cattle off the islands in the Bay from under the guns of Admiral Graves and his squadron; and who, on the night of the thirteenth of August 1776, had conveyed the American army safe and sound across the East River after their defeat in front of Brooklyn. They had been recruited from that seafaring population of Marblehead, which was thrown out of work by the Act of Parliament excluding the New England colonies from participation in the Newfoundland Fisheries. The rank and file were mariners all; clad in blue round jackets, and in those loose short trousers which, (as a student of Gillray's caricatures will remember,) formed the distinguishing dress of shipmen at a time when every landsman still wore breeches and long stockings. They carried rifles; and had shown themselves good soldiers in a shrewd skirmish on Westchester peninsula. The regiment had been raised by Colonel John Glover, who before the Revolution owned a number of vessels manned by the seamen whom he afterwards led to war Small of stature, but brisk and stout-hearted, he had now been promoted to the charge of a brigade. He continued, however, to keep a close and loving eye on his sailors; and he was well supported and seconded by his regimental officers, who at this period of the campaign were as one to six of the privates. A critic from the middle colonies, very sparing indeed of any compliment to New Englanders, admitted that Colonel Glover's officers had mixed with the world, and knew how to make themselves respected and obeyed. The men, (this gentleman said,) were deficient in polish, but afforded a notable example in all the essentials of discipline.[1] One of their captains was John Blunt, a New Hampshire shipmaster, who had often taken his trading schooner up the Delaware to the head of the tide at

---

[1] *Memoirs* by Alexander Graydon of Pennsylvania. There is an account of Glover's regiment in William Stryker's *Battles of Trenton and Princeton*. The numbers and composition of Washington's army are given by that excellent author in minute, and most interesting, detail.

Trenton, and who now was making himself familiar with the higher stretch of river which lay between that point and Coryel's Ferry.[1]

Not in Glover's regiment only, but throughout the Continental army, Captains and Lieutenants were in excessive proportion to the soldiers whom they commanded. Six of the brigades contained between them, present and fit for service, four thousand men and five hundred officers. This immense multitude of commissioned people included some bad characters, and many who could show few military attributes except their title and their epaulettes; but none the less the very pick of the nation was there. Great numbers of respectable and prosperous colonists had abandoned their trades and their professions in order to see the Republic through its early perils. Men of this class had stood proof against the infection of despondency and timidity which, when the star of the Revolution began to decline, had thinned the Provincial army. Those of them who were not invalided to their homes, or prostrated on the mattresses of Philadelphian hospitals, had remained steadfast and indefatigable at their appointed station in Washington's dwindling ranks. And while older citizens, at the bidding of duty, reluctantly sacrificed family life and profitable avocations, there had been a joyous exodus from school and college of all that was most ambitious and keen-witted in America. The army on the Delaware contained not a few striplings of exceptional talents, and with a shining future. We are told that the New York company of artillery " was a model of discipline; its captain a mere boy, with small, slender, and delicate frame, who, with cocked hat pulled down over his eyes, and apparently lost in thought, marched beside his cannon, patting it every now and then as if it were a favourite horse or pet plaything." This was Alexander Hamilton; indubitably the most brilliant, and

[1] The places mentioned in this chapter, and in the next, may all be found in the Map of New Jersey, and of New York and its Environs, at the end of the volume

perhaps the most tragic, figure in all the historical gallery of American statesmen   After the peace he was foremost among the political architects who planned and constructed the fabric of her stable and stately Constitution ; and, as a fitting crown to his military career, he was invited by Washington, at the siege of Yorktown, to lead an assault which was the final and decisive onslaught of the entire war.   In December 1777 the precocity of Hamilton's genius had gone beyond the stage of mere promise.   He was not yet of age ; but his reputation as an eloquent, and still more as a thoughtful and convincing, speaker had been already made.   The two pamphlets which, when just turned eighteen, he had put forth in reply to the Westchester Farmer, were ascribed at the time to more than one public man of high mark and recognised authority, and are still read with admiration by the best judges of polemical literature [1]

Another distinguished regimental officer, for the present attached to the infantry, was a cousin, although no very near one, of the Commander-in-Chief   Captain William Washington always took his share of a fight on foot, but Virginian gentlemen were then seen at their best in the saddle.   Before very long he was famous as the leader of cavalry who taught American troopers to charge home, and who, by an almost infallible discernment in timing the moment for an onset, gained one crushing victory, and saved two stubborn battles from degenerating into ruinous defeats.   His imperturbable valour, and remarkable bodily strength, went, (as is not unusual in such natures,) with an excess of diffidence

[1] Hamilton's *Full Vindication of Congress*, and his *Farmer Refuted*, were attributed by some to John Jay, and by others to William Livingston. "There are displayed in these papers a power of reasoning and sarcasm, a knowledge of the principles of government and of the English Constitution, and a grasp of the merits of the whole controversy, that would have done honor to any man, at any age   .   They show great maturity, — a more remarkable maturity than has ever been exhibited by any other person, at so early an age, in the same department of thought "   This passage, written by George Ticknor Curtis, is quoted, with concurrence, by Professor Tyler in his *Literary History*

whenever he was called upon to face the less familiar, and to him far more redoubtable, ordeals of civic life. Picton, the hero of heroes, — who for forty-eight hours concealed what was almost certainly a mortal wound in order not to be prevented by the surgeons from leading his division at Waterloo, — twice excited respectful compassion by the evident distress with which he rose to respond when he was thanked in his place in the House of Commons. And so, when the war was over, and William Washington's friends desired to nominate him for the Governorship of the State, he gave them that which he pronounced to be an unsurmountable reason for declining the proffered honour. He reminded them how, as holder of such an office, — an office, moreover, in which no less an orator than Patrick Henry had been among his predecessors, — he would undoubtedly be expected to speak in public. "In that case," he said, "I know that, without gaining credit in your estimation, the consciousness of inferiority would humble me in my own. I cannot make a speech."[1]

The junior officer in William Washington's company was a lad even younger than Hamilton, and not his equal, (as indeed very few were,) in intellectual endowments or in personal charm. And yet, if in the course of ages both their memories were to perish, that of Lieutenant Monroe would in all likelihood be the last forgotten of the two; for he was the James Monroe who in December 1823, as fifth President of the United States, enunciated the policy which defeated the machinations of the Holy Alliance, and which deprived Spain of her American colonies. The famous doctrine, wherewith his surname is indissolubly associated, has been frequently revived and reasserted with marked effects upon the history of the world; and a very great deal more will have to be written about it before that history attains the closing chapter. As time proceeds, and the giant Republic grows increasingly conscious of its strength, fresh occasions will arise, or be made, for the

[1] Garden's *Anecdotes of the American Revolution;* Vol. I., page 61.

use, or misuse, of the most formidable and far-reaching of all diplomatic weapons ; and during generations, and even centuries, to come, the name of Captain Washington's subaltern in the Third Virginian Continental Infantry may still be a word of disagreeable import among the Chancelleries of Europe.

General Washington's troops, in numbers and in equipment, bore very little resemblance to the army of a nation which, in the lifetime of some there present, would order the combined autocrats of Eastern and Central Europe to forbear from meddling, and force them to recognize the Western Hemisphere as an inviolable sanctuary of freedom and self-government. Very few indeed of his regiments were as much as two hundred strong, and some of them could only muster from forty to ninety privates. The Third Virginian, (to take a specimen instance,) had a hundred and sixty enlisted men around the colours ; while no fewer than four hundred and fifty were reported as sick, or on extra duty, or on furlough, — which was often only another word for absence without leave. Regulars and militia together, it is probable that about eight thousand Americans stood in arms over a front of thirty miles along the Pennsylvanian shore of the Delaware.[1] It was a force which in military parlance might have been stated at six thousand five hundred bayonets, were it not that one soldier out of every three was still unprovided with that very essential weapon. The Philadelphia Associators, fresh from homes close at hand and stocked with comforts, were in good condition for a winter campaign ; but it was less well with the Continental regulars who had been

[1] This is the calculation of William S. Stryker, himself a professional soldier, and a skilled examiner of records. On the twenty-second of December, 1776, a "Return of the Forces encamped on the banks of the Delaware, under the command of His Excellency George Washington Esq., Commander-in-Chief of the Forces of the United States of America," gives 4704 Rank and File present for duty. But some of the regiments from the Northern army, the large body of Philadelphia militia, and apparently a few other smaller contingents, were not included in the Return

marching and fighting ever since the middle of August. Many among them were barefoot; and Washington was reduced to send round the Pennsylvania villages to beg or buy old clothes and blankets for his freezing soldiers. But at any rate they *were* soldiers, — true metal that had been tried in the fire; from whose ranks the cowards and sluggards had all deserted, while the feeble in body had been eliminated by the searching hardships of those cruel months. They were clad like scarecrows: but each of them carried a gun whose tricks he knew, with the barrel as clean as oiled rag could make it; and in that camp rags were plenty. They now were somewhat rested; for they slept sound under a tight roof, behind a broad river; and, for the first time during many a long day, they had enough to eat. Robert Morris, who was working with the zeal and devotion of ten fair-weather administrators, confessed that the transport and commissariat had been seriously deranged ever since Congress had retired to Baltimore [1] But the hamlet of Newtown, which contained Washington's head-quarters, lay only a few leagues distant from Philadelphia; and the townsmen of that hospitable capital, on both sides of politics, loved to regale those who agreed with them in opinions. Provision-waggons came and went through the mud and snow with a regularity which showed that Benjamin Franklin, when he sailed for France, had not taken all the resource and energy of his adopted city with him. The veterans of Haerlem and of White Plains had never lost their courage; and now they got back their buoyancy. They were tired of being told that they had practised the back-step long enough.[2] Their fancy was not captivated by the prospect of recommencing a retreat over vile log-roads, far away from any chance of good victuals; and they were more

---

[1] Robert Morris to Colonel Cadwalader; *American Archives.*

[2] "Where are your good ladies? My love and best compliments to them, and desire that they will take care of themselves, lest our retrograde soldiers should run them down. I wish you would introduce a new step into your army. I am sure they are perfect in the back-step by this time." William Shippen to Richard Henry Lee, December 1776.

inclined to push forward across the Delaware before the Hessians had killed all the turkeys, and burned up all the dry billets of wood, in the province of New Jersey.

These men entertained very definite notions about the cause which had brought them from their ploughs, from their dairies, and from the counters of their stores. They had learned to read at school; and they retained the habit in after life, instead of breaking off their education at that precise point of childhood when the intellect unfolds itself to the appreciation of the delight and instruction which books afford " In many towns," (we are told,) "and in every city, they have public libraries. Not a tradesman but will find time to read. He is amused with voyages and travels, and becomes acquainted with the geography, customs, and commerce of other countries. He reads political disquisitions, and learns the outlines of his rights as a man and a citizen."[1] Nor was that the case with townsmen only; for already good books were treasured, and slashing newspapers eagerly sought, by farmers and rural mechanics, who in the long Northern winter had more time for study and reflection than the people who lived in the streets of a city. Leisure, indeed, was not abundant in Washington's army on the Delaware; but the minds of his soldiers were profoundly stirred, and the full significance of national politics was brought before their eyes in a very visible and concrete shape. Nothing ever arouses so lively an interest in literary productions as personal intercourse with those who create them. The writers who had most successfully evoked a martial spirit in America did not lie open to the taunt which, since wars first began, has been levelled against those who instigate others to fight, but who will not fight themselves; — a taunt which the ancients embodied in the fable of the trumpeter who begged for quarter on the plea that he never had killed anyone with his own

---

[1] " Letter written by a foreigner on his Travels , " by Francis Hopkinson. *American Archives* for December 1776.

sword. During the earlier operations in the campaign the author of the "Answer to a Westchester Farmer" might have been seen loading and pointing in the thick of the fire, or trudging contentedly at the head of his battery while his charger helped to drag the cannon; and any Patriot in uniform, when he had done his turn of sentry, and felt inclined for some conversation on public affairs, might exchange ideas with a still more celebrated pamphleteer, who occupied a humbler military station than Alexander Hamilton in that exceptionally constituted army.

Thomas Paine, in the very flush of his influence and reputation, had shouldered a knapsack, and joined the Flying Camp as a Pennsylvania militiaman. General Greene made him one of his aides-de-camp; but an appointment on that staff, during those weeks, carried with it very little either of privilege or luxury. In the flight from Fort Lee Paine lost his baggage and his private papers;[1] but he had kept, or borrowed, a pen He began to write at Newark, the first stage in the calamitous retreat; and he worked all night at every halting-place until his new pamphlet was completed. It was published in Philadelphia on the nineteenth of December, under the title of "The Crisis," and at once flew like wildfire through all towns and villages of the Confederacy. In Europe the piece attracted less attention than had been paid to its predecessor; for, whereas "Common Sense" had been a reasoned exposition of state policy, "The Crisis" was an impassioned appeal to arms. That circumstance, however, endowed Paine's glowing rhetoric with a special value in the estimation of Americans. To their mind's eye the little work was adorned by an imaginary frontispiece of a soldier writing by the watch-fire's light, with his comrades slumber-

---

[1] A letter written from the British army relates that on this occasion "the rebels fled like scared rabbits, leaving some poor pork, a few greasy proclamations, and some of that scoundrel 'Common Sense' man's letters; which we can read at our leisure, now that we have got one of 'the impregnable redoubts' of Mr. Washington's to quarter in."

ing round him, and it was among those comrades that
the author found his warmest admirers and his most
convinced disciples. The privates were called together
in groups to hear "The Crisis" read; and it would
have borne the test of reading aloud even before a
more exacting audience. "These are the times that
try men's souls. The summer soldier and the sunshine
patriot will, in this crisis, shrink from the service of his
country; but he, that stands it now, deserves the love
and thanks of man and woman."[1]

Such were the first words of that thrilling exhortation; and what followed was of a piece with the opening sentences. Americans in the army were especially
pleased by the parallel drawn between their commander
and the last King of England who had been a famous
warrior. William the Third, (it was said,) never appeared to full advantage but in difficulty and danger.
"The character fits General Washington. There is a
natural firmness in some minds which cannot be un-
locked by trifles. I reckon it among public blessings
that God hath blessed him with uninterrupted health,
and given him a mind that can flourish upon care." If
to applaud that sentiment was flattery on the part of
Washington's soldiers, it was none the less a tribute
which honoured those who paid it, and proved that they
had not degenerated from their forefathers. The
nation from which they issued, — of which, only six
months before, they formed a part, — in peril and
disaster is slow to blame those of its servants who have
honestly and faithfully done their best at home and in
the field; and no other trait in the British character
inspires foreigners with more genuine respect and
admiration, not unmixed with envy. Washington deserved the confidence of his supporters; for he set an
example of the manner in which men should think and
act when their country is in grave peril. While labouring with all his powers to recapture success, he steadily

[1] Moncure Conway's *Life of Thomas Paine;* Vol. I, chapter vii
Tyler's *Literary History;* chapter xxiv., sections 1 and 2.

trained his mind to contemplate the very worst that could possibly befall. Asked what he would do if Philadelphia were taken, he is reported to have answered that he would retreat beyond the Susquehanna River, and thence, if necessary, into the Alleghany Mountains.[1] He had penetrated the inward meaning of the secret which, in the last extremity of fortune, sustains the brave, "who resign themselves to everything in thought, but in action resign themselves never." [2]

[1] *The Life of Washington* by Jared Sparks ; chapter ix.
[2] "Il faut par la pensée se résigner à tout, et dans l'action ne se résigner jamais."

CHAPTER XXIII

RALL AND VON DONOP. TRENTON. PRINCETON

BEFORE Washington retired into the forests which lay west of the Susquehanna he intended to see whether something might not yet be done on the east of the Delaware. That region afforded a possible and, (to his judgement,) a promising field of action now that the British general had withdrawn his head-quarters to New York, and disposed the bulk of his troops in cantonments over the five northern counties of New Jersey. The situation was fairly enough described in a letter by a Virginian colonel, who wrote that in December 1776 General Howe held a mortgage on the American army, but had decided not to foreclose. Years afterwards, when both the immediate and the secondary consequences of his untoward decision were patent to the world, Sir William Howe discoursed to the House of Commons about the operations of that winter at considerable length, and with apparent frankness. He owned that the left wing of his cantonments in New Jersey had been dangerously extended towards the southward. He defended himself, however, on the score of his desire to protect a district containing many inhabitants, who had committed themselves to the Royal cause on the faith of his own express invitation; and the assertion of this honourable motive was neither an excuse nor an after-thought.[1] He was blamed, (so

---

[1] On the twentieth of December, 1776, — nearly a week before Trenton, — Howe wrote thus to Lord George Germaine. "The chain, I own, is rather too extensive ; but I was induced to occupy Burlington, to cover the county of Monmouth in which there are many loyal inhabitants ; and, trusting to the general submission of the country to the Southward of this chain, and to the strength of the corps placed in the advanced posts, I conclude the troops will be in perfect security."

he acknowledged,) for having entrusted the post of
danger to other than British troops; but he pleaded
that our German auxiliaries had all along been stationed
on the left of his line, and that to shift them from that
position would have been an imputation upon their
courage and discipline which up to that time they had
not deserved. During the Seven Years' War, (so he
reminded Parliament, and few had a better right to
speak about that war than William Howe,) the Hessians
had been reputed to be as good soldiers as any in
Prince Ferdinand's army. But, while profuse in his
self-justification on all minor and collateral charges,
Howe put the main question aside in silence. He did
not explain why he had checked the rush of his victorious campaign; had deliberately surrendered the power
of bringing on a combat at his own time and place;
and, by breaking up his force into isolated and stationary fragments, had handed over the advantage of the
offensive to Washington.

The six brigades of Royal troops quartered in the
Jerseys were put in charge of Major General Grant,
who located himself at New Brunswick on the Raritan
river, as nearly as possible in the centre of his command. The shore of the Delaware, facing the whole
extent of the position where Washington's army lay,
was occupied by a Hessian division under the orders of
Colonel Von Donop. He was an exceedingly valiant
officer who, within a year afterwards, died very nobly
for a cause which in his own view was not worthy of
so great a sacrifice Von Donop, with the insight of
a genuine soldier, recognised that both opponents must
have had their say in the matter before a campaign
could be declared closed; and he found no reason to
believe that the Americans were a party to the bargain
He foresaw that all his regiments, acting together, were
none too many to ensure their own safety; and he
urged that the entire division should be massed, and
kept on the alert, in a position suited for defence, and
not very near the enemy. The town of Trenton he

regarded as too exposed for security ; and any body of troops, which might be quartered there, was in his view a forlorn hope. But Colonel Rall, — as the reward of his undoubted services at White Plains, in front of Brooklyn, and particularly at Fort Washington, — claimed the command of a brigade, with head-quarters of his own   Howe let himself be talked over, and Rall was placed at Trenton with three fine regiments of Hessian infantry. The officers of his corps for the most part regarded their adversaries with the disdain of professional soldiers for irregular levies, and of petty aristocrats for hard-working, self-supporting citizens. German letters and diaries, during this period of the war, were impregnated by ideas then potent in Europe, but which never had, — and, it is to be hoped, never will have, — any vogue whatever in America. Some very curious observations, made by these gentlemen after Putnam's defeat on Long Island, have been preserved for the instruction of posterity. Among the prisoners, (they wrote,) were many so-called colonels and lieutenant-colonels, who in reality were nothing but tradesmen and mechanics, tailors, shoemakers, and barbers ; and some of them had been well knocked about by the German grenadiers, who would by no means consent to treat such people with the tenderness due to commissioned officers. General Putnam was a butcher by profession ; much such another as butcher Fischer at Rinteln in North Hesse. Their artillery was miserable, mostly of iron, and mounted on ship-carriages. As for the privates, these wretched creatures merited pity rather than fear. No regiment was properly uniformed. Every man had a common gun, such as the citizens of Cassel marched out with at Whitsuntide, which it took him a quarter of an hour to load , and he would always be glad to surrender his fire-arms, and himself too, if only he were not afraid of being hanged for a rebel.[1]

[1] Many extracts to this effect from German military publications are given in Mr Lowell's book on the Hessians.

Insolence and over-confidence were not discouraged by the Brigadier in command, who was a brave, proud, and stupid man. Imbued with the densest prejudices incidental either to his class or to his calling, he neglected the most ordinary precautions against a foe whose defects he ridiculed, and to whose very remarkable military qualities, which were not exactly those of the Potsdam guard-parade, he was wilfully and incurably blind. Colonel Rall's present circumstances by no means justified his self-complacency, for the position which his force occupied was extremely hazardous. Some of his junior officers displayed a zeal, and an interest in the realities of soldiering, which put the indolence and recklessness of their chief to shame; for no fewer than three Hessian lieutenants have left each of them a plan of Trenton which would do credit to any modern Staff College. The place was within a few hundred yards of a navigable river, of which the Americans had the undisputed command; but Colonel Rall's most serious danger was in the opposite quarter. Several high roads, leading from the interior of the province and from the crossing-places further up the stream, converged upon a spot at the northern entrance of Trenton where a single battery of hostile cannon could sweep, from end to end, the two broad straight streets which constituted the village. That spot, moreover, was to rear of the Hessians, planted fair and square across their communications, and, if it was seized and maintained by a superior American force, nothing could save their brigade from a total and irretrievable overthrow.[1] The more intelligent German officers felt relief and satisfaction when Von Donop paid a visit to Trenton in order to examine the ground with his own eyes. He directed Colonel Rall to raise a small fortification at the Ferry, and, as a matter of prime necessity, to erect a redoubt, with flanking angles

[1] The scale of the map at the end of this volume has been calculated to show the battle-fields of Trenton, and of Long Island, sufficiently for the purposes of the reader.

for cannon, at the meeting of the roads to the north of the village. Rall made a show of acquiescence, and ordered faggots to be prepared for the construction of a battery; but, after Von Donop's departure, he stayed his hand, and his six field-pieces, instead of being mounted in embrasures where they might protect the approaches, were all parked near the middle of the town in a graveyard at the back of the English Church

Rall's three regiments were distributed among the public buildings and places of worship, or in the private dwellings of King's Street and Queen's Street in the proportion of a company to every five or six houses. The men, though snugly lodged, were allowed very little time to themselves. A capable officer, Lieutenant Andreas Wiederhold, has recounted the proceedings of that fortnight at Trenton in terms which indicate a deep feeling of shame and resentment.[1] The soldiers, he wrote, were harassed with watches, detachments, and pickets without purpose and without end   The cannon were drawn forth every day, and paraded about the town seemingly only to make a stir and uproar. Whether his men kept their muskets clean and bright, and their ammunition in good order, was of little moment to Colonel Rall; but of the regimental bandsmen he never could either see or hear enough. The officer on guard for the day must march round and round the churchyard in front of the Commandant's windows, with his men and musicians looking for all the world like a Roman Catholic procession, " and wanting only the cross, the banner, and the chanting choristers, at their head." Rall amused himself far into the night, and slept late of a morning. "When we came from parade," said Wiederhold, "at ten o'clock to his quarters, we had many times to wait half an hour because he had not finished his usual bath." At length, emboldened by the arrival of a renewed and pressing

[1] Wiederhold died in Cassel in 1803, where he was Inspector of the Arsenal

message from Von Donop, some of Rall's subordinates, both young and old, implored him to commence intrenching without delay; but they got nothing from him except some clumsy banter. Major Von Dechow, who commanded the Knyphausen regiment, was an old officer of Frederic the Great. Though severely wounded at Fort Washington, he had dragged himself back to take a share with his comrades in the perils which he foresaw to be impending. His earnest but respectful expostulations were encountered, on the part of Colonel Rall, with a bad imitation of those epigrams that were frequent in the mouth of the great captain under whom Von Dechow had formerly served[1] A superior officer's satire, however pointless, does not admit of retort; and silence was imposed upon proud and gallant men by the implication that they were afraid of a parcel of cowardly rebels, whom a bayonet-charge over open ground would at once send to the right-about. Lieutenant Colonel Scheffer, of the Von Lossberg regiment, was actually worried into a fit of illness by the folly that he was compelled to witness, and by the prospect of a calamity which hourly grew more definite and inevitable.

The river in front of the Hessian position was hostile water. At the cardinal moment of the war a large portion of our naval, as well as of our military, strength had been diverted from that central and vital enterprise on which the two combined services had hitherto been engaged, and sent on a distant and subsidiary expedition to Rhode Island. The full unwisdom of that policy now became apparent. There were British schooners and gunboats lying superfluous and useless in Narragansett Bay which ought to have been employed, on very active service indeed, between the right and left banks of the Delaware. Lord Howe, with his brother's

---

[1] "Let them come," said Rall. "We want no trenches. We will go at them with the bayonet." "Colonel," answered Von Dechow, "an intrenchment costs nothing. If it does not help, it can do no harm." And then he held his peace.

army to help him on land, might easily ere this have broken up the chevaux-de-frise which guarded the course of the stream at a point forty miles below Trenton. Much harder tasks have not seldom proved to be within the competence of the Royal navy; and, when once our smaller vessels had penetrated above the obstructions in the neighbourhood of Philadelphia, the river would have been our own. English lieutenants and senior midshipmen, — the like of Edward Pellew, and the other young fellows who had handled the sloops and bomb-ketches under fire at Valcour Island, — would very soon have sunk or taken all the craft that floated on the upper reaches of the Delaware, with decisive effect on the result of the campaign. It might indeed be objected that the current of a river only a few hundred yards wide was a dangerous cruising-ground, as long as one of the shores continued to be in the occupation of the enemy; but a practical refutation of that argument was afforded by an American sailor. If the western bank of the Delaware remained in the power of General Washington, the eastern bank was strongly held by the Royal forces. And yet Commodore Seymour, of the Continental navy, ranged freely up and down with his row-galleys and gondolas; landed wherever he chose; searched suspected houses; made prisoners of formidable Tory partisans; and expelled the German outposts from every ferry, quay, farm, and village that was situated within cannon-range of his decks.[1]

Nothing British or Loyalist could slip across to Pennsylvania except by stealth, and at imminent risk of death or captivity. On the other hand parties of

---

[1] The Loyalists of Burlington, through the mouth of their Tory mayor, entreated Colonel Von Donop to take away his troops, as otherwise the American flotilla would proceed to a bombardment of the town. Von Donop hesitated to comply with their request, and Commodore Seymour discharged a few round-shot, which injured no one, but effectually cleared the place of the Hessians. This Mayor of Burlington was Mr. John Lawrence, the father of James Lawrence who, as Captain of the Chesapeake, was killed in her duel with the Shannon.

Americans, — thirty, seventy, and, on occasion, even four hundred strong, — boated over to New Jersey as openly as if they were a troop of graziers repairing in time of peace to a mart or a cattle-fair; attacked outlying pickets; cut off foragers; and killed dragoons who were carrying messages from one Royal commander to another. These roving bands were supplied with information, and forewarned of danger, by Jersey farmers and townsmen who already had had more than enough of their German champions and defenders. Rall's correspondence with Colonel Von Donop at Bordentown, with General Grant at New Brunswick, and with General Leslie at Princeton, — whenever he could contrive to get a letter through, — soon became a doleful record of alarms, anxieties, and misfortunes. At length, after a pair of orderlies had lost, the one his horse, and the other his life, Rall sent an officer, escorted by a hundred men and a piece of artillery, to admonish Leslie that communication between Trenton and Princeton would soon be impracticable unless the wing of a regiment was stationed at the intermediate village of Maidenhead. It was a signal evidence that the use of metaphors, often misleading in politics, may sometimes be absolutely fatal in war. Before ever the packet, bearing Sir William Howe's despatch of the twentieth of December, had got past Sandy Hook on her way to England, the brigade at Trenton, which that roseate epistle pictured as one of a strong and continuous chain of posts erected for the protection of a loyal district, was already, in fact and in truth, a beleaguered garrison abandoned to its own resources in the midst of a bitterly disaffected population.

Washington was apprised of all that took place on the opposite side of the Delaware. The collection of secret intelligence, throughout the war, was a department which he kept in his own hands, and to which he devoted everything that he possessed of industry, acuteness, and discretion. In the utmost penury of the Philadelphian treasury, — when the paper issued by

Congress had become so discredited that a pound of sugar cost fifty shillings, and a single garment from a tailor's shop sold for a thousand dollars in currency,[1] — Washington always made a point of having by him a small supply of hard money to pay for early and accurate information about the movements and, if possible, the intentions of the enemy. He doled out that precious metal to his officers, all the continent over, in sums of twenty, and twenty-five, guineas at a time. He sent them phials of invisible ink for confidential correspondence, and directions how to use it; together with minute instructions as to the individuals who should be employed, and the assumed names by which they were severally called.[2] The methods and doings, and even the identity, of some among his most trusted agents were known to himself, and to himself alone. Their personal risk was awful; for a detected spy, in either camp, suffered instant, certain, and shameful death, in obedience to the stern military code which all nations equally recognised. But there was a danger which American citizens feared yet worse than the gallows It was indispensable for them, (so Washington himself expressed it,) to bear the suspicion of being thought inimical to the national cause; nor was it in their power to assert their innocence, because their future usefulness would be destroyed if once they disclosed themselves as partisans of the Revolution.[3] These men implicitly relied upon their general's promise that, when the war was over, their true story should be made known to

---

[1] *The Pennsylvania Magazine of History and Biography* for April 1901; page 21.

[2] Washington to the President of Congress, August 25, 1778; and September 4, 1778. To Benjamin Tallmadge, September 24, 1779; and again February 5, 1780. These entries are specimens. References to the same subject in Washington's letters are far too numerous to quote The receipts and expenditure on Secret Services are carefully entered in his accounts During the eighteen months which followed the evacuation of Boston he disbursed under this head some fifteen hundred pounds.

[3] Washington to Governor Livingston ; Valley Forge, January 20, 1778.

the world ; and that, if they perished in his service, he would see their memory righted.[1]

Of such was John Honeyman ; a veteran who had been in Wolfe's body-guard at the battle of Quebec, but who had convinced himself that the interests of America were not, at the present juncture, served by Sir William Howe and Governor Tryon, and still less by Lieutenant General Von Heister and his Hessians Honeyman, whose real sentiments were carefully concealed, passed among his country neighbours by the appellation of the Tory Traitor. He gained his livelihood as a butcher and cattle-dealer ; and during the third week of December he was constantly in and around Trenton, procuring beeves from the farmers, and bringing them into the town for slaughter. When he had seen and heard enough to form a judgement, he got himself captured by some American scouts, who strapped him to a horse, and carried him to the head-quarters of their army at Newtown. There the Commander-in-Chief examined him in private for the space of half an hour, and then ordered him to be imprisoned and brought before a court-martial on the morrow, but, when morning came, Honeyman had vanished. Eighteen months

[1] Lafayette gradually acquired a personal influence over the American soldiery only second to that of Washington. In September 1781 he persuaded one Morgan, a private in a New Jersey regiment, to take his life in his hands, enter Yorktown in the character of a deserter, and learn what he could concerning the situation of the garrison Morgan consented with great reluctance. " He told the general that he would go, on one condition ; which was that, in case any disaster should happen to him, the general should make the true state of the case known, and have the particulars published in the New Jersey gazettes, that no reproach might come upon his family and friends."

Lafayette assented. Morgan did his errand, and returned safe, bringing over no fewer than seven real deserters with him. Lafayette offered him money and promotion ; but he refused both. He believed himself, (he said,) to be a good soldier He might not make so good a sergeant, and he preferred to remain where he would be the most useful to his country. Since, however, the general wished to oblige him, he had a favour to ask While he was away, some one had taken his gun. He set great store by it, and would be particularly pleased to have it once again Nearly half a century afterwards Lafayette related the story as an anecdote in every respect characteristic of the Revolutionary soldier

afterwards some prominent Whigs arraigned him before
the Magistrates as having aided and comforted the
enemies of New Jersey in the evil days when that State
was occupied by the invader; but in the end Honeyman
surmounted all his perils, and long out-lived his unpopularity.   He died in the odour of patriotism, at the ripe
age of ninety-three.

That conversation on a winter night between Washington and John Honeyman settled the fate of Colonel
Rall and the brigade which he commanded.[1]   The
faulty disposition of the Hessians inside Trenton, and
the absence there of all due caution and preparation,
were now intimately known to the American general;
and he had informed himself quite sufficiently about the
state of things prevailing in the district outside the confines of the village.   It was his constant custom to send
across the British lines a number of horsemen, habited
like well-to-do rustic folk, and to keep them riding
backwards and forwards through and through the
country, making their mental notes leisurely and coolly,
and with all but assured impunity.[2]   In this respect,
from the nature of the case, Washington possessed a
great advantage over the Royal generals.   The spies
accredited by Sir William Howe and Sir Henry Clinton
had unusual hazards and difficulties to encounter; and,
unless they shirked the business of their mission, their
careers were for the most part very brief.   Washington's army contained regiments from all the States;
and within the precincts of his camp there was sure to
be at least one native of any given county and township in the Confederacy.   If the Royal spy was of colonial origin, it was long odds that some rebel militiaman
or another would recognise him for a fellow-townsman
and a Loyalist; and, if he was an Englishman, he had
to undergo that searching catechism of personal inqui-
ries which, then and long afterwards, in peace and war

[1] In Stryker's *Trenton and Princeton* a narrative is given of Honeyman's proceedings during December 1776.

[2] Washington to Major General Putnam; January 5, 1777.

alike, it was the pleasure of every true American to inflict upon a stranger for the gratification of his own curiosity. But Washington's corporals and sergeants, —who even in their uniforms looked much more like agriculturists than military men, — when got up as harmless civilians could make the round of British bivouacs without fear of meeting any one who knew their faces, their antecedents, or their political opinions, and they were safer still in the company of Hessians, none of whom could so much as tell a Yankee from a Carolinian. The Revolutionary emissaries wandered at ease through the cantonments of Grant, and Leslie, and Von Donop; talking Toryism, peddling tobacco, and picking up valuable materials for observation at every turn. Their general was soon absolutely certified that, if he moved forward quietly and rapidly, he would have at least three clear and uninterrupted days within which to arrange the accounts of Colonel Rall and his regiments. General Grant had under his own hand at Brunswick considerably less than a thousand men; round Princeton the troops were dispersed in winter quarters, and had given over the very idea of further movements until spring arrived; while in Burlington County the Royal soldiers were reported as " scattered through all the farmers' houses, — eight, ten, twelve, and fifteen in a house, — and rambling over the whole country "[1]

Washington's opportunity had come; and not a moment too soon. He already had confessed to his brother that " the game was pretty nearly up," owing to the defection of the middle colonies from the American cause, to the ruinous policy of short enlistments, and the too great dependence which had been placed on the militia.[2] Every clause of that melancholy sentence was correct in all particulars. Governor Tryon exultingly wrote to Lord George Germaine that in the

---

[1] Colonel Reed to General Washington ; Bristol, December 22, 1776.
[2] Letter to John Augustine Washington ; Camp near the Falls of Trenton, December 18, 1776.

colony of New York loyalty towards the Crown was no longer a passive or a timorous sentiment. One day he had mustered under the Royal standard eight hundred and twenty armed inhabitants of Queen's County; and on another the oath of allegiance was administered to almost as many of the Suffolk Militia. Not a murmur of discontent could be heard throughout the whole crowd which witnessed that imposing ceremony. General George Clinton, on the other hand, who governed, in the interest of the Revolution, as much of the province of New York as Howe had not reconquered, informed the State Convention that his men had gone away, and still were going, without leave and in great numbers. He doubted, (he said,) whether he had strength enough to bring them back even though he should leave his lines undefended, and employ his whole remaining force to hunt up and recover the defaulters.[1] It is certain that the entire, and the almost immediate, dissolution of the Provincial forces was serenely anticipated at the British head-quarters in New York city. Washington himself fully believed that his adversary was only waiting till the ice bore, and the Continental troops had melted away, in order to draw his brigades once more together, and advance upon Philadelphia.[2] That fear was not chimerical; for by the end of the first fortnight in January the Delaware was frozen so hard that, if Sir William Howe had still been in fighting mood, (which, for good reasons, he no longer was,) he might

[1] General Clinton to the President of the Convention of New York; December 28, 1776.

"Our people here are many of them in the utmost distress about their families, and other affairs at home, at this severe season. Their complaints are most desperate, and I am afraid many women and children, together with their cattle, will suffer, if not perish, and am sorry to Inform you that, In spite of all our Efforts, I am convinc'd the Melitia will go home Bodily, Before three Days, the consequence of which is obvious to Every man of the least desernment." Colonel Allison to General George Clinton; Tappan, December 27, 1776. The news of Trenton had not, by then, penetrated to the Hudson river.

[2] General Washington to Colonel Reed, December 23, 1776.

have marched his infantry across the river in extended order of battle.

One hope remained to comfort the mind, and stimulate the faculties, of the American commander. A single brilliant and indisputable success, all the more surely in proportion as it was unexpected, would reanimate the spirit of the nation, decide waverers, recall absentees to arms, and set the embers of the Revolution once more in a blaze. As early as the fourteenth of December Washington, in no less than three letters, expressed that conviction, and declared his intention to act upon it.[1] The announcement, however, was made in general terms; and he thenceforward kept his own counsel. From the time when specific information about the distribution of his enemy's forces began to reach him, and his own scheme of action took definite shape, all further allusion to the subject disappeared even from his most familiar correspondence. At last, on the twenty-third of December, when his views were clear and his plans thought out, he wrote thus to the Adjutant General of the army. "Christmas-day at night, one hour before day, is the time fixed for our attempt on Trenton. For Heaven's sake keep this to yourself, as the discovery of it may prove fatal to us, — our numbers, sorry am I to say, being less than I had any conception of. But necessity, dire necessity, will, nay must, justify an attempt."

On Christmas Eve, General Greene requested the family with whom he lodged to leave their house in his charge for the night. When the coast was clear, Wash-

---

[1] One of these letters was addressed to General Heath, and another to General Gates. In the third, Washington wrote to Governor Trumbull of Connecticut about the troops whom Schuyler had sent down from Albany and Ticonderoga "By coming on they may in conjunction with my present force, and that under General Lee, enable us to attempt a stroke upon the forces of the enemy, who lie a good deal scattered, and to all appearance in a state of security. A lucky blow in this quarter would be fatal to them, and would most certainly rouse the spirits of the people, which are quite sunk by our late misfortunes"

ington and his principal officers came in to supper; and, before they left the table, all their preparations were complete Colonel Cadwalader, — himself a Philadelphian, — was to take the Philadelphian Associators, and a brigade of New Englanders, across the Delaware in the neighbourhood of Bristol, and beat up Von Donop's cantonments at Bordentown.[1] General Ewing, with something under a thousand militiamen, was bidden to pass the river at Trenton Ferry, and station his troops on the southern bank of the Assunpink Creek. Washington himself, meanwhile, purposed to traverse the stream at a higher point, and advance against Colonel Rall's position from the northwest quarter. His force consisted of twenty-four hundred Continental veterans under Greene and Sullivan, and no fewer than eighteen cannon. So large a mass of artillery was a grievous incumbrance on this night march, undertaken with intent to surprise an enemy covered by a nearly impassable current; but the future showed that the arrangement had been dictated by just foresight Each of the seven brigades was to be furnished with two good guides. Every officer in the column was to set his watch by Washington's, and to fasten a piece of white paper conspicuously in his hat. Every man carried cooked provisions for three days; a blanket to cover him if ever he found leisure to lie down , a new flint screwed into the hammer of his piece, and forty rounds of ammunition which, whatever might be the case later on, were at all events to be dry when the expedition started. An express rider was despatched to summon Doctor

[1] This was a brother of that Colonel Cadwalader who was taken at Fort Washington, and who was released by Sir William Howe in return for civilities shown by the Colonel's father to General Prescott when a prisoner in Philadelphia Washington, in terms of unwonted vivacity, expressed an apprehension lest the Continental officers might "kick up some dust" at being placed under the command of a brigadier from the militia. He accordingly desired General Horatio Gates to lead the force which was destined to attack Von Donop ; but Gates pleaded illness, and went off to Baltimore, where he put himself in touch with the less respectable Members of Congress, and laid the foundation of an intrigue directed against the leadership of Washington.

Shippen and his assistants from the hospital at Bethlehem, with orders to accompany the march, and be close
at hand when the firing began. The pass-word for the
ensuing evening was "Victory or Death"; and there
was hardly a soldier in the ranks who did not understand
why that phrase had been chosen

The weather was frightful. Intense cold set in on
the twentieth of December; and the Delaware, from
bank to bank, swam thick with frozen blocks, which
were already piled into a mass lower down the river
where the stream was affected by the tides. Ewing
found himself unable to cross at Trenton Ferry. Cadwalader tried first above Bristol, and then below; but
he encountered a solid field of ice, three hundred feet
in breadth, between the open water and the Jersey
shore, and though, by dint of great exertions, he at
length landed a part of his infantry, they came too late,
and the event was decided without him. Washington's
own difficulties were somewhat less, and he had more
perfect appliances wherewith to surmount them; but
the task which awaited him was rude enough. At two
in the afternoon on Christmas day his little battalions
stepped off from their quarters; and before sunset the
whole force was assembled on the shore in front of
McKenky's Ferry. Those who were behind time could
easily trace the route which their comrades had followed; "for the snow was tinged here and there with
blood from the feet of the men who wore broken shoes."
It had confidently been hoped that the troops would
have been transported across the river by midnight, so
that they might have the rest of the darkness for their
march to Trenton, and be in a position for commencing
an attack with the earliest gleam of dawn. But the
Delaware ran high and strong; the cold was sharp to
the point of torture; and about eleven o'clock a bewil-
dering tempest of sleet and hail was hurled athwart the
channel on a fierce, bitter wind. Huge jagged cakes
of ice, troublesome from the first, were a more dangerous obstacle at each successive crossing. During

nine mortal hours the Marblehead fishermen contended with the gale and the flood. Captain Blunt of
Portsmouth saw the boat-loads off, timed the journeys
to and fro, and instructed the steersmen as to the
allowance which should be made for the force of the
current. Colonel Knox shouted directions to the troops
in stentorian accents, which were heard through the
roaring of the storm, and never left his station on the
Pennsylvanian bank until he had assured himself that
not an ammunition cart or an artillery horse remained
on the wrong side of the river. Even at that unnatural
hour, and in those inclement surroundings, the Americans found a hearty welcome on the Jersey shore. The
township of Hopewell, in that province, was one of the
two districts which had suffered most cruelly from the
devastations of the Hessians. A hint had got abroad
that Washington was expected ; and all the able-bodied
men turned out from their ransacked homes to meet
him. They hauled up the great Durham boats through
the shallow water, they helped to coax the horses, and
turn the spokes of the cannon-wheels, down extemporised bridges which gave access from the vessels to
the shore; and every one of them either accompanied
or preceded the army to the field of action. Some
were guides Others went on ahead, secure from suspicion in their farming clothes, to spy out, and report
upon, the amount of vigilance displayed by the outlying Hessian pickets. One, an old miller, — whom the
Germans had imprisoned, but who escaped, costumed
as a woodsman with an axe on his shoulder, after
having been under the same roof as Colonel Rall, —
brought to Washington the very latest news from the
interior of Trenton.

As the storm increased, — and as the night, with its
priceless advantages for an assailant, slipped away, —
the American commander sate, tranquil and silent, amid
an anxious and despondent group of generals. It was
not till four o'clock on the Thursday morning that the
army was formed up for the march upon Trenton.

The scene was cheerless, more especially for the younger privates, who were already very near the end of the small stock of vital energy which a long campaign had left them. Dead-beat and footsore, they slipped and stumbled amid the frozen slush, drenched through and through by the merciless hail. Their officers walked among them, teaching them, by precept and example,[1] to cover the locks of their muskets in their blankets, or beneath their coat-skirts; reminding them of worse times; and promising them a fair and speedy chance to retrieve their past defeats Half-way to Trenton a halt was called, and the soldiers took a hasty meal, while Washington breakfasted in the saddle When the order was given to re-form the ranks, many were already asleep at the road side, and could with difficulty be got once more upon their feet. The two divisions pursued separate routes. Sullivan led three brigades along the lower road, nearest to the river; and Greene, with four brigades, came by the Pennington highway. A detachment of artillerymen went with the advanced parties, carrying spikes and hammers to disable, and drag-ropes to secure, the enemy's cannon. On both roads four field-pieces travelled in front of the infantry, and the others followed at intervals, well forward in the line of march. Colonel Knox had brought all his guns for use, even at the risk of losing some few of them by capture. Washington rode along on his chestnut-sorrel charger, sunk in thought, but from time to time calling to his men, "Press on; press on, boys" The first signs of daylight now began to appear; and all hope of surprising the Hessians in their beds was perforce abandoned.[2] The boldest felt that they had better make the most of that sunrise, as they might never see another. No one was sanguine

---

[1] The American regimental officers carried fusees; and some, who knew that they could use a rifle with advantage, had provided themselves with that weapon.

[2] Stryker's *Trenton and Princeton.* His account of the passage over the Delaware, and of the night march, is excellent throughout.

enough to anticipate, what was indeed the case, that the hardest, and even the most perilous, section of their enterprise had already been accomplished.

The preliminary arrangements for the expedition, though made with all possible secrecy and circumspection, had been elaborate and comprehensive. They embraced a large extent of country, and inevitably challenged the observation of hostile eyes. Colonel Rall had not been at the pains to send spies into the American lines; but two deserters from the Continental army informed him that the Philadelphian militia were assembling, and that Washington's soldiers were employed in cooking enough rations for several days A Tory farmer from Pennsylvania brought word that Trenton would certainly be attacked at an early moment; and on the twenty-fourth of December General Grant wrote from Brunswick that he had "got into a good line of intelligence," and had learned enough to assure himself that the Hessians ought at once to put themselves on their guard German officers, who had very good reasons for avoiding the possible contingency of having the packages and bundles in their private waggons overhauled by an American victor, suggested to Colonel Rall that the baggage might be transferred to a place of safety; but he replied that whoever could capture him, and his brigade, might take the baggage as well If the rebels, (he said,) came across the Delaware, the best they could hope for was a good retreat And so the Germans set themselves down to enjoy their Christmas; with kindly thoughts, doubtless, of those whom they had left behind them in Franconia and Westphalia; but with no pity or compunction for the cold hearths, and bare larders, of many a New Jersey family.[1] About seven in the evening on Christmas day a noise of firing

---

[1] A great deal has been written about the drunken revels of the Hessians, but all the evidence goes to show that they were badly off for liquor that Christmas. The officers were distressed about the price of Madeira, which was three and sixpence a bottle. Rall exerted himself

suddenly broke out on the north of the town, and all the three regiments were mustered for battle. It was little more than a false alarm. An American scouting party had surprised the outposts, and had wounded half a dozen Hessians without any loss to themselves. Rall came to the conclusion that this was the aggressive movement with reference to which General Grant had cautioned him. The troops were dismissed, and returned to their merry-making; and he himself repaired as guest to a jovial supper, where he stopped over his cards and wine until the late winter morning had nearly come. In the course of that night, a Loyalist from across the river knocked at the door of the house where the festival was in progress, and asked to see the Colonel. Refused admittance, he wrote a few lines, and gave injunctions that they should at once be delivered to Rall, who slipped the note into his pocket unread. Not many hours afterwards when, as a dying man, he had been undressed for the last time, this scrap of paper was found in his clothes, and he learned the nature of the neglected warning with resignation and contrition.

On the evening of Christmas day, when the alarm had subsided, but before the brigade was dispersed to quarters, Major von Dechow earnestly adjured his commanding officer to send out strong patrols along all the roads, and as far as the ferries; but Rall answered that morning would be time enough. A half troop of English Light Dragoons had been attached to his command, and some of them were usually employed in reconnoitring the vicinity; but on the twenty-sixth of December that precaution was omitted. Three infantry privates only went off to scout, and, after walking a short distance into the country, they returned long before daybreak with the report that nothing was stirring. One company of the Von Lossberg regiment

to procure spruce-beer, or small beer, for his soldiers, but not very successfully; and, at the best, those beverages were poor drink for the countrymen of King Gambrinus.

was stationed on the Pennington road, a quarter of a mile outside Trenton; and at nearly the same distance further on was the advance-post, which on this occasion was held by a score of the Von Knyphausens under Lieutenant Wiederhold. This young gentleman was a smart officer, especially when criticising his superiors after things had happened; but at the place, and the moment, of all others, he himself was not sufficiently alive to the danger. Chancing to step out of the house at a quarter to eight in the morning, he saw a number of men coming through the edge of the woods about two hundred yards away. They were General Greene's skirmishers; and the main column was close behind The fight at once began, — fast, furious, and unceasing from the earliest minute to the last. Before the officers in charge of Rall's outposts had time to look about them, the Americans were thick in their front Along both roads the tide of battle surged with extraordinary violence. The Hessian pickets on the Pennington highway were rolled up, and driven back into the town, a great deal the worse for the collision. Sullivan, in the quarter towards the river, without losing a man of his own, beat in a picket of fifty chasseurs. Hunters and gamekeepers from the German forests, they passed in Europe for dead shots at stags and poachers; but they aimed badly when their target was a backwoodsman with the butt of a rifle at his shoulder. The tactical movements, on which success or failure depended, were conducted with rare precision and marvellous celerity. Even if grass could have grown in such weather, there would have been no great crop of it that day beneath the feet of Washington's people. Greene's two leading brigades filed steadily and swiftly past the northern entrance of Trenton, and formed up in a continuous line extending from the Princeton highway to the Assunpink Creek. His third brigade, which General Mercer commanded, turned off the road by which they had hitherto travelled, got into touch with Sullivan, and assailed the western skirts of the village; while Lord

Stirling, who hitherto had marched at the tail of the column, drew up his slender, but well-tried, battalions of Southern infantry opposite the junction of the two principal streets, on the very spot which Von Donop had marked out as a site for the redoubt that never had been erected.

The net had been drawn, almost without an interstice, around the devoted village before the garrison was arrayed for battle. Their brigade adjutant looked into Rall's chamber at six o'clock, and again at seven; but on both occasions he found its occupant sleeping heavily. When the rattle of small arms arose outside the town, he a third time knocked loudly at the front door; and the colonel, roused at last, flung on his uniform, and was instantaneously in the street. Fiery soldier that he always was, nothing except the prospect of a fight would have drawn him out of his bed without a grumble. He at once set his troops in such order as was permitted by the hurry, and by the fatal disadvantage of the restricted locality within which he was now reduced to manœuvre. His own regiment fell in some distance down King Street, which was the western of the two thoroughfares; and the Von Lossbergs mustered in Church Alley, at the back of the poplar trees, with orders to clear Queen Street of the rebels. Von Dechow drew up his battalion to the rearward, at a right angle with the rest of the brigade, and faced Sullivan in the southern quarter of the town. But the streets of Trenton, with round-shot already bounding along the causeways, were ill suited for an assembling-ground. Colonel Knox had placed his guns in line as fast as they arrived at the cross-roads, and gave them the range himself; and the Americans had pushed forward so briskly that Alexander Hamilton, — who marched with the reserve, and was therefore the last to unlimber, — discharged shell with deadly effect into the leading company of the Von Lossberg regiment as it emerged from Church Alley. Of effective response on the other side there was none whatever. The Von Knyphausen cannon got among the Von Lossberg ranks; while the Von Loss-berg cannon remained throughout the affair with the Von Knyphausen battalion, and made a very poor his-tory. For all the damage that they wrought, the Ger-man field-pieces might have remained in the arsenal at Cassel, since their fire was at once dominated by the American gunners, who aimed as scrupulously and coolly as if they were shooting at a mark to win a prize for their battery. By the time that the four Hes-sian cannon which pointed northwards had discharged twenty rounds between them, they had lost half their horses; many of their artillerymen had been struck down; and the remainder were running for their lives.

Meanwhile the town was filling up rapidly with American marksmen, who were busy and efficient in a theatre of action which exactly suited their favourite mode of warfare. The streets were bordered by hand-some and commodious houses, standing in enclosed plots of ground, which in summer time were shaded by abundance of elm, and black-oak, and hickory.[1] The fences, dividing one property from another, were lined more thickly every minute by skirmishers, who pelted with musketry the groups of Hessians, huddled up behind the tenements for shelter from the grape-shot which scoured the street. The riflemen, — a privileged class, who went their own way in battle, — ensconced themselves under cover from the rain in cellars[2] or in upper chambers; wiped their priming-pans dry, and took deliberate shots at every German uniform which showed itself round a corner. Mercer's troops, who had penetrated within the confines of Trenton from the

[1] A traveller, who visited Trenton more than a quarter of a century before the battle, described the houses as comfortably built of stone below, with an upper-floor of wood; standing flush to the street, but apart from each other, and with larger or smaller gardens to the rear of them *Travels in North America*, by Professor Peter Kalm, in Volume XII. of Pinkerton's Collection. Professor Kalm may fairly be called the Swedish Arthur Young.

[2] Professor Kalm especially noticed the cellars at Trenton, which apparently were a feature of the place.

west, fired sharply, and close at hand, into the flank
of the Hessians through the pales of a large tan-yard.
After no long while Stirling gave the word, and
launched his infantry, at a run, down both roads towards
the centre of the village If the German officers had
so poor an opinion of generals and colonels who were
tradesmen and mechanics, this was the time to prove
it; for Knox was a Boston bookseller; Stirling had
kept a shop; and Nathanael Greene, when it came to
forging an anchor, could hold his own among any gang
of hammermen in Rhode Island. The moment, however, was one when social distinctions are apt to be in
abeyance. William Washington's Virginians charged
for the guns in King Street. Their stalwart captain
was shot through both his hands, and Lieutenant
Monroe had an artery cut by a ball If surgical aid
had not been promptly forthcoming, he might have
died then and there; and his doctrine, which in any
case could hardly fail to have been invented, would
have borne some different title. But the guns were
taken. Rall's own regiment fired two volleys, and then
broke and fell back, throwing the left wing of the
Von Lossbergs into great confusion. A mighty clamour
came from their rear, where Sullivan's division was
pushing the Von Knyphausens in hopeless rout across
the southern districts of the town. Colonel Stark,
who held the rail-fence at Bunker's Hill, commanded
the leading regiment, — as active in attack as he had
then been obstinate in defence. The names of his
people recall the battles of the Old Testament; and
they were not behindhand with the Israelites in their
zeal to smite an adversary. Fifteen or sixteen New
Hampshire men from Derryfield kept constantly to the
front, under Sergeant Ephraim Stevens, and Captain
Ebenezer Frye; a very corpulent officer who had
retained his girth through all the hardship and star-
vation of the Jersey retreat They are said to have
taken prisoners sixty Hessians, who afterwards professed to have been puzzled and misled as to the

number of their captors by the headlong and desperate
character of the onset.   The streets were thick to suf-
focation with the smoke of gunpowder.   The sleet came
down more dense and blinding than ever.   The narrow
spaces resounded with the roar of cannon and musket,
with shrieks and exclamations, with vehement cheering,
and a great deal of swearing in two languages.   Words
of command were thick in the air, for among Washington's troops there was an excited captain or subaltern to every ten or twelve privates; and some of
the German officers exerted themselves bravely and
strenuously, although they nowhere could induce their
men to stand.   Doors and windows on the ground-floor
were beaten in; and the dwellings were used as for-
tresses by the American riflemen, or as asylums by
Hessians who sought refuge and concealment beneath
Tory roofs   Colonel Knox, with all else that he had to
occupy his attention, found time to bestow a compassionate
thought upon the residents of Trenton and their hapless
families.[1]   The scene, terrible to civilian householders,
was too much for the nerves of a good many professional
soldiers   Several hundreds of the garrison fled across
the bridge over the Assunpink Creek, which still was open,
and made their way safe to Bordentown.   The calamity
which they left behind them was so overwhelming that
their timely retreat, instead of being censured or punished,
was accounted to them for righteousness.[2]

The Hessian Commander began to be aware that,
unless he could extricate his brigade from the streets
and by-lanes of the town, it would soon be destroyed
piecemeal.   He had at first been dazed and mystified
by the suddenness and multiplicity of the American

---

[1] "The attack on Trenton was a most horrid scene to the poor
inhabitants.   War, my Lucy, is not a humane trade."   General Knox to
his wife ; January 2, 1777.

[2] "The number of men who succeeded in escaping plainly shows
what the rest could have done if the officers remaining had done their
duty, and not put aside the obligations they were under to me, to the honour
of my troops, and to their own reputation."   Letter of April 1777, from
the Landgrave of Hesse Cassel to Lieutenant General von Knyphausen.

attacks; but he now recovered his presence of mind, and saw his course plain before him   Having withdrawn the Rall and Von Lossberg regiments to the open ground east of the village, he ordered them to face about, and advance in extended line against what had now become the American position.   Their ranks were re-formed; their colours were displayed conspicuously in the centre of each battalion, and the band struck up a tune.   The moment had arrived for trying the efficacy of that assault with the bayonet which was the gallant veteran's ideal of warfare.   It was all in vain. His own regiment would not face the rifles.   The Von Lossbergs, — who alone of the Hessians on that day did well, or even respectably, — lost several officers and thirty men, without anywhere getting into thrusting distance of an enemy   Rall fell from his horse with two frightful wounds; and his troops abandoned the fray, and retired to an apple-orchard just beyond the Friends' Meeting House on the eastern edge of the village.   The surviving field-officers recognised that all was over.   Their men would not go forward ; and the means for standing successfully on the defensive were altogether wanting.   Wet had spoiled the muskets ; and towards the close of the affair there were a great many more misfires than explosions.   The braver soldiers were seen chipping away at their flints amid a shower of bullets, and then pulling their triggers again and again without effect.   Artillery, in those days, was the proper weapon for bad weather; but the German cannon had all been captured or disabled.   Washington, on the other hand, had provided himself with field-pieces in double the ordinary proportion to the numbers of his infantry; and he had committed them to the charge of an officer who utilised them to the very utmost.   Colonel Knox, who had thriven in business by industry and assiduity, laid claim to no other qualities in his capacity of an artilleryman,[1] and he took good

---

[1] " Will it give you satisfaction or pleasure in being informed that the Congress have created me a general officer, with the entire command

care at Trenton that no man in his command should be idle, and no gun-muzzle silent, as long as any profitable work remained to be executed.

Knox hurried up his batteries from the point where they had been stationed at the commencement of the action, and cannonaded the Hessians, who shielded themselves, as best they could, among the trees of the orchard. Greene had kept in reserve two entire brigades, posted on his extreme left, in express view of some such contingency as now occurred, and they moved forward in serried ranks, with loaded arms, eager to take their part in the victory. The Germans saw themselves threatened by a semicircle of field-guns; while a thousand fresh and untouched troops of the Continental line were bearing down upon them within a distance of sixty paces. The American infantry forbore from shooting, and the artillery-fire ceased; for both parties knew that the fight was ended, and neither of them desired that the butchery should begin. The Hessian standards were lowered, the muskets were grounded; "and the officers placed their hats on the points of their swords, and held them up in token of submission."[1] Some few hundred yards away to the southward the Von Knyphausen regiment was helplessly recoiling from the conflict in quest of safety. Major von Dechow, mortally hurt, had fallen into American hands; and his senior captain attempted to escape, with the remnant of his command, by the bridge over the Assunpink Creek. If the roads which led to the ferries had been properly patrolled by cavalry, the whole garrison, forewarned in time, might have made good their retreat across that bridge long before Washington had arrived within several miles of the town. It was now too late; for Sullivan, who never in his life made a finer figure than on that morning, had already secured the

of the artillery? If so, I shall be happy. People are more lavish in their praises of my poor endeavours than they deserve. All the merit I can claim is industry." General Knox to his wife, January 2, 1777

[1] Stryker's *Trenton and Princeton.*

pass with infantry and cannon. Two field-pieces, which the Von Knyphausens dragged along with them, sank in the mud, and were abandoned to the advancing enemy The march of the column was obstructed by a train of waggons, piled up with plunder, which had been brought thus far, but no further, on the way to Germany; and a throng of camp-followers, male and female, — shrieking, and rushing to and fro as the shot flew about them, — spread panic and disorder in the ranks. Under cover of the thick underbrush that fringed the stream some captains and lieutenants, with a few hardy privates, endeavoured to discover a passage through the creek; sounding the bottom with their spontoons, and wading up to their necks in the ice-cold water. The stoutest fellows swam across to freedom; but others were drowned; and Sullivan's leading brigade, active in pursuit, was now almost within pistol-shot The Germans were called upon to surrender at discretion; and, after a protracted parley, they consented to obey. As the Hessian regiment threw down their firelocks, "the patriot troops tossed their hats in the air; a great shout resounded through the village, and the battle of Trenton was closed."[1]

Rall's forces, when the affair commenced, had been sixteen hundred strong.[2] Their killed and wounded

[1] Stryker's *Trenton and Princeton.*
Colonel Knox gave his wife an excellent account of the affair in brief, interspersed with touches of affection not out of place even in such a story "About half a mile from the town," he wrote, " was an advanced guard on each road, consisting of a captain's guard. These we forced, and entered the town with them pell-mell, and here succeeded a scene of war of which I had often conceived, but never saw before The hurry, fright, and confusion of the enemy was not unlike that which will be when the last trump shall sound. They endeavoured to form in the streets, the head of which we had previously the possession of with cannon and howitzers. These, in the twinkling of an eye, cleared the streets The backs of the houses were resorted to for shelter. These proved ineffectual. The musketry soon dislodged them. Finally they were driven through the town into the open plains beyond."

[2] Each of the three line regiments contained on an average four hundred and eighty men and officers, and there were, in addition, the Chasseurs, the detachment of artillery, and some British dragoons.

were above a hundred, of whom two-thirds belonged to the Von Lossberg regiment. The Americans captured six field-pieces; a thousand fine muskets, forty sound horses; fifteen standards, twelve brass-barrel drums, and all the clarionets and hautboys, together with forty hogsheads of rum. Among the prisoners were thirty regimental officers, ninety-two Sergeants, twenty-nine musicians, and seven hundred and forty privates; as well as a Provost Marshal, whose office must of late have been a sinecure, for the buildings occupied by the Germans contained a large assortment of miscellaneous property which had not been honestly come by. Washington gave directions that the casks of rum should at once be staved in, and the liquor emptied on the ground; and he invited the inhabitants of New Jersey to reclaim any goods of which they had been despoiled. Those farmers from Hopewell Township, who had come to his assistance empty-handed, might now carry back with them their fireplaces and kitchen-furniture to help their wives and children through what remained of the savage winter. The Hessians, in their hour of humiliation, made a resplendent show. Their regimental flags were of white silk, worked in gold with haughty devices to which the occasion lent an ironical meaning.[1] The soldiers were described by an eye-witness as hearty-looking and well-clad, with large knapsacks, and spatterdashes on their legs. The Rall battalion in dark blue, the Von Lossbergs in scarlet, the Von Knyphausens in neat and seemly black, and the artillerymen in blue coats with crimson lapels and white borders, were all in singular contrast to the dingy threadbare summer clothing, and naked feet, of their captors

[1] The Von Lossberg banner bore the words "Pro Principe et Patriâ;" and some Americans knew enough Latin to wonder what were the patriotic interests which had brought Hessians to fight on the Delaware. Another regiment, which had shown no appetite for battle, displayed a Lion rampant, surmounted by the motto "Nescit Pericula." The captured standards are reported as fifteen in General von Heister's official despatch to the Prince of Hesse The general probably included the guidons of companies as well as the regimental flags.

Washington gathered up his prizes; collected his troops; and issued orders to start forthwith upon the homeward journey. Before his departure, accompanied by General Greene, he waited upon Colonel Rall; took his parole of honour, which was a sad and very superfluous ceremony; spoke to him kindly and most respectfully; and assured him, in reply to his anxious request, that the prisoners should be humanely and considerately treated. Rall did not survive the morrow; and Von Dechow died within a few hours of his chief. Washington's troops reached the ferry, where they had left their vessels, in time to commence the return passage over the Delaware before nightfall. The weather had not mended A boatful of German officers came very near being swamped in the freezing current; and tradition relates that three Americans died outright of cold. The victors arrived at their respective quarters dropping with sleep,[1] having marched and fought continuously for six-and-thirty, forty, and in some cases for fifty, hours. That was a long and a severe ordeal; and yet it may be doubted whether so small a number of men ever employed so short a space of time with greater and more lasting results upon the history of the world.

One circumstance in the affair was strange almost to

---

[1] The good people of the house, in which a young New England captain lodged, had prepared for him a large dish of hasty pudding , but he fell asleep over his supper, and awoke next morning with the spoon still in his hand.

David How was at Trenton ; and his journal represents that famous passage of arms under its most elementary aspects.

"Dec 24. We have ben Drawing Cateridges And provisions in order for a Scout.

"25 This Day at 12 a Clock we Marched Down the River about 12 miles. In the Night we Crossed the River Dullerway With a large Body of men And Field Pieces

"26 This morning at 4 a Clock we set off with our Field pieces and Marched 8 miles to Trenton whare we ware Atacked by a Number of Hushing and we Toock 1000 of them besides killed Some Then we marched back and got to the River at Night and got over all the Hushing.

"27. This morning we Crossed the River and come to our Camp at Noon.

"28. This Day we have ben washing Our things "

a miracle. The incidents at Trenton have been described by German military writers in narratives marked externally by the same professional minuteness and fidelity which characterise the Official Accounts of recent wars issued, in our own generation, by the Staff Department at Berlin. These narratives solemnly and specifically report how in the battle of Trenton this regiment deployed, and advanced firing; and how that regiment retired to take up a less exposed position; and how one captain or another, at such a minute in such an hour, rallied his company, and brought it once more into action, at the corner of a certain street. And in the end we learn that, as the net result of all those prolonged and complicated operations, not a single American was killed in the course of the whole engagement. Two privates were wounded, and two officers; of whom the more severely hurt was alive, and in the White House, forty-eight years afterwards. The watchword "Victory or Death" proved to be, for Washington's followers, a literal, an exact, and, (in the ultimate event,) a most cheerful and satisfactoiy alternative Excuses were put forward by some among the vanquished who were not wise enough to leave ill alone. They talked of the Germans as out-numbered; and undoubtedly Washington had eight hundred more men than Rall; but, as long as the adversaries were still at grips, and while the possession of Trenton was being disputed within the confines of Trenton itself, the town contained at least as many Hessians as Americans. The rain, (it was further alleged,) fell so heavily that the German muskets would not go off. It cannot, however, be forgotten that Washington's men, and their firelocks likewise, had for nine consecutive hours been exposed to a constant downpour without any protection whatsoever; while Rall's troops came forth to battle from weather-tight quarters, as warm as rooms are kept by soldiers when they are burning fuel which belongs to other people.

The explanation, of what otherwise is inexplicable,

rests not on military or material, but on moral, grounds. Washington, in a General Order of congratulation addressed to his soldiers, observed that he had previously been in many actions, but always had perceived some misbehaviour in some individuals. At Trenton, however, he had seen none. Too much praise, (a contemporary remarked,) could not be given to the Continental troops "His Excellency was pleased at their undaunted courage. Not a soul was found skulking; but all were fierce for battle."[1] Americans were fierce for battle, because they understood what the battle was about; but in the opposite ranks there was a great lack of knowledge, and very little ardour The Germans who made such a poor affair of street-fighting in Trenton were not born less brave than those countrymen of theirs who attacked the villages in front of Lutzen in 1813, and who in 1815 defended Ligny and St. Amand with the extreme of heroism. But Blucher's infantry were contending for their fatherland; whereas the dullest fusilier in Rall's regiments, beneath all the pipe-clay of his cross-belts, felt an uneasy consciousness that he was enlisted on what, likely enough, was the wrong side of a dispute that did not in any way concern himself or his nation. The Hessian officers never attempted to justify their presence under arms in New Jersey by any public or patriotic motive They admitted quite frankly, in the hearing of Lord Stirling, that they had not conceived it their duty to inquire which of the two parties in the American controversy was right. By far the most ably reasoned defence of German interference in the war between Britain and her colonies is given in a letter of the Freiherr von Gemmingen, a Minister to the Margrave of Anspach. "The Margrave," this statesman wrote, "is determined to set his affairs in order, and to pay all his own debts, and those of his predecessors; so the good that may come out of such a treaty of subsidy will far outweigh the hatefulness of the business. . . . The matter will naturally be looked on in

[1] *American Archives* for December 1776.

the most unfavourable light by people who do not understand an affair of State as a whole. But as soon as such people see foreign money flowing into our poor country, — as soon as they see us paying its debts with the means that come pouring in, — they will acknowledge that the troops, whose business is to fight the enemies of the state, have conquered our worst enemy, namely our debts. Even the lowest soldier shipped to America will come back with his savings, and be proud to have worked for his country and for his own advantage."[1] In plain words, Anspachers, and Waldeckers, and Hessians crossed the Atlantic in order to fill the empty treasuries of their rulers, and to draw increased pay and allowances for themselves; and the calamities which there befell them were accepted by public-minded and self-respecting men, all the world over, with feelings ranging between lively satisfaction and contemptuous indifference.

In England the Hessians met with the same sort of sympathy as a crowd in a market-place, where a fair stand-up fight is going on, would accord to a stranger who took five shillings to trip up one of the combatants, and got knocked down for his pains. Our bluff countrymen in those days had a strong prejudice against foreigners, more especially foreigners who lived on English money; and they loved George the Third's German mercenaries as little as their grandfathers had liked and revered George the First's German mistresses. On the continent of Europe, — outside the precincts of those petty Courts which had habitually and traditionally made a profit by selling their subjects to the War Offices of neighbouring powers,[2] — national opinion had been deeply and sincerely outraged by the revival of that hateful traffic, on a vast scale, for the prosecution

[1] This letter is quoted in the second chapter of Mr. Lowell's *Hessians*.
[2] In 1782 a pamphlet, attributed to a Minister of the Landgrave of Hesse, was published in French and German. The writer there stated, by way of defence for his royal patron, that the letting-out of Hessians for foreign service, so far from being an innovation, was the tenth occasion of the kind since the beginning of the century.

of a policy alien to every legitimate European interest. The poet Schiller, before the war closed, gave forcible expression to the shame and indignation which filled every true German heart; and the drama in which he denounced and satirised royal dealers in human life, — with such point and vigour that friends to whom he showed the piece had not dared confess to having read it in private, — when brought openly upon the stage was acted amid a tumult of applause.

Some dim perception of the disgust and humiliation, which were inspired in all honest men by the cruel and ignoble system, gradually filtered down to the unfortunate creatures who were the victims of it; and the news from Trenton, as may well be imagined, made the trade of crimping none the easier. In March 1777 two regiments from Anspach and Bayreuth were put into boats at Ochsenfurth, — a little walled town which then belonged to the Bishop of Wurtzburg, — for water-carriage down the Main and the Rhine to a port of embarkation in Holland. This flock of country lads, (we are informed,) were shivering with cold, and sickened by the smell of the closely packed barges which, in their simplicity, they thought were to carry them, without change of ship, across the ocean to America. They broke out into mutiny, "a poor helpless mutiny, without a plan, without a leader. At daybreak some of the soldiers of the Anspach regiment, whose boat was near the bank, laid a plank to the shore, and walked over it They then dragged other boats to land; and in an hour the miserable crowd of cold and hungry men was on shore, storming with anger, and refusing to yield to the threats and promises of its officers." [1] Some chasseurs were ordered to fire upon the deserters from the surrounding hills; and on this occasion they shot more accurately than when they confronted a skirmish-line of American riflemen. The Bishop of Wurtzburg sent hussars and dragoons to quell the riot, and was subsequently thanked by Lord North's government for

[1] Lowell's *Hessians*, chapter v. Stephan Popp's *Journal;* 1777-1783.

his friendly and spirited conduct. The Margrave of Anspach himself, who had been fetched in hot haste, accompanied the flotilla down the rivers, and never lost sight of the goods which he had undertaken to deliver until they were duly consigned on board the British transports. Then, with conscience clear and pocket well lined, he started gaily on a trip to Paris, having already arranged for sending another batch of recruits down stream in the course of that autumn. He had written to his uncle, — who was no less than Frederic the Great, — asking that these troops might be permitted to pass through a corner of the Prussian dominions; but he esteemed the request a mere formality, and travelled off to France without waiting for an answer. Frederic was not a bishop; and, in language which was to his credit both as a soldier and a German ruler, he returned his nephew a flat refusal.[1]   The princes whose capitals lay to the south of Magdeburg and Berlin were thenceforward reduced to despatch their contingents by a circuitous route, which traversed several independent States, and the territories of some free cities. The commander of the Anhalt Zerbst regiment, in particular, found it almost impossible to bring his recruits along. Local sympathy was everywhere excited, and actively exerted, on behalf of the youths who filed through town and village in a weary woebegone procession; and, before the seacoast came in view, three out of every eight had made good their escape from servitude.

The victory at Trenton was hailed with joy and triumph by the great majority of Americans, who had been profoundly incensed against the foreign soldiers of the Crown. They reproached them, (wrote a British

---

[1] "Monsieur my Nephew!

"I own to your Most Serene Highness that I never think of the present war in America without being struck by the eagerness of some German princes to sacrifice their troops in a quarrel which does not concern them My astonishment increases when I remember in ancient history the wise and general aversion of our ancestors to wasting German blood for the defence of foreign rights, which even became a law in the German state."

So the letter began , and the rest was of a piece.

historian,) with the highest degree of moral turpitude for quitting their homes in the Old World to butcher a people in the New World from whom they never had received the smallest injury; but who, on the contrary, had for a century past afforded an asylum to their harassed and oppressed countrymen, when they fled across the seas in multitudes to enjoy the blessings of a liberty most generously held out to them.[1] When it became known that Great Britain was hiring Hessians and Brunswickers to suppress freedom in her colonies, the Americans loudly condemned what they regarded as German ingratitude; and their anger had since then been exacerbated by the plunder and devastation of New Jersey. Washington's soldiers, on the western bank of the Delaware, had waited in a state of white rage for an opportunity to get at the throats of those who had perpetrated the outrages; but, when the fight ended, and the delinquents were at their mercy, their wrath cooled down, and their good nature reasserted itself in all its plenitude. Their commander set the example of generosity Going even beyond the promise which he had given to his dying foe, Washington ordered that the portmanteaus of the Hessian officers, and the knapsacks of the soldiers, should be made over to them unsearched and unopened. As soon as a dinner could be cooked, he entertained the colonels and majors at his quarters; while captains and lieutenants were turned over to the care of Lord Stirling. Retaining a pleasant recollection of General von Heister's courtesy when he himself had been a prisoner after the battle of Long Island, Stirling surpassed his own reputation as a bountiful host, and promptly repressed a sour-visaged Lutheran pastor from Hanover who thought fit to harangue the company, in their own tongue, about the

---

[1] "History of Europe" in the *Annual Register* for 1777, chapter 1 That argument went strongly home to the Pennsylvanian emigrants of German descent, upon whom the Revolution, as the earliest of its boons, had conferred the enjoyment of full political freedom, and who were almost to a man, devoted adherents of the popular party.

iniquities of George the Third, and the justice of the American case as put forward in the Declaration of Independence.[1]   After having given their parole, the Hessian officers were conveyed to Philadelphia in comfortable equipages, were driven to the sign of The Indian Queen, and there set down to "a grand supper, with plenty of punch and wine, at the expense of Congress."   These official attentions were liberally supplemented by private hospitality in the cities which they successively visited   They respectfully admired the beauty, the elegance, and the joyous unembarrassed bearing of Virginian ladies; and some of them noted with satisfaction that their own musical accomplishments, which were not rated highly in Germany, procured them much social consideration in America.[2]

The rank and file of Rall's brigade acquired the good will of the captors by their docility, their mild and even tempers, and their freedom from political bitterness, — a virtue which was based on the solid foundation of absolute and entire political ignorance.   They had been poor soldiers at Trenton; but they made most excellent prisoners.   When they were passed southwards across the Pennsylvanian border, a difficulty occurred about the provision of an escort; and the officer in command trusted the Hessians to find their own way up the Shenandoah valley by themselves.   Three stages onwards, and at the appointed hour, each one answered to

[1] "I had the honour," (so Stirling told Governor Livingston,) "to make two regiments of them surrender prisoners of war, and to treat them in such a style as will make the rest of them more willing to surrender than to fight."

[2] At Fredericksburg sixteen ladies organised a surprise party, which visited the Hessian officers at their quarters, and stayed from half past three till ten o'clock in the evening.   The Germans regaled their guests, — who included Washington's niece and his sister, — with coffee, chocolate, cakes, claret, and even with tea; and gave them an entertainment of vocal and instrumental music.   "In Europe," said Wiederhold, "we should not have got much honour; but here we passed for masters." Such amenities, in time of war, have often been deprecated on the ground that women should not consort with those who have slain their countrymen in battle.   American ladies probably held that that consideration did not apply in the case of the Hessians who fought at Trenton.

his name in the roll-call, and was rewarded with a glass of brandy. They were scattered in detachments among the townships on either bank of the Potomac, where they lived peaceable and contented, with no desire whatever to go back to the war, and not impatient even for their return to Germany. Their minds were at ease; for their pay was running up on the books of the British War Office; and, as far as they were concerned, that was the one and only object for which they had come to America. They were on friendly and familiar terms with the inhabitants of the country, assisting them in their industries, sharing their festivities, and most certainly abstaining from all obtrusive manifestations of Tory sentiment. Those among them who had an aptitude for mechanics were allowed to take service with an ironmaster of Hessian birth who owned a large forge and foundry in New Jersey, where they helped to make gun-carriages and cannon-balls for General Washington's artillery. Colonel Rall's bandsmen remained in Philadelphia, and they must have got their clarionets and hautboys back, for they are stated to have performed at the Fourth of July celebration which followed six months after the date of Trenton.

Americans were the less vindictive in their feeling towards the Hessians because they had ceased to be afraid of them. The Seven Years' War had exalted to a very high point the military reputation of those who had been engaged in it; and it was currently believed that German strategists and tacticians possessed certain tricks of their trade which lay beyond the reach of citizen soldiers. "Our officers," John Adams wrote, "do not seem sufficiently sensible of the importance of an observation of the King of Prussia, that stratagem, ambuscade, and ambush are the sublimest chapters in the art of war. Regular forces are never surprised. They are masters of rules for guarding themselves in every situation and contingency. The old officers among them are full of resources, wiles, artifices, and strata-

gems, to deceive, decoy, and over-reach their adversaries."[1] That exaggerated estimate of German craft
and subtlety did not survive Trenton. It thenceforward
was evident that Hessian and Hanoverian colonels, —
without a Prince Ferdinand of Brunswick, or a Prince
Henry of Prussia, to command them, and when opposed
to an Anglo-Saxon enemy, — were not all of them so
many Mollendorfs and Seidlitzes. The German grenadier had hitherto been a terrible bugbear in the
imagination of ordinary Americans. Coarse engravings
had been widely circulated representing him with long
mustachios, an enormous pigtail, and a head-dress
closely resembling an episcopal mitre, cocked forward
at a minatory angle over his beetling brows; and the
vast panoply of war, which encumbered his person on
march and in action, was popularly regarded as an indication of his superhuman strength. After the close of
the campaign, however, the employers, as well as the
antagonists, of the German mercenary had begun to
perceive that the secret of being formidable in battle
depends not on looking ferocious, but on aiming correctly. That all-important truth at last penetrated the
convictions of the British War Office. When it was
ascertained that at Fort Washington, where they behaved well, the Hessians had killed very few Americans,
— and that at Trenton, where they behaved ill, they
had killed no Americans at all, — the authorities in
Whitehall directed their agents on the Continent of
Europe to enrol recruits, if such could be found, who
knew something about the use of the musket which
they carried. The Americans, on their part, who were
a practical people, had mastered the fact that they
ran no great danger to life or limb even within a few
score yards of the Hessian muzzles. They still treated
with respect a foreign regiment, when it stood in the
line of battle, flanked and backed by an array of British
bayonets. But, — whether they were Continental regulars, or minute-men, or armed farmers in their shirt-

[1] John Adams to William Tudor; Philadelphia, August 29, 1776.

sleeves, — they advanced to the attack, wherever they got a German force by itself, in disdainful and assured anticipation of an easy victory.

The ruler of Hesse Cassel was deeply mortified He could entertain no illusion as to the conduct of his soldiers. Under the treaties made with the British Government the German princes were paid a fixed sum for each of their subjects who was killed outright, while three wounded men reckoned as one dead ; [1] and the Landgrave, therefore, needed only to glance at the credit side of his account-books in order to learn that his troops had laid down their arms after losing only six per cent. of their strength in battle. He recalled General von Heister; and he ordered the officer next in command not to rest until a long series of brave acts had expunged the memory of a most unfortunate affair.[2] The guilty regiments, (so their sovereign declared,) should never receive any flags again until the day when they captured from the enemy as many standards as they had surrendered in such a disgraceful manner.

That day never came. In the course of the succeeding autumn Colonel von Donop, intent on wiping off the disgrace of Trenton, obtained leave to assault Fort Mercer at the head of a force composed exclusively of Hessians ; but the attempt failed, and the brave German fell mortally wounded amid a great carnage of his followers. Earlier in the same year, at Bennington in the Hampshire Grants, Colonel Stark hastily mustered the inhabitants of the country-side, routed Burgoyne's Brunswickers, and captured them by many hundreds in a battle which proved to be the turning-point of the

[1] In the Treaties made by His Majesty the King of Great Britain with the Duke of Brunswick, and the Hereditary Prince of Hesse Cassel, Reigning Count of Hanau, it was expressly stipulated that for every footsoldier killed there should be paid "thirty crowns Banco, the crown reckoned at fifty three sols of Holland " In the Treaty with the Landgrave of Hesse Cassel the principle was asserted, but the details were left unspecified.

[2] The Landgrave of Hesse Cassel to Lieutenant General von Knyphausen ; Cassel, April 7, 1777. Von Heister, two months after his return, died of sorrow and disappointment.

Saratoga campaign, which was the turning-point of the whole war. Such was the fate of the only two German contingents that possessed the martial traditions, the corporate spirit, and the robust organisation of long-established armies. It was evident that George the Third could expect little, — and he most undoubtedly obtained nothing, — from the fragmentary and extemporised rabbles of unwilling peasants who had been pressed upon his acceptance by the minor potentates of Franconia. Industrious plunderers,[1] and soldiers of no account, that wretched infantry went through the war, (whatever might be the case as to their honour,) with their bayonets unstained The military record of the Anhalt Zerbst battalion was farcical; the Waldeckers all of them surrendered in detachments; and the Anspach and Bayreuth regiments were captured bodily at Yorktown. Seldom has public money been worse laid out than in the case of Lord North's Continental subsidies. The unpopularity of that policy in England, the disapprobation of Europe, and the irremediable alienation of American loyalty, far over-balanced any military advantage which accrued from the extravagantly remunerated services of the German mercenaries.

Washington had caught the occasion by the forelock, at a moment when, unless his grasp had held firm, all would have been over with himself and his cause. A few days before Christmas he informed Robert Morris that Sir William Howe, in order to prosecute his designs

---

[1] In March 1780 a raiding expedition pillaged the rich and beautiful village of Hackensac, which was entirely undefended. Some Americans came in arms to the rescue ; and the spoilers ran " My own booty," wrote an Anspach musketeer, " which I brought safely back, consisted of two silver watches, three sets of silver buckles, a pair of woman's cotton stockings, a pair of man's mixed summer stockings, two shirts and four chemises of fine English linen, two fine table-cloths, one silver table-spoon and one teaspoon, five Spanish dollars and six York shillings in money. The other part, namely eleven pieces of fine linen and over two dozen silk handkerchiefs, with six silver plates and a silver drinking-mug, which were tied together in a bundle, I had to throw away on account of our hurried march, and leave them to the enemy that was pursuing us."

against Philadelphia, was only waiting for the Delaware to freeze, and for that first of January 1777 when the American army would disband itself. You might as well, (said Washington,) attempt to stop the winds from blowing, or the sun in its diurnal revolution, as to prevent the soldiers from going home when their time was up. In another important direction the outlook was most discouraging. " It is mortifying to me," Morris wrote to President Hancock, " when I am obliged to tell you disagreeable things; but I am compelled to inform Congress that the Continental currency keeps losing its credit. Many people refuse openly and avowedly to receive it; and several citizens, that retired into the country, must have starved if their own private credit had not procured them the common necessaries of life, when nothing could be got for your money." [1] General Lee was known to be in pecuniary distress; and Congress had procured a hundred of the pieces which went by the name of a half-johannes, in order to relieve the immediate necessities of the distinguished prisoner. Washington was entrusted with the disbursement of this slender hoard; and it was all the specie which his military chest contained. He was already bare of money, and by the week's end the greater part of his troops would have disappeared, when his cannon opened fire on Trenton, and the saving mercy came.

Then at last, and at once, the prospect brightened. Wherever, and whenever, the thrice-welcome news arrived, the whole Confederacy was astir. From one State and another the authorities sent in word that every man should march who could be prevailed upon to move. In Connecticut, — where Jonathan Trumbull ruled with the despotic power which at a national crisis is accorded to conspicuous energy and tried probity, — it was reported on the twenty-eighth of December that some hundreds of substantial freeholders, many of them not belonging to the militia, had engaged with a generous ardour to

[1] Robert Morris to the President of Congress at Baltimore; Philadelphia, December 23, 1776.

serve for two months at least, until the four Continental battalions, which the State was bound to furnish, had been equipped and disciplined. Several Colonels and Majors, setting considerations of rank aside, had readily accepted the command of companies. On the same day Washington was informed that Pennsylvania had at length been fairly roused, and was coming in great numbers to His Excellency's support [1] The encouraging assurance proceeded from General Mifflin himself. That admirable recruiting officer had been working hard amid gloom and discouragement; but the light had broken through the clouds, a single day of sunshine enabled him to complete the harvest; and he returned from his labours, bringing his sheaves with him. Before ever the year ended, sixteen hundred more Pennsylvanian militiamen had been sent across the Bristol Ferry to Burlington and Bordentown. Washington's most pressing care, however, was not so much to obtain additional regiments as to preserve those which he had already. "The Continental troops," (he wrote to Robert Morris,) "are all at liberty. I wish to push our success to keep up the panick, and have promised them a bounty of ten dollars, if they will continue for one month. If it be possible, Sir, to give us assistance, do it. Borrow money where it can be done. We are doing it upon our private credit. Every man of interest, every lover of his country, must strain his credit upon such an occasion" [2]

Washington led the way by pledging his own estate, for all that it would bear, in case Congress should neglect, or refuse, to make his promise of a bounty good. Colonel Stark, and other hard-fighting officers who likewise were men of substance, did not show themselves behindhand with their chief in patriotism and disinterestedness; and four hundred and ten Spanish dollars, two crowns, ten shillings and sixpence in English coin, and a French half-crown, were contributed as a unique and precious oblation by Robert Morris That

---

[1] *American Archives* for the later days of December 1776.
[2] Washington to Robert Morris; Trenton, December 31, 1776

was all the gold and silver which the great financier could scrape together in Philadelphia; but on the first of January he sent Washington fifty thousand dollars in paper, collected among his private friends, or drawn out of his own pocket; and he accompanied the gift with a cheerful, fraternal letter which it must have done the General's heart good to read.[1] Boston meanwhile, — safe within her own borders, and mindful of those whose turn it now was to hazard their lives for the principles which she had been the first to proclaim, and the foremost to defend, — sent a plentiful assortment of shoes and stockings, and of still more essential garments, to clothe the destitute New England regiments.

With these material resources in hand, the most persuasive and influential officers united in exhorting their soldiers to remain a while longer in the ranks, and of eloquence, in that army, there was a larger supply than of creature-comforts or solid cash   Washington spoke his best; and Knox also; while every regiment had an opportunity of hearing General Mifflin harangue, " mounted on a noble-looking horse, in a coat made of rose-coloured blanket, with a large fur cap on his head " The man whose words, — winged by his own noble, and even sublime, example, — flew most directly and surely to the mark, was the commander of the Massachusetts and Rhode Island brigade.   Colonel Daniel Hitchcock, a Master of Arts of Yale College, was an accomplished gentleman, and as fine a classical scholar as the erudition of the colonies could then produce.   In the last stage of consumption, he still might look forward to another fortnight of existence among the snow-gusts of that chilling winter; and his men heard him eagerly and sadly when he adjured them not to desert him until he had the satisfaction of striking one more blow for America.   A great number of them assured him that

---

[1] " If further supplies of money," Morris wrote, " are necessary, you may depend on my exertions either in a public or private capacity.   The year Seventeen seventy six is over;   and I am heartily glad of it, and hope you, nor America, will be plagued with such another."

he might count upon having his own soldiers round him
to the last; and the New England brigade set the rest
of the army an example which Washington described
as an extraordinary mark of their attachment to their
country. The militia, (so the Commander-in-Chief
wrote,) were pouring in from all quarters, and only
wanted a firm body of troops, inured to danger, to lead
them on.[1] He did not pitch his hopes too high; and
he was tolerably contented when more than half his
Continental veterans agreed to stay six weeks beyond
their term of enlistment; for that period would see the
Republic through the gravest of the peril.[2] Congress,
schooled by misfortune, had authorised Washington to
raise, organise, and equip a large additional body of
regular troops, and had invested him with supreme
military powers for the furtherance of that object.
Those powers were already being employed to such
purpose that, if he could hold his own for one or two
months longer, he would find himself at the head of
a force which, in comparison with anything he had yet
commanded, might almost be termed a standing army.

On the morning of Monday, the thirtieth of December, Washington passed the Delaware, in order to try
conclusions with a better prepared, and a much stouter,

[1] Washington to the officer commanding at Morristown, December 30,
1776; to the President of Congress, January 1, 1777; to the Committee
of Congress remaining in Philadelphia, January 1, 1777.

[2] David How's battalion was approached, like the others, with the offer
of a bounty.

"Dec. 31. The General ordered all to parade And see How many
wood Stay 6 Weaks Longer and a Grate Part of the Army Stays for that
time

"January 1. This fore noon we have ben Drawing our wages and
Sauce money. This after Noon we set out For New England marched
4 miles. Staid at night there."

It is plain that How himself insisted on his right to leave the colours,
and go home. Nine months afterwards he turned out once more, "to
march to General Gates his assistance," and arrived in time to witness the
capitulation of Burgoyne. That, so far as is known, was his last service.
Having taken part at Bunker's Hill, at the capture of Boston, at Trenton,
and at Saratoga, he had done his share towards the manufacture of
history.

adversary than the Germans whom he had overthrown at Trenton His head-quarters were transferred to that village; where all his levies, new and old, had been directed to muster. Stirling was left in charge on the Pennsylvanian bank of the river, temporarily crippled by a well-earned attack of rheumatism; that scourge of elderly generals who have enjoyed life freely, but who do not shrink from hardship and exposure in the field Within three days Washington had collected round him five thousand men and forty pieces of artillery. His army was a medley of unequally sized and very dissimilar fragments, of which the best were the smallest. Of Haslet's eight hundred Delawares only a hundred remained; and the Marylanders, who had marched to Long Island a thousand strong, had been reduced, there and elsewhere, to less than eight-score effective soldiers. The militia regiments on the other hand, none of which had been embodied during more than a fortnight, were full to overflowing, and made up quite half the numbers, though very much less than half the strength, of Washington's army. Different, indeed, was the character and the composition of that force which was being hurried forward to recover New Jersey for the Crown, and to retrieve the credit of the Royal arms When Colonel Rall's defeat became known in New York, time was not squandered, nor pains spared. The finest of the English regiments were sent off as fast as they could be got into travelling order, and pushed quickly towards the Delaware, gathering up the garrisons which were stationed along their line of march. Lord Cornwallis, whose baggage was already on board for England, gave up all thought of that voyage; started for the front on the first morning of the New Year; covered fifty miles of road at the pace of a fox-hunter on the way to a distant meet; and by nightfall was already at Princeton, at the head of eight thousand magnificent soldiers, and a powerful train of cannon Before daylight next morning he set the bulk of his troops in motion for an immediate advance on Trenton; while a

strong rear-guard remained behind at Princeton, with
orders to rejoin the main army early on the morrow.

It was a bad prospect for Washington; but he had
very carefully weighed the alternative dangers which
beset him; and he had made up his mind, at any risk
whatsoever, to hold his ground to the east of the
Delaware. He was firmly resolved on no account to
abandon those inhabitants of New Jersey who had
hailed his recent victory as the signal of their own
deliverance, and had openly and definitively cast in
their lot with the Revolution.[1] Trenton, however, (as
Washington, in the course of the past week, had bril-
liantly and conclusively proved,) was not a defensible
post He therefore established himself on the flank of
the village, and disposed his army in line of battle over
a space of three miles along the southern shore of the
Assunpink Creek, with his left resting on the Delaware
river. Time was of moment to him; for his force was
not yet completely assembled, and his more remote detachments were still coming into camp during the whole
forenoon of the second of January. He accordingly
despatched a body of picked troops towards Maidenhead, with orders to delay the enemy's march, and
stave off the impending general engagement during at
least four-and-twenty hours His injunctions were faithfully and scrupulously obeyed. Cornwallis advanced
in three columns along, and alongside, the Princeton highway. The English light infantry swarmed on
ahead, together with a strong party of Hessian chasseurs attached to the command of Colonel von Donop,
who always knew the trick of making his soldiers fight.
But the Americans had by now acquired the self-respect
and the self-possession of veterans who would be
equally ashamed to fail in their duty by remissness,
or by rashness to sacrifice in killed and wounded a

---

[1] "Our situation was most critical, and our force small To remove
immediately was again destroying every dawn of hope which had begun
to revive in the breasts of the Jersey militia." Washington to the
President of Congress; January 5, 1777.

heavier toll than the performance of that duty unavoidably exacted. They disputed each turn of the
road, and every thicket and ravine which lay to the
right or the left of it. Once at least the British artillery had to be fetched up from the rear in order to
dislodge them from a position of advantage. Both
sides, as is usual in an affair of that nature, imagined
that they were destroying a great number of their
opponents, and knew that they were losing very few of
their own people,[1] but, although the Americans had
not shot down many adversaries, they had killed much
time. The British advance guard which, without displaying any backwardness, had consumed eight hours
in traversing just as many miles, did not reach the
houses of Trenton until four in the evening, after
which, in the first week of January, there is little daylight left.

Cornwallis, when on active service, was an early
riser; and he was sure to be at work the next morning
as soon as he left his bed. So able a soldier could be
under no doubt as to what it was incumbent on him to
do. A front attack on the hostile position was altogether out of the question. Except in a very few places
the Assunpink was too deep for wading, as the Von
Knyphausens had learned to their cost; the bridge, and
all the fords, were protected by earthworks; and the
passage of the stream was commanded by more than
three times as many muskets, and six times as many
cannon, as had swept the slope in front of Bunker's
Hill. But Cornwallis had a superior force of well-
trained troops, who manœuvred with promptitude and
precision; and it would be an easy matter for him to
turn the right flank of the enemy in the direction of
Allenstown, and force them into a combat on equal
terms and in the open country. A full half of the

---

[1] Two or three American officers were wounded, and some of their
men were killed. The Hessians lost fifteen, including a chasseur whose
ghost, according to the negroes of the neighbourhood, walked the
Maidenhead woods for many years afterwards.

K 2

Americans were militiamen, badly drilled, and new to
warfare; whereas none of Cornwallis's regiments were
much below the average quality of the Royal army, —
and that average was very high.   Most military critics
hold that, in a pitched battle, Washington would probably have been beaten ; and they all of them are agreed
that, if beaten, he would have been utterly ruined.[1]

The situation was alarming, but of the class with
which Washington had always been singularly capable
of dealing.   He rapidly thought out a scheme by which
he might extricate his troops from the front of peril
without discouraging or humiliating them, and might
attain the fruits of victory more cheaply than at the
price of a bloody and dubious encounter with the whole
of the Royal army.[2]   His objects were very clear before
him ; and there was no bungling or hesitation in the
methods which he adopted in order to ensure success.
Cornwallis and his staff noticed a display of activity in
the American lines which, to their view, augured a deep
anxiety on Washington's part as to the issue of the impending battle   Camp fires, fed with cedar rails from
the fences round, were blazing all along the bank-top,
and all through the night.   Sentinels challenged; and
strong parties of infantry paced up and down the fore-
ground of the position until morning broke.   Especially
observable was the industry with which the American
engineers employed the interval of darkness for strength-
ening the fortification at the bridge.   The British pickets
could distinctly hear the voices of workmen, the blows
of axes, and the rattle of frozen earth as it was tossed

---

[1] General Knox put the case very frankly in a letter to his wife
" The situation," he wrote, " was strong to be sure, but hazardous on this
account, that, had our right been defeated, the defeat of the left would
almost have been an inevitable consequence, and the whole thrown into
confusion, or pushed into the Delaware, as it was impassable by boats."

[2] Washington gave President Hancock his reason for marching on
Princeton in a sentence of involved construction, but perfectly plain in
meaning.   "One thing I was certain of, that it would avoid the appearance of a retreat, (which was of consequence, or to run the hazard of the
whole army being cut off;) whilst we might by a fortunate stroke withdraw General Howe from Trenton, and give some reputation to our arms."

out of the ditches by the spade. But the real business
of the night was conducted elsewhere. The heaviest
American cannon, and all the stores and baggage, were
packed off to Bordentown and Burlington, and at one
in the morning the army commenced a movement the
nature and the direction of which had been disclosed to
no one below the rank of Brigadier. So strictly was the
secret kept that officers, who had taken up their quarters
in farmhouses to rear of the bivouacs, were left to have
their sleep out, and next day found difficulty in rejoin-
ing their regiments.[1] Orders were given in a whisper;
muskets were gingerly handled, and footfalls lightly
planted; and the tires of the gun-wheels had all been
carefully wrapped in strips of cloth. A hard frost made
the muddy causeways passable for artillery; and the
frequent forests through which those causeways led did
not confuse or impede the progress of the expedition.
An army containing so many Indian fighters, from the
Commander-in-Chief downwards, was at home among
the woods in night-time; and the journey proceeded
from start to finish without mishap or misadventure.
Washington steered his course with an inclination
towards the east, and then gradually worked round to
the northwest, until at daybreak he struck the Princeton
highway a mile and a half to the southward of that
town He came out exactly where he intended; but he
lighted upon something which he had not anticipated;
for marching down the road across his front was a
column of red-coated infantry.

Cornwallis had left at Princeton for the night three
regiments of the British line, with two guns, and a small
force of light dragoons. Some of these troops were
now pushing on for Trenton, to take their part in the
expected battle, with a haste which was to the credit of
their courage, and an absence of caution that was a

---

[1] Chapter xv. of Stryker's *Trenton and Princeton*. The account there
given of Washington's flank-march is illustrated by the local knowledge
of a neighbour, and the oral traditions accessible to the member of an old
Revolutionary family.

practical and most indisputable compliment to the craft
and secrecy of Washington's strategy. The British,
(so General Knox wrote,) were as much astonished as
if an army had dropped perpendicularly upon them
from the clouds;[1] but, though amazed, they were not
confounded. They at once faced about, deployed into
line, and came valiantly, and even jauntily, forwards.
Colonel Mawhood, of the Seventeenth Foot, who was
their acting Brigadier, rode among them on a small
brown pony, with two favourite spaniels bounding
before him. The Americans were cold and hungry, and
worn out by toil and want of sleep. The English were
fresh and well breakfasted; but that was the sole advantage which they enjoyed; for they were outnumbered
four to one, and their scanty force was dispersed in
three segments. The Fortieth regiment had remained
in Princeton to guard the stores; the Fifty-fifth, though
already on the road, was a mile to the rear; and Colonel
Mawhood had under his hand little besides his own battalion. During the first few minutes the odds were not
unequal. In the van of the American army was a weak
brigade of Continental infantry, under the command
of General Mercer, — a man of mature years, with a
varied, an eventful, and a most honourable career behind
him. He served as surgeon in Prince Charles's army
at Culloden; he had borne arms with distinction in
French and Indian warfare; and before the Revolution
he was a physician, noted throughout Virginia for his
skill and gentleness. Both parties raced for the possession of an orchard which lay midway between them.
The Americans reached it first, but the English
appeared to want it the most. Three volleys were
exchanged across a space of forty yards, and then
Colonel Mawhood led on his people at a run. It was
a bayonet-charge of another sort from that of poor
Colonel Rall. The Continental soldiers broke and fled;
but some of the officers remained at their post, and died
very staunchly. Two New Jersey field-pieces were

[1] General Knox to his wife; Morristown, January 7, 1777.

captured, and the captain in charge of them was killed at his guns. Mercer himself used his sword until he fell covered with wounds. Those who witnessed the behaviour of the Seventeenth Foot on that occasion might well ask themselves what would have happened if Cornwallis had hurled not one, but twelve or fifteen, of such regiments against the right wing of the American army while it was enclosed and entrapped between the ice-laden flood of the Delaware, and the unfordable Assunpink Creek.

The British followed in pursuit; but they found themselves in presence of numerous reinforcements which were flocking in towards the sound of the firing. Immediately to their front was a great mass of the Philadelphia Associators. These unpractised soldiers, civilians of yesterday, were thrown into disorder by the backward rush of their defeated countrymen; but they were recalled to their duty by the strenuous exertions of some gallant men who did not ask themselves whether that lead-swept spot of ground was the precise place to which their special business called them. Captain William Shippen, a naval officer of the Delaware squadron, there got his death-wound; and Colonel Haslet dropped with a bullet through his brain. In his pocket was an order directing him to go home on recruiting service, which he had divulged to no one, and had silently disobeyed. Washington himself rode forward between the opposing lines, until he was within thirty paces of the hostile muzzles. His friends disapproved the action as an excess of rashness; but it was a matter on which, like Wolfe before him, and Wellington after him, he had no conscience whatsoever[1] The veterans from Rhode Island and Massachusetts, whom Colonel Hitchcock brought into action in soldierly array, showed

---

[1] One of our generals, in the Peninsular war, had been too reckless of his own safety under fire "Lord Wellington," wrote Sir George Larpent, "blames his exposing himself, with what face I know not." That was a fine compliment to the valour of the Commander-in-Chief; and very pithily turned.

a steadfast countenance; the Philadelphia Associators warmed to their work, and Mercer's soldiers began to come back, as soon as there was a nucleus of discipline and martial resolution on which to rally; and the whole space in front, and in flank, of the English regiment was rapidly thronged with as many militiamen, regulars, and riflemen from the Western frontier, as could find room to ply their firelocks. The adversaries were separated by so short a distance that they could hear each other speak during the moments which elapsed before the roar of musketry commenced.[1] A Pennsylvanian battery was brought almost within pistol range, and the guns were discharged with such terrible effect as to shock those American officers who observed the ravages of the grape-shot It was the old story. During the early portion of the war it had sometimes not been easy to induce the country-bred troops to stand; but, whenever they held their ground, their fire was extraordinarily destructive. The line of British infantry, a bare four hundred to begin with, must very soon have been annihilated. No military object could be promoted by such a tragedy; enough had been done for honour; and Colonel Mawhood turned his attention to the task of saving the remnant of his battalion. He abandoned the two cannon which he had taken, and two others of his own, and made off in the direction of Trenton, covering his retreat, as best he might, with a handful of cavalry.[2]

According to those who professed to have taken the time by their watches, all this desperate fighting was crowded into fifteen minutes; and in that quarter of an hour the affair had been decided. When Colonel Mawhood retired from the field, the rest of the British

---

[1] As the First Virginians were being got into position, Captain John Fleming called out, "Gentlemen, dress the line" "We will dress you," a British private retorted; and Fleming was killed the next instant.

[2] "In this trying and dangerous situation the brave commander, and his equally brave regiment, have gained immortal honour." That sentence, from the "History of Europe" in the *Annual Register*, expressed the unanimous opinion of Colonel Mawhood's countrymen.

force would have done well at once to march away in the opposite direction; but they now were entirely cut off from their commanding officer, and they had no orders. Without artillery, and on ground not adapted for effectual defence, they very speedily had upon their hands the whole of Washington's army. General Sullivan, who led the right wing of the Americans, advanced vigorously against Princeton, and drove the Fifty-fifth and Fortieth regiments in a northerly direction through and beyond the town, killing a few, and capturing large numbers of prisoners. An attempt at resistance was made in and around the College. Even in that quarter there was very little bloodshed, but some profanation; for young Alexander Hamilton, with the irreverence of a student fresh from a rival place of education, planted his guns on the sacred grass of the academical Campus, and fired a six-pound shot which is said to have passed through the head of King George the Second's portrait in the Chapel. The buildings were soon encompassed by an overwhelming force, and their garrison surrendered at discretion.

When the town had been cleared, Washington came to an almost instant resolution as to the course which it behoved him to pursue. If he had been able to dispose of six or eight hundred troops with some spring and alertness left in them, he would, (he said,) have made a forced march on Brunswick, which contained the magazines belonging to the British army of occupation, as well as their military chest, with seventy thousand pounds inside it.[1] But his soldiers, who had carried their arms during forty continuous hours of bitter weather, were falling asleep on the frozen ground; and there was no time allowed them to snatch a rest or cook a meal. As soon as the sun tinged with light the fog of early morning, Cornwallis discovered the trick which had been played him on the Assunpink Creek; and he marched at top-speed towards the dis-

[1] Washington to the President of Congress; Pluckemin, January 5, 1777

tant boom of the cannon, — that most distracting of all
music in the ears of those who themselves ought by
rights to be taking an active part in the concert. While
Washington's rear-guard was still within sight of Princeton, the British light infantry were already at the southern entrance of the village; and the Americans would
have been overtaken by their pursuers before ever they
reached Brunswick. There, by all the rules of war, they
should have encountered Sir William Howe and his
New York army, and they would have been caught
between two fires, either of which was quite as hot as
they could endure. At a point five miles beyond Princeton, Washington turned due north out of the Brunswick road; lay that night at Somerset Court House,
and marched thence, by Pluckemin, to the central, the
convenient, and the very defensible position of Morristown. There he established his troops securely, and,
(by comparison with their experiences during the first
ten weeks of winter,) not uncomfortably. Undisturbed
by the adversary, — and in daily communication with
Albany, Philadelphia, and New England, — he abode
during the next four months at his head-quarters in the
Jerseys; a thankful, a somewhat hopeful, and an exceedingly busy man.[1]

Howe, giving no names or details, stated the British
loss at about two hundred and twenty. Washington
reported to Congress that upwards of a hundred of the
enemy were left dead on the field, and that he had in
custody near three hundred prisoners, of whom fourteen
bore commissions. Thirty Americans were returned as
wounded. The same number of their privates were
killed, and seven of their officers.[2] The fighting had
been so close and fierce that a very large proportion of
the casualties were fatal; and yet, during the whole of

[1] Between the seventh of January and the twenty-eighth of May, 1777,
every single one of Washington's despatches is addressed from Morristown

[2] General Mercer lived till the Sunday week after the battle, and suffered cruelly up to the very last. When the firing ceased, Washington
shook hands with Colonel Hitchcock at the head of the New England

the operations which had taken place since Washington crossed the Delaware on Christmas night, not two hundred lives were sacrificed in both the armies together. More often than enough in the world's history twenty thousand men have been slaughtered in a single battle; and far less has come of it, at the moment, or thereafter.

Howe, in his published despatch, made very light indeed of the disaster at Princeton; but he was too old a soldier to neglect the lesson which the events of the past ten days had taught him. He at length perceived that, so long as Washington's army was in existence, his own tactics would have to be governed by military, and not by political, considerations. It had been a premature act to quarter his troops in detached cantonments over an extensive district for the purpose of overawing populations of doubtful fidelity, or of safeguarding a loyal province; and New Jersey was no longer friendly, nor even neutral. "Howe," wrote John Adams, "will repent his mad march through the Jerseys. The people of that Commonwealth begin to raise their spirits exceedingly, and to be firmer than ever. They are actuated by resentment now; and resentment coinciding with principle is a very powerful motive."[1] A Delaware captain, who was following the army, and who kept his eyes about him, prophesied that Jersey would henceforward be the most Whiggish colony on the Continent. The very Quakers, (he said,) declared for taking up arms; for the distress of the country was beyond imagination, and everyone had been stripped without distinction.[2] The proceedings of the Hessians, moreover, suffered by contrast. Washington's conduct in disposing of their booty has been faithfully described by an honest Tory, who would have travelled many

brigade, and thanked him in the hearing of his soldiers. The colonel then went quietly home to Rhode Island, and died in ten days, — killed at Princeton, if his family cared to claim that honour.

[1] John Adams to his wife; Baltimore, February 17, 1777.

[2] Captain Thomas Rodney, from near Princeton; December 30, 1777. The letter is in the *American Archives.*

miles to see him executed for a rebel. The American commander, (so this gentleman related,) advertised for all persons to come in, and prove their property in the stolen goods; and to all such as made out a title the effects were delivered. " This act gained him the hearts of the people. It gave him an influence, a popularity, and a character in New Jersey of which he made the most proper use." [1]

The news of Trenton spread confusion and perplexity through all the townships where Royal troops were stationed; and the ferment was redoubled when it became known that Washington had marched across the rear of Cornwallis, and had sorely maltreated three of his regiments.[2] Sir William Howe's chain of posts at once came clanking and clattering down. Hackensac and Elizabeth Town, — in the very heart of the district which he had undertaken to protect, — were captured by the Americans, together with much baggage and many prisoners; a band of minute-men killed or took a detachment of fifty Waldeckers, and a score of New Jersey light-horsemen intercepted a train of Royal waggons laden with woollen clothing which was most acceptable among the tents at Morristown. All this happened in the first week of January; and Howe, passing from the extreme of temerity to a redundance of caution, collected his New Jersey army of occupation into two large garrisons of five thousand men apiece, and planted them respectively at Brunswick and Perth Amboy, within

---

[1] Jones's *History of New York;* Vol I, chapter viii. There are some interesting remarks, relative to New Jersey, in the *Annual Register* for 1777. "As soon as fortune turned," (so the passage runs,) "and the means were in their power, the sufferers of all parties, the well-disposed to the Royal cause as well as the neutrals and the wavering, now rose as a man to revenge their personal injuries and particular oppressions, and, — being goaded by a keener spur than any which a public cause, or general motive, could have excited, — became its bitterest and most determined enemies."

[2] Colonel Enoch Markham's journal supplies a vivid picture of the disorder which prevailed in rear of the British lines when the New Year opened. Extracts are given in the first Appendix at the end of this volume.

touch of each other, and out of all opportunity for striking a blow against the enemy. He contented himself
with securing the banks of the Raritan for a stretch of
ten miles above the mouth of the river; and he abandoned all the rest of the province to the audacious and
indefatigable enterprise of the Revolutionary partisans
The rural folk put themselves at the service of Washington's flying columns in the capacity of scouts, mes-
sengers, and informants;[1] and the more adventurous
among them transacted much business on their own
account at the expense of the British regimental messes.
They surprised convoys; they cut off foragers; they
detected and emptied outlying repositories of food and
fuel. " Not a stick of wood," we are told, "not a spear
of grass, or a kernel of corn, could the troops in New
Jersey procure without fighting for it, unless it was sent
from New York;" and in New York nothing grew, and
everything had to be fetched from England or Ireland
at a vast expense, and very much the less palatable on
account of the distance over which it had travelled. By
the end of March 1777, the London diners learned with
compassion that their friends in Sir William Howe's
army were reduced to salt provisions, and to ammunition
bread which notoriously was almost uneatable.[2] Captain
Harris of the Fifth Foot, — a valiant trencherman, like
most young fellows who are marked out for eminence
in war or politics, — complained that our reverses had
occasioned such shifting of quarters as to render the
prospect of passing the winter in ease and luxury totally
dark; inasmuch as those supplies which had been pro-

---

[1] Jones's *History of New York;* Vol. I., chapter viii
[2] Horace Walpole to the Revd. William Mason, Strawberry Hill,
March 28, 1777 The garrison of New York, (said Walpole,) had not
even, for a relish to their salt beef, the twenty thousand pounds' worth
of pickles which had been sent them when they were besieged in Boston.
"It is highly unpleasant," (so George the Third wrote to Lord North
on New Year's day, 1777,) "to see the contractors have continued
delivering such bad biscuit and flour after the repeated directions given
by the Board of Treasury, but I trust Sir William Howe is now in
possession of so extensive a country that he will not require to be entirely
provided from Europe."

curable for money, and at very moderate prices, had
now to be gathered at the point of the sword, and, what
was worse, with very great fatigue.[1]

Sir William Howe, for the time being, had lost his
hold on the mainland of America ; and his second campaign, like his first, had gone to water. The most important results, however, of Trenton and Princeton were
not of a local or a temporary character. The permanent
and paramount consequence of those masterly operations
was the establishment of Washington's military reputation, and the increased weight of his political and
administrative authority throughout every State of the
Confederacy, and up to the very latest hour of the war.
A commander, patient and intrepid in adversity, and
silent under calumny, — who never attempts to gloss
over his reverses, or to explain away his mistakes, —
reaps the reward of his honesty and self-control tenfold,
and a hundredfold, when, out of a cloud of gloom and
peril, success at length comes. No one then questions
the truth as he tells it in his despatches ; men are
inclined to over-rate, rather than to depreciate and to
decry, the advantages he has gained ; and few grudge
the full credit of victory to a general who has always
accepted the entire responsibility for failure. The withdrawal of Sir William Howe from his advanced positions
in New Jersey proved to be, in the case of Washington,
what the retreat of Massena from before the lines of

---

[1] *Life of Lord Harris, G.C.B.* The distress in New York grew ever
more severe as the war proceeded. " How people exist in this town,"
(Lord Carlisle wrote,) " is to the greatest degree wonderful. All the
necessaries of life are dear beyond conception. Meat is from fifteen to
seventeen pence a pound, and everything else in proportion. My weekly
bills come to as much as the house-account at Castle Howard when we
have the most company " Lord Carlisle to Lady Carlisle ; New York,
September 22, 1778

The contents of the three last pages, (in addition to what is derived
from British and Loyalist sources,) are mainly taken from the *Public
Papers* of General George Clinton, from Heath's *Diary*, and from
Washington's *Correspondence*. There is likewise an important passage
in a letter from Robert Morris to the American Envoys in Paris of
March 28, 1777.

Torres Vedras was in relation to the personal fortunes, and the public usefulness, of Wellington. Any more exact parallel in the story of two exalted careers it would be difficult to name. From Trenton onwards, Washington was recognised as a far-sighted and skilful general all Europe over, — by the great military nobles in the Empress Catherine's court, by French Marshals and Ministers, in the King's cabinet at Potsdam, at Madrid, at Vienna, and in London. He had shown himself, (said Horace Walpole,) both a Fabius and a Camillus; and his march through the British lines was allowed to be a prodigy of leadership.[1] That was the talk in England; and the Englishman who, of all others, most warmly appreciated Washington's strategy in New Jersey during that fortnight of midwinter was one who had had the very best opportunity for judging of it After the capitulation at Yorktown, in October 1781, a dinner was given at the American head-quarters to the principal officers in the British, the French, and the Continental armies. Cornwallis, — exaggerating to himself, it may be, the obligations of old-fashioned courtesy and chivalry, — took his seat at the board, and responded thus to a toast which Washington had proposed "When the illustrious part that your Excellency has borne in this long and arduous contest becomes matter of history, fame will gather your brightest laurels rather from the banks of the Delaware than from those of the Chesapeake." At that moment, and before that audience, Washington's generalship in the Chesapeake campaign must have represented an exceptionally high standard of comparison.

In such estimation was Washington held by foreigners, whether they were declared enemies, or benevolent neutrals, or potential and probable allies; and he thenceforward had all his own countrymen for admirers, except those very few who did not as yet altogether renounce the ambition of being popularly regarded as his rivals. The enhanced influence which he derived

[1] Walpole to Mann, Strawberry Hill, April 3, 1777

from prosperity came at the precise conjuncture when that influence could be utilised with the greatest possible effect. On the twentieth of December he had addressed to the President of Congress a long and earnest exposition of the evils arising from the plan of short enlistments in the Continental armies; from a low average of professional capacity in the commissioned ranks; from the weakness of the artillery, and the entire absence of cavalry and of scientific officers. Congress, in reply, invested him with "full, ample, and complete powers" to raise sixteen additional battalions of infantry, three thousand light-horse, three regiments of artillery, and a corps of engineers; to call upon any of the States for such aid of the militia as he should deem necessary; to displace and appoint all officers beneath the rank of Brigadier; to take, at a fair price, all supplies of provisions, or articles of equipment, which he might require for the use of the army; and to arrest, confine, and send for trial in the Civil Courts, any persons whatsoever who were disaffected to the American cause. This dictatorship,— for it was nothing less,— was extended over the old Roman period of six months; and Congress specifically announced that the step was taken in perfect reliance on the wisdom, the vigour, and the uprightness of General Washington. It was handsomely worded ; but the force of the compliment lay not so much in the phrasing, as in the timing, of the Resolution. Although a final decision was not taken until the day after Trenton, Washington's letter had been read and considered, and a committee had been appointed to prepare an answer, before the issue of that battle was known in Baltimore. Such an expression of confidence, unstintedly and unanimously accorded during the closing hours of the very darkest season in American history, will remain on record through all ages as a tribute to the man, and not to his fortune.

That fortune had now turned. After a year and a half's intense and continual study of Sir William Howe,

Washington had read his character, and understood his ways. Divining with certainty that the British general would leave him in peace during the rest of the winter and well forward into the spring, he set himself calmly to the task of reinforcing and remaking the Continental army. Congress, acting on his advice, had sanctioned the enlistment of soldiers for a term of three years, or for the duration of the war; and the sixteen new battalions were to be formed of men taken indiscriminately from all or any of the States. The last provision was much to the mind of Washington, who, (to use his own language,) had laboured to discourage all kinds of local attachments and distinctions throughout the army, " denominating the whole by the greater name of American." [1] That sentiment, in the early days of the Revolution, was not congenial to the national tastes and temperament. In the view of a New Englander, or a Pennsylvanian, the ideal regiment was a provincial corps where he was at home among friends and neighbours; where discipline was loose, and furloughs might be had for the asking, or even for the taking, and where the period of service was terminable within the twelvemonth. Previously to Trenton it would have been impossible to exact the strict conditions indispensable for the solidity of a regular army; but the name of Washington was now endowed with a power to inspire and attract his younger fellow-countrymen, and he succeeded in engaging a considerable supply, although not a sufficiency, of recruits who bound themselves to see the war through. If they came in slowly, they came steadily; and those who presented themselves were for the most part well worth retaining.

Washington still had plenty of room in his ranks for privates; but the case was otherwise with regard to his officers The muster-rolls showed a superfluity of captains and lieutenants, and a veritable glut of colonels There were good and bad among them; but their indi-

---

[1] Washington to the President of Congress, Camp above Trenton Falls, December 20, 1776.

vidual worth had been severely and decisively tested on Long Island and at White Plains, in the Jersey retreat, and amid the hardships of the Canadian expedition. Washington had an intimate personal acquaintance with those brigades which he had led in battle; he knew for himself whether an officer sought, or shunned, work and danger; and he spared no pains to ascertain the merits and defects of those who had served in distant parts of the Continent under other generals.[1] Absolute trust was reposed in his justice and impartiality, his authority no one ventured to dispute; and there seldom, or never, has been a fairer opportunity for the exercise of that unflinching and enlightened selection which is the keystone of warlike efficiency. The labour of reorganisation was carried forward under dire pressure; but it was not scamped or hurried. Before the end of the ensuing summer a very censorious critic was at his post of observation when the American Commander-in-Chief marched down the main street of Philadelphia at the head of nine or ten thousand of his troops. Though indifferently dressed, (so this witness remarked,) they held well-burnished arms, and carried them like soldiers; and they looked as if they might have faced an equal number of their redoubtable adversaries with a reasonable prospect of success.[2] That opinion was justified, in the

---

[1] The *American Archives* contain a curious report to the New York Convention, made at the close of 1776 by a committee appointed for the purpose of revising the list of officers in the State Contingent. The work was done conscientiously and rigidly, and some of the entries are in remarkably plain and unvarnished English "Not so careful and attentive as could be wished." "A sober officer, but rather too old" "Too heavy and inactive for an officer." "Too heavy and illiterate for an officer" "Of too rough a make for an officer; better qualified for the Navy than the Army." "A very low-lived fellow." "A good officer, but of a sickly constitution, and had better quit the service." "Wanting in authority to make a good officer. He has deceived the Convention by enlisting the men for six and nine months, instead of during the war." "These three lieutenants wish to decline the service. They will be no loss to it." Many of the names are noted as excellent, creditable, and promising, but it is evident that there had been little time to pick and choose among the candidates for commissions during the stress and hurry which accompanied the outbreak of hostilities.

[2] *Pennsylvanian Memoirs;* chapter xii.

five years which were to come, by a long series of battles honourably lost, or arduously won. The military force which Washington brought into shape at Morris-town, — waxing or waning in numbers, but constantly improving in quality, — followed him obediently, reso-lutely, and devotedly as long as their country had occasion for a general and an army.

CHAPTER XXIV

FEARS FOR ENGLISH LIBERTY. THE NEWSPAPERS. NORTH AND SOUTH BRITAIN

THE events, which took place during those stirring months in the regions watered by the Delaware and Hudson rivers, form a plain and straightforward narrative; but the story of what was passing in England is more complicated, and far more difficult to tell. For that was no affair of marches and counter-marches, of skirmishes, and panics, and surprises The conflict there was in the senate, the market-place, and the newspaper; in the interior of every household, and within the breast of every thinking citizen. Before the year 1777 was six weeks old it became plain that the hour had arrived when it was incumbent upon all men to form an opinion of their own, to profess it frankly, and to abide by it courageously. Up to this time many had concerned themselves but little with the rights and wrongs of the quarrel, or with the expediency of an appeal to arms. The Government, which was supposed to know, had proclaimed that the colonists were contemptible as antagonists, that the war would be short and cheap, and that the cost of it would very soon be covered, several times over, by the produce of taxes which Americans would never again refuse to pay when once they had been well beaten; and quiet people, who liked being governed, had believed the Government. Some, indeed, among the Peers and members of Parliament who supported the Cabinet had long ago admitted to each other, in whispers and sealed letters, that they had begun to be desperately uneasy. "Administration," (wrote Lord Carlisle to George Selwyn as early as the winter of 1775,) "is in a great scrape. Their measures never can succeed. We, who have voted for them, have a right to complain, for they have deceived us, and, I suppose, themselves."[1] The same disheartening conviction was now brought home to every private individual who could spare five minutes a day to the consideration of public affairs. After eight years of military occupation, and twenty-one months of very hard fighting, America was far from being conquered, and farther yet from being convinced that her interest lay in submission to the demands of the British Parliament.

The situation was clearly understood, and temperately but unanswerably exposed, by discerning onlookers in either country. An American Whig, at the very moment when the prospects of his own cause were darkest, made a cool and careful estimate of the English chances. "Their whole hope of success," he said, "depends upon frequent and decisive victories, gained before our army is disciplined. The expense of feeding and paying great fleets and armies, at such a distance, is too enormous for any nation on earth to bear for a great while. It is said that ninety thousand tons of shipping are employed in their service constantly, at thirteen shillings and four pence a ton per month. When our soldiers are enlisted for the war, discipline must daily increase. Our army can be recruited after a defeat, while our enemies must cross the Atlantic to repair a misfortune. Have we felt a tenth part of the hardships the States of Holland suffered at the hands of Spain, or does our case look half so difficult? States are not conquered by victories. After a succession of splendid victories obtained over France by the Duke of Marlborough, in each of which more men were slain than in the whole of this war, still that kingdom made a formidable resistance, and obtained an honourable peace."[2]

---

[1] *George Selwyn and his Contemporaries;* Vol. III., page 114, of the Edition of 1844.

[2] American newspaper article of December 24, 1776; signed "Perseverance."

That was written in December 1776, when all the victories which hitherto marked the campaign had been
scored by the British.   After Trenton and Princeton
were fought, and Howe had retired from the Jerseys,
the same views were yet more powerfully enforced by a
Londoner.   " The small scale of our maps deceived us ;
and, as the word ' America ' takes up no more room than
the word ' Yorkshire,' we seem to think the territories
they represent are much of the same bigness ; though
Charleston is as far from Boston as London from Venice.
Braddock might tell the difficulties of this loose, rugged
country, were he living.   Amherst might still do it.   Yet
these officers found a willing people to help them, and
General Howe finds nothing willing.   We have undertaken a war against farmers and farmhouses, scattered
through a wild waste of continent, and shall soon hear
of our General being obliged to garrison woods, to scale
mountains, to wait for boats and pontoons at rivers, and
to have his convoys and escorts as large as armies.   These,
and a thousand such difficulties, will rise on us at the
next stage of the war.   I say the next stage, because we
have hitherto spent one campaign, and some millions, in
losing one landing-place at Boston , and, at the charge
of seven millions and a second campaign, we have replaced it with two other landing-places at Rhode Island
and New York.   I am entirely of opinion with Voltaire
that every great conqueror must be a great politician.
Something more is required, than the mere mechanical
business of fighting, in composing revolts and bringing
back things to their former order." [1]

The keenest eye in Europe already foresaw the inevitable issue.   Frederic of Prussia had won and lost many
battles, and had learned not to over-rate the importance
of any single defeat or victory.   He had followed Washington, through the vicissitudes of the protracted struggle, with the insight and sympathy of one who himself
had striven against fearful odds ; who had committed
grievous mistakes, and had profited by his lesson ; and

[1] Letter from London of February 1777.

who had at length emerged, secure and successful, from
a flood of war in which both friends and enemies, for
years together, felt assured that nothing could save him
from being overwhelmed. With such an experience he
did not need to wait for Saratoga and Yorktown in order
to be convinced that Great Britain had involved herself
in a hopeless task All the information which he had
received, (so he wrote in the first half of March 1777,)
went to show that the colonies would attain, and keep,
their independence.[1] That was how the future was regarded by the greatest warrior of the age ; and the facts
of the case, as he knew them, were the property of all
the world. Civilians, who had never seen a cannon fired,
but who could use their common sense, had plenty of
material on which to build an estimate of the military
probabilities. Abundant and most discouraging intelligence appeared in private letters from officers in
America, which were freely published in the English
journals, and even those who took in the " London
Gazette," and no other newspaper, might find very serious matter for reflection as they read between the lines
of Sir William Howe's despatches.

There was, however, an aspect of the question which
occupied and concerned our ancestors far more deeply
than any purely military considerations. It must never
be forgotten that many Englishmen from the first, — and
in the end a decided, and indeed a very large, majority
among them, — regarded the contest which was being
fought out in America not as a foreign war, but as a
civil war in which English liberty was the stake. They
held that a policy had been deliberately initiated, and
during half a generation had been resolutely pursued, of
which the avowed object was to make the Royal power
dominant in the State ; and the historians in highest
repute, who since have treated of those times, unreservedly maintain the same view. That policy had now prevailed ; and Personal Government, from a mischievous
theory, had grown into a portentous reality. The vic-

[1] Le Roi Frédéric au Comte de Maltzan ; Potsdam, 13 mars, 1777.

tory of the Crown had been preceded by an epoch of
continuous and bitter strife, every stage in which was
marked by deplorable incidents. The publication through
the press of opinions obnoxious to the Court had been
punished with unsparing severity.   The right of con-
stituents to elect a person of their choice had been denied in words, and repeatedly violated in practice.   The
benches of the Lords and the Commons swarmed with
an ever increasing band of placemen and pensioners
subsidised by the King ; and these gentlemen well knew
the work which their paymaster expected of them. Their
vocation was to harass any minister who conceived that
he owed a duty to the people as well as to the Sovereign ; and to betray and ruin him if he proved incor-
rigible in his notions of patriotism.   The most famous
English statesmen, — all, it is not too much to say, who
are now remembered with pride by Englishmen of every
party, — were shut out from the opportunity, and even
from the hope, of office, and our national qualities of
manliness and independence had come to be a standing
disqualification for employment in the nation's service.
At last the Cabinet had picked a quarrel with the colonies over the very same question which convulsed England in the days of Strafford and the ship-money.   In
order to vindicate the doctrine that taxation might be
imposed without representation, the servants of the
Crown, or rather its bondsmen, (for the Prime Minister,
and the most respectable of his colleagues, were in this
matter acting under compulsion, and against their consciences,) had undertaken to coerce the communities in
America with fire and sword, and to visit individuals with
the extreme penalties of rebellion   It followed, as a
natural and certain consequence, that the party, which
resented the encroachments of the Crown at home, sincerely and universally entertained a belief which influenced their whole view of the colonial controversy   That
belief had been placed on record, in quiet but expressive
language, by a nobleman who, in his honoured age, lived
among us as the last of the old Whigs.   Lord Albemarle

distinctly states that in 1774, and for some years afterwards, the Opposition were possessed by "a deep and
well-grounded conviction that, if despotism were once
established in America, arbitrary government would at
least be attempted in the mother-country." [1]

Those apprehensions were shared by men whose
judgement cannot lightly be set aside, and the strength
of whose patriotism was many degrees above proof.
Chatham, when he spoke in public, dwelt mainly upon
the rights of the colonists, the duty of England, and the
appalling military dangers which would result to the
Empire if those rights were invaded and that duty ig-
nored. With the instinct of a great orator, he did not
willingly introduce fresh debateable matter into a controversy where he had so many sufficient and self-evident
arguments ready to his hand; but his private correspondence clearly indicates that the keenness of his emotion,
and the warmth of his advocacy, were closely connected
with a profound belief that, if America were subjugated,
Britain would not long be free. Would to Heaven, (he
wrote,) that England was not doomed to bind round her
own hands, and wear patiently, the chains which she
was forging for her colonies! And then he quoted, with
telling effect, the passage in which Juvenal described
how the spread of servility among the Roman people,
and the corruption of their public spirit, avenged the
wrongs of the subject world upon the conquerors themselves. [2]

The fears which Chatham acknowledged were confessed likewise by the only man, then alive, whose
authority stands on a level with his own. In the early
spring of 1777 Burke affirmed that the American war
had done more in a very few years, than all other causes
could have done in a century, to prepare the minds of

---

[1] Those words are found in the tenth chapter of the second volume of
Lord Rockingham's Memoirs Lord Albemarle, who had played trap-ball
with Charles Fox, lived to hold an extemporised levée of London society
on the seventy-fifth anniversary of the day when he carried the colours on
to the field of Waterloo.

[2] The Earl of Chatham to Mr. Sheriff Sayre; Hayes, August 28, 1774.

the English people for the introduction of arbitrary government. The successive steps of the process, by which
that result was being brought about, are set forth in the
last five paragraphs of the Letter to the Sheriffs of Bristol with the fullness and exactness of a political philosopher, and the incisive vigour of a practical statesman.
Those paragraphs, indeed, are too long to quote; and it
would be a literary crime to abridge or to paraphrase
them; but the conclusions at which Burke had arrived
are more briefly and roughly stated in a couple of sentences wherein he thus commented on the American
rebellion. "We cannot," he wrote, "amidst the excesses
and abuses which have happened, help respecting the
spirit and principles operating in these commotions.
Those principles bear so close a resemblance to those
which support the most valuable part of our constitution, that we cannot think of extirpating them in any
part of His Majesty's dominions without admitting consequences, and establishing precedents, the most dangerous to the liberties of this kingdom." [1]

Horace Walpole, with whom the chief men of both
parties freely conversed, had no doubt whither the road
led which the stronger, and the worse, members of the
Cabinet joyfully followed; and down which the less
perverse, and the more timid, were irresistibly driven.
He never was easy about the political future of his
country, until North's Government fell, and the danger
disappeared. During the winter when Howe and
Washington were contending in the Jerseys, Walpole
complained that his life at present consisted in being
wished joy over the defeat and slaughter of fellow-
countrymen, who were fighting for his liberty as well
as for their own. Thirty months afterwards he spoke
still more gloomily. It was bad enough, (he said,) to

---

[1] The manuscript, which is in Mr. Burke's handwriting, is thus dock-
eted by the fourth Earl Fitzwilliam "Probably this was intended as an
amendment to the Address to be moved after the campaign of 1776" In
that case, the paper must have been drafted at the precise point of time
which this narrative has now reached.

be at war with France and Spain because we would not be content to let America send us half the wealth of the world in her own way, instead of in the way that pleased George Grenville and Charles Townshend. But the subversion of a happy Constitution, by the hands of domestic enemies, was a worse fate than any which we could suffer from the foreigner; and that fate, unless the nation recovered its senses, only too surely awaited us. Walpole emphatically declared that the freedom of England had become endangered, and her glory began to decline, from the moment that she " ran wild after a phantasm of absolute power " over colonies whose liberty was the source of her own greatness.[1]

It was an ominous circumstance that the Jacobites and the Nonjurors were open-mouthed against America, and, one and all, were ardent supporters of the war The members of that party, which professed the doctrine of passive obedience, had transferred their allegiance to George the Third, honestly and undisguisedly, from the moment that he made manifest his intention to select his own ministers and govern for himself. They stood by the Court, (as readers of Junius are aware,) throughout every turn of the conflict which raged around the Middlesex Election. They were frequently taunted, in very good prose and extremely poor verse, with having deserted the shrine of their ancient loyalty; but the course of action which they adopted was to the credit of their common-sense and their consistency. The Jacobites of 1775 were not dreamers, nor dilettantes. Only half a life-time before that date they had been formidable enough to shake the State to the very foundation; and, now that they had suited themselves to their altered circumstances, they were a redoubtable party again. Men who had been Jacobites in their youth, and who were the friends of arbitrary government still, constituted a strong minority in the Corporations of

---

[1] Walpole to the Countess of Ossory, Jan. 26, 1777. Walpole to Sir Horace Mann, June 16, 1779; and to the Countess of Ossory, June 22, 1779.

some towns, and a majority among the Justices of the Peace on not a few Petty Sessional benches in the northern counties. They did not amuse themselves with a ritual of wreaths and rosettes, or trouble themselves about the Christian name of the monarch whose health they drank. Their creed was a serious and genuine devotion to the principles in accord with which they thought that the country ought to be administered. If they could not have a Stuart, they were willing to accept a Hanoverian who pursued the Stuart policy; and they were quite ready to put their money on the White Horse, so long as he galloped in what they conceived to be the right direction. When once the American war broke out, it became evident to them that there were no lengths to which the King was not prepared to go: and there were most certainly none to which they themselves would not eagerly follow.[1] Testimony to that effect was given by a witness who knew, as well as anybody, what the Jacobites were thinking. In one of the last letters which he wrote, David Hume, with the solemnity of a dying man, prophesied that, if the Court carried the day in America, the English Constitution would infallibly perish.[2]

Historians, who understand their business, when seeking to ascertain the trend of national opinion at any crisis in our history, have always laid stress upon the confidential reports of foreign emissaries accredited to St. James's, and on the conclusions which were

---

[1] "The Scots address and fight now with as much zeal in the cause of the House of Brunswick as they did, during the last reigns, in that of the House of Stuart. This proves that it is not the name, but the cause, for which they fight. The Scots are in hopes that extinguishing the very name of English liberty in America will secure the destruction of the constitution in old England. In the present auspicious reign they think themselves nearer the completion of their wishes, and are therefore more insolent, and more ardent, in the pursuit." Extract from the *Gazetteer and New Daily Advertiser* of 1776.

[2] *Histoire de l'Action Commune de la France et de l'Amérique pour l'Indépendance des États-Unis*, par George Bancroft. Tome III., page 200. The Paris version of this work is described as "Traduit et annoté par le Comte Adolphe de Circourt, accompagné de Documents Inédits."

borne in upon the mind of the potentate to whom those reports were addressed. Our knowledge of English feeling, during the years that preceded our own Great Revolution, is largely derived from the secret correspondence of the French Ambassador at the Court of James the Second; and, in like manner, the correspondence of the Prussian Minister in London, at the time of the Declaration of Independence, throws an important light upon British politics. Indeed, of the two diplomatists, Frederic the Great's envoy is the safer guide. The Count de Maltzan was better qualified to distinguish between material facts, and party gossip, than de Barillon, who habitually dabbled in political intrigues at Westminster; and Frederic, in a very different degree from Louis the Fourteenth, was an employer to whom it was much less safe to tell a doctored and flattering tale than a disagreeable truth.

Frederic had observed every turn of the constitutional struggle in England as closely as he watched the variation in numbers of the Austrian or Russian armies, and with as good cause, and he now was firmly persuaded that the fears of Burke and Chatham with regard to the precarious condition of our public liberty were not exaggerated It might have been supposed that the prospect would have left him indifferent; for assuredly he had no desire to set up a Parliamentary opposition at Berlin, or convert his own Kingdom into a limited monarchy. But he was in the habit of looking to results; and, in his eyes, the suitable form of government for any country was that, and only that, which produced strong and capable administration The England, which Frederic the Great desired to see, was an England taking a continuous and intelligent interest in Continental movements; commanding the esteem and confidence of her neighbours, and able, with all her enormous resources well in hand, to make her influence decisively felt But, under her then rulers, our country was a cipher in Europe; distracted by internal dissension, and spending in a foolish quarrel with her own colonies the strength which had so recently made her the arbitress of the world, and which, — at the rate that she was lavishing men, money, and reputation, — might soon be hardly sufficient for the protection of her own coasts and arsenals

Frederic, moreover, had a special grudge of his own against the system of government which had of late been inaugurated in England. That nation, under the inspiration of Lord Chatham, — the statesman who now was the prime assertor of its imperilled liberties, — had fought the earlier campaigns of the Seven Years' War side by side with Prussia, and had helped her, in her dire extremity, with a supply of British gold which was only less welcome than the assistance of the British sword But when George the Third ascended the throne, and as soon as he could get a minister to his mind, he tore up that glorious treaty of alliance ; stopped the payment of a subsidy which to the English Treasury was a pittance, but which seemed a mountain of wealth to the thrifty Prussian War Office ; and, in the hottest moment of the chase, threw Frederic over to the wolves. Those wolves, in the end, found him a tough morsel ; but he never even pretended to forget that the first overt act of Personal Government in England had been to play him a trick which came very near to be his ruin. Detestation of Lord Bute, and of Lord Bute's Royal patron, and a very genuine love and admiration for Chatham, rendered the Prussian King an earnest and far-seeing friend of British constitutional freedom. If the nation, (such was the tenor of his predictions,) allowed the Sovereign to act according to his good pleasure, and abandoned the colonies to the lot which he destined for them, that lot would sooner or later be shared by England ; for the policy of George the Third was the same everywhere, and he was pursuing despotic courses in all portions of his dominions. " It appears," Frederic wrote, " from all I hear, that the ancient British spirit has almost entirely eclipsed itself, and that everything tends to a change in the form of government, so that the old constitution will exist only in the surface, and the nation in effect will be nearer slavery than in any preceding reign." [1]

Those were strong words from a ruler who was an autocrat, and who fully purposed to remain one; but the danger which threatened English liberty aroused uneasiness in a still more singular quarter than the Royal cabinet at Potsdam Frederic, after all, was at peace with our country, although it did not break his heart to find her in a scrape; whereas France was an active, and erelong an open, enemy. The French Government, sore from recent losses and humiliations, greeted with delight the rebellion of our colonists; supplied them almost from the first with money and military stores; seized the opportunity of our difficulty to declare hostilities, which were prosecuted with what, for the French, was unwonted, and even unexampled, energy; and laboured to unite Europe in a coalition against the British Empire. And yet there were Frenchmen, and many Frenchmen, who never ceased to reverence England as a country which held up to the contemplation of mankind an example of the material and moral advantages arising from stable and rational self-government; and which, for more than two centuries, had been a champion of liberty outside her own borders. Their prayer, or, (more strictly speaking,) their hope and aspiration, — for advanced thinkers in France were not much given to praying, — was that England might cease to be forgetful of her high mission, and might bethink herself, before it grew too late, that in destroying the freedom of others she was striking at her own

These ideas are reflected in letters addressed to Lord Shelburne by the Abbé Morellet when war between France and England was already imminent; and a later part of the same correspondence proves that, after four years of fierce and dubious fighting, solicitude for

---

[1] Le Roi Frédéric au Comte de Maltzan, 14 août, 1775, (en chiffres;) 18 décembre, 1775; 26 juin, 1777.

the honour of our country had not been extinguished in
the hearts of some generous enemies.   The fall of Lord
North in 1782 was hailed by enlightened Parisians with
a satisfaction inspired by the most laudable motives.
They felt joy and relief because there would be an end
of bloodshed; because the highest civilisation, of which
France and England were the chief repositories, would no
longer be divided against itself ; but above and beyond
all, because liberty would henceforward be secure in
the one great country of Europe which was constitutionally governed.   "Yes, my Lord," cried Morellet,
"in spite of the war that divides us, I am glad to see
your country better administered   I rejoice, in my
quality of citizen of the world, that a great people should
resume their true place; should regain a clear view of
their real interests ; and should employ their resources,
not in the pursuit of an end which cannot be attained,
but for the conservation of that wealth and influence
which are naturally their due, and which, for the sake
of the world at large, it is all-important that they should
continue to possess.   If the independence of America
had perished, your constitution would have been overthrown, and your freedom lost."[1]

Among foreigners who vexed themselves about the
perils which overhung the British Constitution the
Whigs in America could no longer be reckoned.   As
the war went forward, and their sacrifices and sufferings
increased, the colonists, (and none could fairly blame
them,) took less and less count of the distinction between the two political parties at Westminster.   They
regarded Britain as one integral and formidable whole;

[1] *Lettres de l'Abbé Morellet, de l'Académie Française, à Lord Shelburne, depuis Marquis de Lansdowne, 1772–1803, avec Introduction et
Notes par Lord Edmond Fitzmaurice*   Paris, Librairie Plon, 1898, pages
110, 189, 191.   The passage in the text reproduces the substance of
Morellet's letter of April 1782, and some of the words, for the words
are many.   Morellet was a decorative artist of a high order, an adept in
dressing up the stern discoveries of British political economists in a shape
to suit the French taste.   When, as in the case before us, he lighted upon
a subject which admitted of sentiment and emotion, he was not sparing of
his ornament.

and the character in which she presented herself at their doors was not such as to command their sympathy Charles Fox, and his eloquent and statesmanlike speeches, were a long way off, while General Burgoyne, with his Brunswickers and his Red Indians, was very near indeed People who were occupied in striving to repel British armies, and in rebuilding towns which British fleets had burned, were left with very little leisure to interest themselves about the preservation of British liberties. But their descendants, who had plenty of time to think the matter over, — and who, indeed, in the department of history, for many years to come thought of very little else, — have gradually arrived at the conclusion that, if the resistance of the colonies had been overpowered, British and Transatlantic freedom would have perished together. That conclusion is, now and again, set forth by living American writers in a tone of just pride, and in language worthy of the theme. Whatever, (we are told,) may be the spirit of the people of the United States to-day, in the eighteenth century the people of the colonies were English to the heart's core. Ever since the new reign began, they had noticed, with growing anxiety, the determination of George the Third to undermine and overthrow the old English structure of genuine national self-government, and real ministerial responsibility. The Englishmen in America rebelled the first, because they were the first to feel the full force of the assault upon liberty. Their Revolution was not an uprising against England, or the English people, or the English Constitution. It was a defensive movement, undertaken in behalf of essential English institutions, against the purpose and effort of a monarch to defeat the political progress of the race, and to turn back the hands of time so that they might mark again the dreary hour before Parliament had delivered us from the Stuarts.[1]

[1] Article by Henry Loomis Nelson, in the New York Journal *Literature* of March 31, 1899

Such, in the deliberate judgement of a succeeding generation, was the aspect of the situation in England during the earlier years of the American war; and such it then seemed to Frenchmen who watched our politics from the safe side of the Channel. It was an aspect necessarily most alarming to contemporary Englishmen who foresaw that the free institutions of their own country might erelong be exposed to a final and successful assault; and who were conscious of being too high-spirited and stout-hearted to shrink, when the day of trial came, from doing their utmost in defence of freedom, however ruinous might be the penalty to themselves and their families. Those anticipations saddened their lives, inspired their public action, and coloured their written and spoken confidences. The Duke of Richmond was a senator of long experience, a man of the world, and a great peer with an enormous stake in the country, his private letters are serious documents of grave authority; and those letters supply posterity with a sample of what was thought and feared by many thousands of humbler, but not less honest and patriotic, people.

In August 1776,—on the day, as it happened, that Howe began to move against the American lines in Long Island, — Richmond wrote to Edmund Burke at great length from Paris. The Duke had repaired to France, for the purpose of looking after his hereditary estate in that country, and of making good his claim to the Dukedom of Aubigny. That proved a burdensome undertaking; for the grant of a peerage, in order to be valid, required to be registered by the Parliament of Paris, and, in the Parliament of Paris, nothing was to be had for nothing. Richmond complained that, "besides the real business itself, the visits, formalities, solicitations, dinners, suppers," and all the rest of the machinery for bringing influence to bear upon every individual concerned, were infinitely wearisome and costly. And yet all the expense of time, trouble, and money was, in his estimation, very well laid out; because, although things were ill managed in France, circumstances might arise when it would be impossible for him to reside at his English home. "Who knows," wrote Richmond, "that a time may not come when a retreat to this country may not be a happy thing to have? We now hold our liberties merely by the magnanimity of the best of kings, who will not make use of the opportunity he has to seize them; for he has it in his power, with the greatest ease and quiet, to imitate the King of Sweden.[1] I have not the least doubt but that his faithful peers and commons would by degrees, — or at once if he liked it better, — vote him complete despotism. I fear I see the time approaching when the English, after having been guilty of every kind of meanness and corruption, will at last own themselves, like the Swedes, unworthy to be free. When that day comes, our situation will be worse than France Young despotism, like a boy broke loose from school, will indulge itself in every excess. Besides, if there is a contest, though it be a feeble one, I, or mine, may be among the proscribed If such an event should happen, and America not be open to receive us, France is some retreat, and a peerage here is something."

British opinion was never unanimous at any stage of the American war; but in what proportion that opinion was divided it is impossible to determine at the distance of a hundred and thirty years. Men of practical experience in politics turn sceptical when told very positively what "the country" thinks with regard to a question even of their own day, and are inclined to ask their informant how large a part of the country has taken him into its confidence. Historians, who have tried to gauge the feeling of our ancestors during the struggle with America, have often paid far too much respect to

---

[1] Gustavus the Third had recently subverted the Constitution in Sweden; not without excuses which were altogether wanting to George the Third when he devised his scheme of Personal Government.

the hasty generalisations of sanguine, or of despondent, partisans. All those who sturdily push their way through the thickets of that ancient controversy find such fruit growing in profusion on every bush. A Whig in Devonshire wrote out to Philadelphia that the whole nation was mad, and that he could scarcely meet one man in twenty who did not wish to see Great Britain, and himself, bankrupt rather than not bring the colonies to the feet of Lord George Germaine. John Wesley, on the other hand, while heartily agreeing that the nation was mad, gave as a proof of it that a great majority of Englishmen, Irishmen, and Scotchmen were exasperated almost to insanity against the King and the King's policy. Anything may be proved on either side by a judicious selection of individual utterances that were made in all good faith, but too frequently from very imperfect knowledge. More profitable results are to be obtained by minute observation of certain facts and circumstances which are beyond dispute ; and the significance of which can be tested by those who, whenever the England of their own lifetime has passed through a period of warlike excitement, have kept their eyes open to what went on around them. Twice in the memory of men over sixty years of age, and once at least in the experience of everyone who reads these volumes, Britain has been engaged in a war on which the interest of the nation was eagerly concentrated All who have noted the features and incidents of the Crimean war, and the Transvaal war, — and who have studied the parallel features and incidents of the years which elapsed between 1774 and 1782, — may estimate for themselves whether the American war, as wars go, was popular or not.

Before commencing that inquiry, there is one preliminary remark which, on the face of the matter, it is permissible to make. The House of Commons, at the last, with the warm and very general approbation of the country, put a stop to hostilities, and recognised the independence of America. The British nation had been tried in the fire before then, and has been tried since, and it has never been the national custom to back out of a just quarrel for no other reason than because Britain, at a given moment, was getting the worst of it. In 1782 our people solemnly and deliberately abandoned the attempt to reconquer America on the ground that it was both wrong and foolish; and that fact, to the mind of everyone who holds the British character in esteem, affords an irresistible proof that a very large section of the people must all along have been fully persuaded that the coercion of our colonists by arms was neither wise nor righteous.

The surest criterion of the popularity attaching to a warlike policy is afforded by the prevailing tone and tendency of the public journals So long as a people have their hearts in a contest, newspapers which oppose the war are few, and for the most part, timid; while the newspapers which support the war are numerous and thriving, and very seldom err by an excess of tolerance when dealing either with critics at home, or with adversaries abroad. Books or pamphlets, however large their number, do not supply an equally important test of national opinion. For on the one hand, it is notorious that Ministers of State in the eighteenth century were in the habit of paying an author to defend them and their proceedings; and, on the other hand, a man who, from public spirit or private spite, is opposed to a Government, thinks little of spending ten or twenty pounds in order that his fellow-citizens should be able to peruse his views in print, however few among them may care to avail themselves of the opportunity. But a newspaper lives by being read, and, in the great majority of cases, none read it, and still fewer buy it, unless they agree with its opinions. The first quarter of a century in George the Third's reign was to a marked degree an age of newspapers. Whatever good or evil the King might have done, he had lent, most unintentionally, an extraordinary impulse to the activity and influence of public journalism. During the long constitutional agi-

tation, of which the Middlesex Election was the outward
and visible symptom, newspapers had played a commanding part.   They had multiplied in number, they
had grown in size; they had perfected themselves in
the art of producing matter acceptable to their readers,
and they had greatly increased their circulation   Between 1760 and 1775 the stamps issued by the Treasury
had risen, from less than nine and a half, to considerably over twelve and a half, millions a year.   In 1776,
— after some experience of a war conducted beneath the
eyes of a vigilant press, — the Cabinet, needing money
much and loving newspapers but little, raised the stamp
duty to the amount of three halfpence on every half
sheet.   Still the sale went upwards; and it was not
until Lord North retired from office, and the long argument between the Crown and the people was thereby
concluded, that the growing demand for newspaper
stamps began to flag, and at length actually fell.

Among London newspapers the largest, the most
attractive, and quite incomparably the most in request,
were opposed to the American policy of the Cabinet.
The " North Briton," indeed, was no longer in existence.
Number Forty-five, the dearest scrap of printed matter
on record, — for it cost the Government, soon or late,
a hundred thousand pounds to suppress it, — had been
burned by the common hangman amid public excitement
so vehement that the hangman himself was with difficulty saved from being burned as well.   But a whole
covey of Phœnixes rose from its ashes, eager to avenge
their defunct predecessor with beak and talon.   The
London " Evening Post," the " Public Advertiser," the
" Morning Chronicle and London Advertiser," and the
" Gazetteer and New Daily Advertiser," gave the Court
and the Bedfords superabundant cause to regret that
they had not left Wilkes and his newspaper alone.

Most of the leading journals, mindful of their origin,
were careful to insert the time-honoured name of " Advertiser " in some corner of their title.   They had commenced existence as advertising sheets, containing little

news and less politics.[1] But it was far otherwise with
the imposing pages which, on every other morning during every week that the American war lasted, came rus-
tling forth from the London presses. They did not
altogether disdain to inform the world where purchasers
might hear of desirable house-property, and seasoned
hunters, and drafts of fox-hound puppies, and pectoral
lozenges for defluxions, and Analeptic Pills for gout, and
Catholic Pills for everything; but they devoted very much
the larger part of their ample space to more flaming and
fascinating topics. Their varied columns teemed with
news which could not be found in the "London Gazette,"
and which the Ministry had frequently the strongest
personal reasons for concealing. In communicated
articles; in spicy paragraphs; in epistles of inordinate
length, signed by old Roman names of the Republican
era, — they flagellated the Prime Minister and every one
of his colleagues, and denounced him for having begun
an unjust war which he was totally incompetent to
conduct.

The "Morning Post and Daily Advertiser" had been
converted into a ministerial paper by Henry Bate, the
editor. Bate was a clergyman by profession, and was
reasonably enough viewed in Whig circles as one who
did not rise to the obligations of his sacred calling, for
very eminent Tories, in his own day and afterwards,
have admitted that at this period of his career he was
nothing better than a bully and a ruffian. Dr. Johnson,
who fought for his Sovereign's policy strenuously, and
even fiercely, but who always fought fair, spoke of Bate
with scathing reprobation; and Mr. Croker, who had
no Whig prejudices, has written an account of the young
man's performances which confirms Johnson's strictures
upon his character.[2] If we except the damaging advo-

[1] Chapter vii of *English Newspapers*, by H R. Fox-Bourne; London,
1897.
[2] "Sir," said Johnson, "I will not allow this man to have merit. No,
Sir; what he has is rather the contrary. I will, indeed, allow him courage; and on this account we so far give him credit. We have more respect
for a man who robs boldly on the highway than for a fellow who jumps

cacy of the "Morning Post," and the official sterility of the "London Gazette," Ministers had not much for which to thank the newspapers. The little "London Chronicle," a square foot in size, treated them with a friendliness tempered by its abhorrence of Lord Bute and the Scotch, whom, (like English mankind in general,) it persisted in regarding as the secret inspirers of George the Third and his Cabinet. The "Public Ledger" announced itself as a political commercial paper, open to all parties and influenced by none; and it bestowed on Lord North an occasional word of praise, accompanied by much good advice which he seldom heeded. And yet even the "Ledger" excused the American invasion of Canada as a step to which the colonists had been driven in self-defence. There were journals which, while they disapproved the war, still continued to speak well of the Government; but in the whole circuit of the London Press no newspaper could be found which adopted the line of being in opposition to the Government, but in favour of the war.

In estimating the balance of British opinion during the American Revolution great importance must be attached to the views expressed by the newspapers; but not less significant was the impunity with which those views were given to the world. It has happened more than once that an Administration, already on the decline, has become powerful and popular when a war broke out, and has retained its advantage so long as that war endured; and, under the Georges, an accession of strength,

---

out of a ditch, and knocks you down behind your back   Courage is a quality so necessary for maintaining virtue that it is always respected, even when it is associated with vice "

This left-handed compliment, — the best that was to be said for Bate, — is to be found in the seventy-ninth chapter of Boswell's *Life of Johnson*, as edited by the Right Honourable John Wilson Croker. Croker gives a short narrative of Bate's proceedings in a note subjoined to the passage. To the end of his days, which were many, " Parson Bate " was a famous patron of the prize-ring, and his prowess had been tested in many chance encounters.   His admirers assure us that the professionals were much relieved by his refusal to step inside the ropes.   Late in life he was made a Baronet. To such base use did that ancient, but unfortunate, order come at last.

and of public favour, meant a great deal more to a Government than it means now. A war ministry then, which had the country with it, was terribly formidable to political opponents at home. It might have seemed likely that, after the colonists had recourse to arms, journalists and pamphleteers who went counter to the royal policy would soon have a very bad time in England; but exactly the opposite result ensued. During the first fourteen years of George the Third, the ministerial censorship of the Press had been continuous, inquisitorial, and harsh almost to barbarity. The most exalted magistrates had placed themselves at the service of the executive with culpable facility, not for the first time in our history Roger North, in his picturesque and instructive family biographies, reports how, throughout the civil dissensions of the seventeenth century, the time of the King's Bench was taken up with factious contentions; and he speaks of that Court as a place where more news than law was stirring. The law, as there laid down by Lord Mansfield in 1763, was fraught with grave consequences to all men who gained their livelihood by writing copy, or by setting up type. Informations began to rain like hail upon authors, editors, publishers, and printers Crushing fines, protracted terms of imprisonment, and the open shame of the pillory, were, for several years to come, the portion of those who criticised the Cabinet in earnest. Their plight would have been hopeless if they had not sometimes found a refuge in the Common Pleas, where the president of the tribunal was Lord Chief Justice Pratt, who subsequently in the House of Peers, as Lord Camden, ably supported Lord Chatham's endeavours to reconcile Great Britain and America Pratt, acting in the true spirit of the law wherever liberty was at hazard, and audaciously advancing the limits of his own jurisdiction when he otherwise could not rescue a victim, nobly vindicated the ancient reputation of his Court.[1] As time went on, the ministerial majority in the

[1] "The parties aggrieved," (so Lord Campbell writes,) "avoided the Court of King's Bench, and sought redress in the Court of Common Pleas

House of Commons joined in the hunt; and Parliamentary Privilege, which had been devised for the protection of freedom, was perverted, amid scenes of scandalous uproar and irregularity, into an engine of tyranny.[1]

Ministers who had pursued such courses in a time of peace, — when they could not excuse their arbitrary measures by the plea of national danger, or the necessity for preserving an appearance of national unanimity, — might have been expected, when a war was raging, to have strained and over-ridden legality more unscrupulously than ever for the purpose of paying out old scores, and repressing fresh ebullitions of hostile criticism. But, though the clamour against the King and his ministers waxed ever more shrill and more pertinacious, the censorship seemed to have lost its nerve, and the Opposition press went forward on its boisterous way unmenaced and almost unmolested. Political trials became infrequent, and, after a while, ceased.[2] The voice of the Attorney-General calling for vengeance, — now upon grave constitutional essayists, or vehement champions of freedom, now upon some miserable bookseller's hack, and the compositors who had deciphered and printed his lucubrations, — was hushed and silent.

from the Lord Chief Justice Pratt. He liberated Wilkes from the Tower on the ground of parliamentary privilege, and, declaring general warrants to be illegal, he obtained from juries very heavy damages for those who had been arrested, and whose papers had been seized, on the suspicion that they were concerned in printing, and publishing, the number of the *North Briton* which had been singled out for prosecution." *Life of Lord Mansfield*, chapter xxxvi.

Roger North's discriminating praise of the Common Pleas under the Stuart dynasty is sanctioned by what was then the highest known authority. "As the Lord Nottingham in one of his speeches expresseth, The law is there at home"

[1] The excesses into which Parliament was betrayed during those evil years, and the zest with which Fox led the riot within its walls, at an age when he ought to have been taking his degree at Oxford, may be seen in the fifth, sixth, and ninth chapters of the *Early History of Charles James Fox*.

[2] John Horne Tooke's trial, on a charge of seditious libel connected with the American controversy, took place as early as the second year of the war. His conviction injured the Ministry much more than it alarmed the Press.

Men wrote what they thought and felt, in such terms as their indignation prompted and their taste permitted. However crude and violent might be the language in which the newspapers couched their invectives, the legal advisers of the Government, when it came to a question of prosecution, were awed and scared by the consciousness that there existed immense multitudes of people for whom diatribes against the Court and the Cabinet could not be too highly flavoured. Absolute liberty of discussion thenceforward prevailed; but, to the honour of English fairness, there was no immunity for gross slander. In the case of a false and foul charge, brought against a public man of either party, our tribunals showed themselves ready, according to the racy old judicial phrase, to lay a lying knave by the heels. The "Morning Post," in 1780, accused the Duke of Richmond of treasonable communication with the French Government. But that statesman's display of kindliness towards British colonists, who would still have been the Duke's fellow-subjects but for an insane policy which he himself had consistently opposed, was no proof of guilty sympathy with a foreign enemy in the view of British jurymen. Nor were they disposed to overlook a flagrant insult offered to one of the real heroes of Minden, in order to gratify politicians who were not ashamed of sitting in the same Cabinet with Lord George Sackville. Bate was found guilty, and was incarcerated for a twelvemonth.

The exemption from maltreatment which Opposition publicists enjoyed was certainly not purchased by their own moderation or discretion. They wrote in a strain, sometimes of jovial impudence, sometimes of powerfully reasoned, and withering, animadversion; and their swoop was never so direct and savage as when they flew at the highest game. In the "North Briton" of the twenty-third of April 1763, Wilkes had commented on a King's Speech in terms very uncomplimentary to the Cabinet, but, wherever the King was mentioned, in decent and measured phrases. While the Speech was pronounced to be the most abandoned instance of official effrontery ever attempted to be imposed on mankind, it was expressly declared to be the production of un-principled Ministers, which in a weak moment had been adopted as his own by a gracious King. At a later time in the annals of journalism, an amiable votary of litera-ture, — whose virtues and weaknesses had rendered him harmless to everybody except himself, — applied to the Prince Regent a jeering epithet which any man of com-mon sense, on the throne or near it, would have read with a contemptuous smile, and dismissed from his memory. And yet Leigh Hunt was heavily fined, and imprisoned for twenty-four months; and George the Third, during ten consecutive years, tried so hard to ruin Wilkes that, in the course of his operations, he came unpleasantly near to upsetting his own throne The promptness and rigour with which attacks upon royalty were punished both before and since, — as com-pared to the boundless license which was permitted at that epoch when the sovereign stood before the nation as a prime instigator, and a resolute supporter, of the American war, — may be taken as a measure of the dis-taste which that war then inspired in a very great number of Englishmen.

From 1775 onward the newspapers went straight for the King. The Empire, (they declared,) was under the direction of a bigoted and vindictive prince, whose administration was odious and corrupt in every part: so that the struggles of a handful of his subjects, made furious by oppression, had proclaimed the weakness of that Empire to the world Those precise words were printed at the beginning of 1776, and towards the end of the year a Christian Soldier addressed George the Third in a sermon of a couple of columns, headed by the first seven verses of the Sixth Chapter in the Wisdom of Solomon. The denunciation against wicked rulers, which those verses contain, was a sufficient sermon in itself ; but the preacher did not shrink from the duty of pressing his text home. "Have you not," he asked the

King, "called your own pretensions the necessity of the State? Have you chosen for your Ministers and Counsellors men of the greatest piety, courage, and understanding? Have you not dreaded to have such around you, because they would not flatter you, and would oppose your unjust passions and your misbecoming designs?" And so the argument continued through a score of interrogatives, any one of which, five years before, or ten years before, would have sent the author, and his printer, and the printer's devils as well, to think out the answer to that string of irreverent queries in the solitude of Newgate

Whenever the Ministry was mentioned in connection with the King, it was not for the purpose of shielding him from responsibility, but in order to upbraid him for having entrusted the government of the country to such a pack of reprobates. There could not, according to one journalist, be anything more unfortunate for a nation than for its Prince not to have one honest man about him. "Americans," wrote another, "are totally indifferent about every change of Ministers which may happen in the Court system. They care not who comes in. They know that a change of men implies nothing more than knaves succeeding to that power which former knaves were fools enough to abuse." The reason why England had come to be ruled by fools and knaves was illustrated by an historical anecdote duly pointed with italics "Mr Waller, the celebrated poet, being in the Closet with James the Second one day, the King asked him how he liked a picture of the Princess of Orange. 'I think,' says Waller, 'she is very like the greatest woman in the world.' 'Whom do you call so?' said the King. 'Queen Elizabeth,' replied the other. 'I wonder, Mr. Waller,' said the King, 'you should think so, as Queen Elizabeth owed all her greatness to the wisdom of her Council' '*And pray, sir,*' says *Waller, 'did you ever know a fool chuse a wise one?*'" [1]

---

[1] The London *Evening Post* of Saturday, September 27, to Tuesday, September 30, 1777.

These passages are a small nosegay of specimens culled from a vast, and not always fragrant, garden Caradoc, and Britannicus, and Publius, and Ximenes, and Eumenes, and A True Whig, and A Friend to Liberty, were often drearily long-winded, and sometimes unconscionably violent; and yet many thousands of our forefathers read their effusions with solemn satisfaction, and never wished them shorter by a sentence, or less strong by a single superlative. Even where an assailant of the King had the grace to veil his attack beneath a guise of irony, he always took good care to make his meaning obvious Before the winter Session of 1776, a contributor to a newspaper, signing himself "Aratus," was at the pains to compose an imaginary Speech from the throne "My Lords and Gentlemen," (so George the Third was represented as saying,) "since the whole world knows how I have been deceived, I have chosen in this public manner to declare that I am now sensible of the errors into which I have been led by evil counsellors. I glory in avowing the disposition of my heart, and, convinced of the generosity and magnanimity of my people, I know they will approve my candour. I have no doubt that they will soon reduce France and Spain to peace, if they should dare to draw the sword against me. An English monarch must always be triumphant when he reigns in the heart of his people."

Odes, as Pindaric as a poet of the antechamber could make them, had long been considered by the French and English Courts to be the appropriate form in which literary incense should be burned before Kings. But George the Third very early learned, — what Louis the Great, to the grievous hurt of his dignity, had been taught by no less skilful a master than Matthew Prior,[1]

[1] "Prior burlesqued, with admirable spirit and pleasantry, the bombastic verses in which Boileau had celebrated the first taking of Namur. The two odes, printed side by side, were read with delight in London; and the critics at Will's pronounced that, in wit as in arms, England had been victorious." Macaulay's *History of England;* chapter xxi.

—that poetry, and official poetry above any, presents a temptation which an idle and malicious humourist finds it impossible to withstand. Regularly as Whitehead's New Year ode, and Birthday ode, were laid on the bookseller's counter, the whole tribe of scribblers betook themselves with never-failing relish to the work of parody. Opposition newspapers, all through the months of January and June, regaled their subscribers with interminable files of halting stanzas. In case the Laureate died, there was only too evidently a large supply of bards who, if they consented to change their political opinions, had every intellectual qualification for succeeding him. Everything which could be said for or against the King, and the King's Friends, and the King's Ministers, found its way into the strophes and antistrophes with which the town was deluged, and in that Amœbean contest it is hard to pronounce whether panegyrists, or detractors, of Royalty were the sorriest rhymers.[1] The Court ode, a sickly and unnatural species of composition from the very first, — whether original, or under the handling of a satirical imitator, — became positively nauseous from endless reiteration.

Incidents not unfrequently occurred which inspired more forcible writers with verses less unreadable, but often grossly and extravagantly unfair. The King was

---

[1] " So firm withal, he's fixed as Fate,
When once resolved, at any rate
   He'll stick to his opinions ;
And, nobly scorning to be crossed,
Has most magnanimously lost
   Three parts of his dominions.

How blest the men he condescends
To honour with the name of Friends !
   Where steadier could he choose him ?
For, from my conscience I believe,
'Tis not in nature to conceive
   The service they'll refuse him."

These are the most presentable lines which can be discovered among the parodies on the Birthday Ode of 1776.

said to have been in the Royal box at the theatre when
the report of a sanguinary battle reached London.

> "At the play when the news of the slaughter arrived!
> What! Pray is the ghost of old Nero revived?
> A Cæsar to grin at a Foote or Macheath,
> While perhaps his own armies are bleeding to death!
>
> .   .   .   .   .
>
> An empire disjoined and a continent lost!
> The zeal of her children converted to hate,
> And the death of the parent involved in its fate;
> Her treasures exhausted, her consequence broke,
> Her credit a jest, and her terrors a joke!"

Those were the circumstances, (so Englishmen were
bidden to observe,) under which poor George the Third,
the most laborious and self-denying of public servants,
had ventured forth for a much needed evening out.
Such a theory of what propriety demanded constituted
a very extensive interference with the King's recrea-
tions; for the time was at hand when never a day
elapsed that some one, in some quarter of the globe,
was not being killed in a war which, after the winter
of 1777, the monarch kept afoot by his own personal
influence against the very general wish of his people, and
the judgement of all prudent members of his Cabinet

In spite of some excesses, absurdities, and affecta-
tions, the best newspapers did much to maintain at a
high level the character of the British Press   The conduct of the war by both belligerents was narrowly
watched, and was criticised from week to week in out-
spoken prose not open to the charge of being either
trivial or calumnious.   There were grave and excellent
writers who constituted themselves the guardians of their
countrymen's honour, on whichever side of the quarrel
those countrymen fought   They censured the arm-
ing of savages by the British War Office, and the
burning of defenceless towns by British frigates; but
they protested, with as warm disapproval, when the
printing establishment of James Rivington, the New

York Loyalist, was sacked by a mob of Whig raiders from Connecticut, and when insults were offered at Philadelphia to Quakers whose scruples would not allow them to take service against the Crown. Newspapers never shrank from expressing an opinion beforehand about strategical operations of the Government; and few were the instances where Lord George Germaine ultimately proved to be in the right, and the newspapers in the wrong. That most illogical test of patriotism which has been insisted upon by unwise rulers, and their flatterers, from the days of Ahab and Micaiah the son of Imlah downwards,[1] had no terrors for Englishmen of a vigorous and valiant generation; and very small attention was paid to ministerial partisans who brought charges of disloyalty against a military critic because he would not prophesy pleasant things

The Opposition newswriters, when the event showed their anticipations of failure to have been accurate, were bold to point the moral. "Who were they who brought His Majesty's army into a place from which it was a triumph to escape? If Boston was not a spot worth defending for its own sake, why did the troops continue there for near two years? Why were they reinforced until they amounted to near twelve thousand men? Why were four generals sent to command them? Why was the Ordnance Office emptied to defend Boston? Why was the Sinking Fund swallowed up? Why were sixty thousand tons of transports employed in that service? Why was the nation almost starved to feed that town? Why was so much brave blood shed at Bunker's Hill?"[2] These are questions which have never yet received an answer.

When, in January 1777, Howe was forced to abandon the Jerseys, and confine himself to the neighbour-

[1] First Kings, chapter xxii, verses 1 to 38. "And the messenger, that was gone to call Micaiah spake unto him, saying, Behold now, the words of the prophets declare good unto the king with one mouth. let thy word, I pray thee, be like the word of one of them, and speak that which is good."

[2] Letter of Valens, July 11, 1776.

hood of New York City, those journalists who had been all along opposed to the expedition were exceedingly frank in their comments. They condemned the General for his faulty tactics, and still less did they spare the Minister. In making out their case against Lord North they appealed to that sound, and not ignoble, principle which had inspired the foreign policy of Burleigh and of Chatham, and had produced the victories won by Drake, and Clive, and Wolfe, and Amherst. On that principle the greatness of Britain was founded; for it consisted in the recognition of some reasonable proportion between the risks and the expense of hostilities, on the one hand, and the importance of the object for the sake of which those hostilities were commenced, on the other. Was Long Island, (the Opposition publicists inquired,) worth one fortieth part of what it had taken to recover it? If England was to reoccupy the whole of the American coast, at the rate it had cost to regain Long Island, would the entire landed estate of the kingdom, if sold to the best bidder, raise enough to pay for that ill-omened conquest?

A certain sense of comradeship between the two great branches of our people, which the war had not extinguished, was manifested in the feelings entertained by many Englishmen in England towards the Revolutionary leaders who had displayed energy and courage, and particularly towards such as had fallen in battle. After the repulse of the Americans before Quebec, Montgomery's body, by General Carleton's order, was borne into the town with every mark of reverence and regret, and buried with military honours. When the tidings of his death reached the House of Commons, the most powerful orators, not on one side only, praised his virtues, and lamented his fate. Burke spoke of him with admiration. Lord North acknowledged that he was brave, able, and humane, and deplored that those generous epithets must be applied to one who had been a rebel; to which Charles Fox retorted that Montgomery was a rebel only in the same sense as were the old Parliament men of a hundred years ago, to whom those he saw around him owed it that they had a House of Commons in which to sit. Some ministerial supporters, — making the usual contribution to debate of senators who are eager to express their view, but afraid to take the floor, — greeted the remark with sarcastic laughter, and that laughter brought up Colonel Barré. He had been with Montgomery where French bullets were flying, and still had one of them embedded in his face; and, (on that occasion, as on others,) when Barré took upon himself to rebuke an impertinence, it was not apt to be repeated A leading journal published its report of the evening's proceeding in a paragraph edged with deep black; and, to judge by the general tone of the press, the same would have been done by other newspapers if the idea had occurred to other editors Close parallels were drawn, in divers odes and sonnets, between the characters of John Hampden and of Richard Montgomery, and between the causes in defence of which they received their death-wounds. There appeared about this time a political pamphlet, thinly disguised as a Dialogue of the Dead; — a species of composition which had been consummately executed by Lucian sixteen centuries ago, and more or less vapidly ever since; until, for the comfort of humanity, in this our own century it has at length ceased to be written at all. The author of this production, who evidently was a staunch partisan of the colonists, professed to relate the first interview between Montgomery, and his former chief, General Wolfe, when they renewed their friendship in the Elysian Fields.[1] Nor were American sym-

---

[1] " It is a happy chance for me, brave Wolfe," (so Montgomery began,) "to find you alone in this solitary walk, since I may, without being interrupted, expatiate with you on the unjust contempt you have shown me from the day of my arrival in this delightful place " That is very well, but not exactly in the style of Lucian The characters in the discussion, besides the two principals, were George Grenville and Charles Townshend, as well as David Hume, who strolled out of a shady valley to join in the talk, and eventually succeeded in reconciling the whole party. Hume had died in August 1776, just in time to take a share in the conversation

pathies confined to those who wrote what was intended
to be perused in the safe seclusion of the study. A
play, dating from the last French war, and containing
a graceful and pathetic allusion to the hero who died
before Quebec, was just then being given in London.
The passage had been written for Wolfe, but the theatre
applied it to Montgomery, "and fairly rocked with
applause."

Washington, from the earliest hour, was handled by
the London newspapers, and in the talk of London
society, after a fashion which could hardly have been
more respectful if his great destinies had already been
accomplished. Indeed, his treatment by English writers and speakers during the war with England is in
strong contrast to the rough usage which, towards the
close of his career and in the heats of the French
Revolution, he frequently experienced from that section
of his own countrymen who were opposed to his foreign
policy. "General Washington," wrote a London journalist in January 1776, "has so much martial dignity in
his deportment that you would distinguish him to be
a General and a Soldier among ten thousand people.
There is not a king in Europe but would look like a
valet-de-chambre by his side." A still more solid compliment was paid to him by Lord Chatham, who knew
well how to address a practical-minded Parliament which
commences business every day by petitioning that its
monarch may be permitted in health and wealth long
to live. "Mr. Washington," said Chatham in the House
of Lords, "who now commands what is called this night
the rebel force, is worth five thousand pounds a year."[1]

The American officer who, at this period of the struggle, had especially caught the fancy of Englishmen, was
Benedict Arnold. His dash and fire, his hairbreadth
escapes, the stories which were afloat about his rollick-
ing and masterful demeanour, his cheerfulness in defeat,
—and, above all, (for so Englishmen are made,) his hard-

[1] Debate on the Address in the House of Lords; Thursday, Nov. 20,
1777.

won successes, — commended him to a people which, next to a trusty servant, loves a gallant enemy. His picture was in shop-windows, and on the walls of many private rooms Since it was pretty clear that the wound which would keep him quiet was not known to surgery, men prayed that he might be captured and brought a prisoner to England; but they would have been sincerely sorry if he had been carried off by death. One of the most severe, and, (if such a supremacy were possible,) quite the worst-rhymed, of all the contemporary pasquinades was addressed to "the partial paragraphist of the Gazette who, after being obliged to recount Colonel Arnold's rapid march, and his bravery and conduct, thought fit to obscure his merit by calling him 'one Arnold.'" Resentment against the carping and jealous attitude of his own Government, — which rankled in Arnold's heart, and at last impelled him to his undoing, — was pointed and intensified by a knowledge that his martial qualities were cordially appreciated by that British adversary who had so thoroughly tested them in the field.

However large might be the number of our countrymen who could not bring themselves to hate Americans, there was one nation, closer at hand, which the great mass of Englishmen made no pretence whatever of loving. The permanent, no less than the ephemeral, literature produced during the first twenty-five years of George the Third's reign was pervaded, to an extent unpleasant and even scandalous, by the animosity with which his subjects south of Tweed regarded his subjects who had been born, but were not content to live, north of that river Englishmen had some excuse for their prejudice against Scotchmen, if only they had indulged it in moderation. Twice in human memory our borders had been penetrated, and our capital threatened, by a host of armed mountaineers; and those warriors, whatever romantic attributes they may possess in the imagination of posterity, most certainly did not impress their

contemporaries as the sort of people by whom a highly
civilised society would willingly be conquered and over
run.   In 1715 a handful of Highlanders, with some
Northumberland fox-hunters for cavalry, had advanced
half-way through Lancashire before they were surrounded and destroyed, and, thirty years later, several
thousand clansmen had marched to Derby, and had
given the Londoners a fright from which not a few
worthy citizens never entirely recovered.

But the Englishmen of 1776 had no need to sharpen
their hatred of the Scotch by repeating to each other
old stories which they had heard from their fathers and
grandfathers.   They themselves had experienced the
calamities and humiliations of a third invasion; and
this time the army of occupation had arrived to stay.
As soon as Lord Bute was Prime Minister, he summoned
southward, (beginning, but by no means ending, with
his own kinsmen and retainers,) a multitude of compatriots to partake of his good fortune.   An assaulting
force, which is active and enterprising, is always esti-
mated above its real numerical strength by the party
of defence.   Pensions, and patent places, and Court
offices with quaint titles and easy salaries, — in the
view of that English governing class whose perquisite
they hitherto had been, — seemed fast becoming the
monopoly of North British peers and North British
members of Parliament.   The sight was all the more
vexatious because a Scotchman of family found means
to save money, and to buy land, from the proceeds of
an office with the aid of which an English nobleman
thought himself fortunate if he could keep the bailiffs
out of his town-house, without even contemplating the
possibility of paying off a farthing of the mortgages
on his country estate.   Untitled Scotchmen, meanwhile,
abounded in the army, in the navy, in the Government
departments, and in India and the colonies.   Wherever
they might be stationed, they did their work admirably,
and, (instead of paying a deputy,) made a point of
doing it themselves.   Idle Englishmen of fashion saw

with dismay that sinecures, the reversion of which they held or hoped for, in the hands of Scotch occupants were sinecures no longer, but, in despite of their industry and public spirit, their shrewdness and frugality, — and even, it is to be feared, all the more on account of those qualities, — the fellow-countrymen of Lord Bute met with the very reverse of gratitude from the nation which they served [1]

Although thirteen long and eventful years had elapsed since Bute vacated office in 1763, he was still the fertile theme of gossip and suspicion. He had, indeed, been far from a popular minister when he stood openly at the sovereign's elbow as chief adviser and prime favourite; but he was not less detested, and much more feared, now that he was supposed, most erroneously and absurdly, to be manipulating the wires from behind the curtains of the throne. It may be doubted whether public opinion has ever been more profoundly affected by a more general and persistent illusion than in the case of the belief that Lord Bute was a motive power of George the Third's policy all the while that the American troubles were brewing, and as long as the war lasted. The Princess Dowager had died several years before a shot was fired; and the last remains of her old friend's political influence had died with her.[2] And yet the legend of an Interior Cabinet

---

[1] The prevalence of these unamiable sentiments is amusingly illustrated by a conversation, the printed report of which remains to all time the very model of artistic treatment. When Johnson and Wilkes, approaching each other from the Antipodes of political opinion, met first at Mr. Dilly's table, a topic had to be found about which they were both agreed, and on which they both were known to talk their very best. By common consent, and with all the greater zest because it was a Scotchman who had brought them together, they at once fell to work against the Scotch.

[2] In July 1778 George the Third wrote to Lord North about the rumour of a political negotiation between the Earl of Chatham and the Earl of Bute. "I have read the narrative," (His Majesty said,) " of what passed between Sir James Wright and Dr. Addington, and am fully convinced of what I suspected before, that the two old Earls, like old coachmen, still loved the smack of the whip." Those were the terms in which the King referred to Lord Bute at a time when, according to Whig newspapers, that nobleman was omnipotent in the secret counsels of the State.

at Buckingham House, where Bute had the first and the last word in every consultation, and where discussions were conducted in a jargon unintelligible to Southron Privy Councillors, was an established article of faith with the majority of patriotic Englishmen. Every odious measure, and every unexpected and exorbitant demand on the Exchequer, was habitually attributed to the machinations of a phantom conclave which passed by the name, sometimes of the Junta, and more often of the Thane's Cabinet. London was reminded several times a week, with a free use of capital letters, that the ruinous and unnaturally wicked conflict in consequence of which English families were mourning the loss of Husbands, Sons, and Brothers was a SCOTCH WAR; engineered by the relentless Bute, and the bloodthirsty Mansfield If once peace were restored, that crafty and cruel Caledonian Judge would no longer be able to harangue the House of Peers about the duty of killing men, and would be reduced, like Domitian, to kill flies.[1] Despatches from Scotch colonial governors had kindled the war; Scotch counsellors had promoted it; Scotch violence had conducted it; and pamphlets from the pens of Scotch gazetteers, — whose necessities had taught them to write, though they could not talk, so as to be understood by Englishmen, — had deluded simple people into believing that the unconditional submission of America was necessary for the honour and safety of Great Britain. Those were the doctrines preached three times a week by Anti-Sejanus, and Historicus, and Politicus, and a whole tribe of able and uncompromising exponents, whose credit with the public steadily grew as hostilities went forward, and

---

[1] Ever since Lord Mansfield uttered his unfortunate sentence about killing Americans, he passed in newspapers by a name the use of which is the most cruel insult that can be offered to a British Judge. In January 1776 it was reported that the distress inside Boston exceeded the possibility of description, and that our troops were eating horse-flesh, and burning the pews for fuel "But the —— goes to the play, and laughs as usual; Jemmy Twitcher sings catches with his mistresses at Huntingdon , and sly old Jeffreys drops hints for shedding more blood."

the cloud of misfortunes thickened. When Burgoyne
had been captured, and when half Europe was on the
eve of joining in an attack upon England, the newspapers authoritatively announced, in paragraphs marked
by a semi-official turn of phrase, that the *private
Cabinet*, of which the Earl of Bute was President, had
met at an Honourable Lady's house, and had finally
resolved to prosecute the war rather than part with
their employments.

Burke, in a sentence which has been quoted in famous debate,[1] laid it down that an indictment cannot
be brought against a nation. Nor, on the other hand,
can a nation commence an action for libel ; or else
Scotland, in any year between the Second and Twenty-
second of George the Third, might have secured exemplary damages from her traducers. The ball of
vituperation, set rolling by Churchill and Wilkes, was
kept in motion by less skilful, but far more unfair and
ill-natured, players, long after Wilkes had grown lazy
and indifferent, and when death had silenced Churchill.
Scotland, and all that appertained to her, was the stock
subject for the gall of the lampooner and the acid of
the caricaturist ; until the most omnivorous collector
of eighteenth-century broadsheets and woodcuts turns
aside in disgust when he espies the syllable " Mac " in
a political ballad, or the flutter of a kilt in the corner
of a coarse engraving. The storm of obloquy rose
perceptibly higher when the American war began, and
waxed more fierce as it proceeded. Sometimes a crafty
adversary, — meeting Scotchmen with their own weapons, and affecting the character of a political economist
whose feelings had been wounded by ministerial extravagance, — put forth a mass of exaggerated statistics

---

[1] That was the quotation with which Mr. Gladstone began his reply
to a chivalrous and heart-felt speech, by Mr. Gathorne Hardy, just before
the division on the Second Reading of the Irish Church Bill. Mr Hardy
had made two yet finer orations in the course of the two preceding years ,
but those, who then heard Mr Gladstone, find it difficult to believe that he
ever had more profoundly and pleasurably stirred his audience than on
that early morning in March 1869.

clustered round a particle of fact. One day it was
affirmed that the Scotch did not pay a fiftieth proportion with the English towards the Revenue, while, upon
the most moderate computation, they enjoyed above
half the emoluments of Government. On another
morning the newspapers published a return of Scotchmen in receipt of public money, accompanied by an
apology to the effect that the catalogue was unavoidably
incomplete. But, even so, the placemen and pensioners,
whose names appeared on the list, were represented as
drawing incomes from the Treasury to the tune of one
hundred thousand a year more than the annual produce
of land-tax from the whole of Scotland.

Anti-ministerial writers vehemently contended that
the continuance of the war, which was ruining the larger
nation, brought nothing except gain to the smaller; and
almost daily proofs were adduced in support of that
assertion.[1] The Prohibitory Act, forbidding importa-
tion from America, had advanced the price of tobacco
seventy per cent. Glasgow merchants, (it was alleged,)
to whom the Chancellor of the Exchequer had dropped
a hint, had laid in great quantities of that commodity,
and were selling at their own prices; since the Junta
would not let slip such a favourable opportunity of ena-
bling Scotch middlemen to fatten on the plunder of English consumers. Government inspectors were said to
have passed without examination all the stores provided
by Scotch contractors, who accordingly supplied the army
with food too bad to be eaten by any except Scotch soldiers, who fed worse at home [2] It was a standing rule,

[1] "A miserable remnant of English nobility, with a few unprincipled
commoners, are cunningly employed to bear the odium of the business,
while embassies, governments, contracts, regiments, and all the profitable
jobs and employments created by the calamities of the war, are without
exception reserved for Murrays, Mackenzies, Stuarts, and Frazers, —
Scotchmen who have been marked as enemies to liberty, and the vile
instruments of two late horrid rebellions." Letter from an Essex Farmer;
July 21, 1776.

[2] "A correspondent asks whether General Howe has any horses to
draw his artillery and waggons, without which he will never get to Philadelphia. The horses sent by Mr. Fordyce are all dead. This is a pretty

(so the story ran,) both at the War Office and the Admiralty, that, when things went wrong, it was never the fault of a Scotchman. The Greyhound frigate, a vessel of a class that in the last war used to capture privateers with thirty-six guns, had been beaten off by an American ship carrying only twenty-six cannon; but the captain was a Scotchman, "and the Ministry would sooner, once in a while, confess Americans to be brave than admit their favourite Scots to lack courage."

South-countrymen, who wished to live out of the taxes, could not be expected to welcome the incursion of a fresh and hungry herd into the very pick of the Treasury pastures. But even those quiet and unaspiring Englishmen, who were honourably contented to carry their labour into the open market, sincerely believed that the bread was taken out of their mouths by Scotch competition, and, if they failed to perceive the injury which was inflicted upon them, it was not for want of telling. A man of spirit, (so they were informed,) would endeavour to explore new lands until times grew better, and would cross the seas on a butcher's tray, if he could not afford a Thames wherry, rather than starve at home under a reign when none except Scotchmen might thrive in England. A correspondent, signing himself Hortulanus, related a sorrowful tale which was calculated to inspire uneasiness in a very large and estimable body of workpeople. He described himself as having been dismissed, with seven English gardeners who had worked under him, by a country gentleman, a kind and good master, who had been perverted by the example of a great person in the neighbourhood. This unpatriotic nobleman, a member of Lord North's Administration, was extremely fond of Scotch architects, Scotch politicians, and Scotch butlers and footmen; and he employed no fewer than

job, but Mr. Fordyce is a Scotchman, and intends to be member for Colchester. He has canvassed the *toone*, and prepared *aw* things in readiness. Contracts are fine things! How many millions of English money will the Scotch profit by in this war?" London Newspaper of October the 11th, 1776.

fourteen of the ten thousand Scotch gardeners who
had ousted Englishmen from all the most expensively
equipped establishments in the south of the island.
Why, (the indignant writer asked,) should men born in
a cold region, where neither plants, fruits, nor flowers,
could flourish, — where the sun could not ripen a grape,
and where half-starved spiders fed upon half-starved
flies, — be preferred to the inhabitants of a country for
which nature was more generous, and the sun more warm
and prolific? "Old as I am and encumbered by a family, I offered to work under these Caledonian favourites;
but my offer was not accepted. The Steward, who
pitied my case, told me I should lead a wretched life
with the Scots, who would consider me, and treat me, as
a foreigner; for it was their usual custom, on getting
into a family, to introduce their own countrymen, and
turn out all the old servants."[1]

Hortulanus, in all probability, never cultivated anything except the flower-pots outside an attic window in
Soho, but he, and plenty like him, had mastered the
easy trick of handling those topics of international prejudice, and trade jealousy, which go straight home to
the apprehensions of common men. The majority of
readers, alarmed and sore, accepted in good faith these
provocative statements, which were often deliberately
invented, or dishonestly over-coloured. They relished
their newspaper all the more when it contained an
appeal to the memory of a prince who, alive or dead,
was incomparably the most popular member of the reigning family throughout the country, and especially in the
capital. It has been wittily said that, from the time
Lord Bute took office, many Englishmen, and most Lon-

---

[1] The letter is in the London *Evening Post* of September 11, 1777.
Macaulay, among his collection of newspapers relating to the American
war, had acquired all the volumes of the London *Evening Post* on which
he could lay his hands That was part of the preparations made for continuing his *History of England* down to a time which was within the memory of men still living, and for relating "how imprudence and obstinacy
broke the ties which bound the North American colonists to the parent
state."

doners, refused to admit any blemish on the fame of the victor of Culloden, and found no fault with his Royal Highness except that he had left too many Camerons and Macphersons to be made gaugers and custom-house officers. Scotchmen, (wrote a vigorous controversialist,) seemed to vie with each other in the business of fettering our fellow-subjects in America, and of subjugating a brave, a loyal, and a free people to absolute slavery and bondage; but their cunning and persistent efforts were really levelled not so much against the liberties of the colonists as against the liberties of Englishmen. " But, alas, since the demise of the Saviour of England, the late worthy Duke of Cumberland, — Wully the Butcher, as the Scotch call him, — an Englishman dare scarce look a Scotchman in the face."[1] Such was the overcharged invective which habitually disfigured the public journals. Our progenitors, it must be admitted, occasionally came rather oddly by opinions which they held very stubbornly; and a vast number of Englishmen were confirmed and rooted in their friendship towards America because with some cause, but out of all measure, they envied and disliked the Scotch.

[1] Letter by Toby Trim; January 29, 1777.

CHAPTER XXV

THE CITY OF LONDON. NEWCASTLE-ON-TYNE. THE NATION AND THE WAR

SINCE the beginning of that century which now was far gone, the City of London, in time of war, had always been a centre of warlike feeling. In 1701 it eagerly rallied to William the Third, whom it did not greatly love, when he proudly and indignantly accepted the challenge of the French King. In 1711 the butchery of Malplaquet had sickened the nation; and the national conscience was revolted by the wanton prolongation of the horrors of a war, the objects of which might long ago have been secured by a prudent and disinterested Cabinet. The new Tory Ministry, which had displaced Godolphin, was actually negotiating with France; and yet the City of London made preparations for greeting Marlborough, as leader of the war-party, with a popular demonstration so aggressive and significant that it was very properly suppressed by the Government in the name of peace and order During the Seven Years' War the Corporation supported Chatham with enthusiasm and devotion. After he fell from power, and was succeeded by ministers who thought that there had been enough fighting, he was honoured, — on his way to the Guildhall, and inside its walls, — with a reception such as no subject has ever experienced in English history. But in 1775 the hostilities in Massachusetts found City opinion sullen and recalcitrant; and that state of mind rapidly developed into angry and determined opposition.

All the four members for London voted steadily against the war from first to last. The Corporation

carried Humble Remonstrances to the foot of the
Throne with so much persistency that George the Third
would almost as willingly have seen at St. James's the
blue and yellow uniforms of Washington's army as the
red gowns, and furred caps, and heavy gold chains of
the City officers.[1] Every successive appearance of that
all too familiar group at the door of his Presence Chamber indicated that he would once more have to listen,
with some show of civility, to a long screed of manly
common sense which he strongly suspected Mr. Alderman Wilkes of having drafted. The Recorder of London wore mourning in public "for the brothers whom
he had lost at Lexington;" and his conduct so far met
the view of those who had elected him that, when he
died no long time after, the Court of Aldermen appointed a successor who notoriously held the same
opinions. Through these trying months John Sawbridge was Chief Magistrate of the City, as well as one
of its parliamentary representatives He was a person
of social consequence; a country gentleman, a Colonel of
Militia in his county, and a high authority in the clubs
of St. James's Street, where he was accounted the best
whist player in town. Wealthy, proud, and honest, he
was beholden to no minister, and afraid of no one. He
had stood up in face of the Government majority at
Westminster, in its most insolent moods, as often and as
sturdily as did Barré, and Savile, and Dowdeswell, and
only less frequently than Edmund Burke and Charles
Fox. The courage and vigour with which, at the Mansion House and in the Commons, Sawbridge thwarted
and rebuked the operations of the Cabinet, secured him
enormous popularity as Lord Mayor, and a safe seat for
life as a member for the City.

Sawbridge strengthened his influence among Liverymen by the somewhat unscrupulous audacity with which

---

[1] "The day before the Sheriffs went to know when the King would
receive the Address, he said to a young man who was hunting with him;
'I must go to town to-morrow to receive those fellows in furs. They will
not be very glad to see me, nor I them.'" *Last Journals*, Dec. 1781.

he asserted the privileges and immunities of the City in
a matter about which almost all citizens were of one
mind.   At the outbreak of hostilities the Board of
Admiralty was even more behindhand in its preparations than the War Office, and with less excuse.   Lord
Barrington, the Secretary at War, had always cherished
a hope that the dispute would be settled by negotiation.
and had done what he dared, (which was not much,) **to**
bring that result about; whereas Sandwich, the First
Lord of the Admiralty, — who was in the inner counsels
of the Government, and the spokesman for his colleagues
in the House of Peers, — had consistently laboured, both in
Parliament and behind the scenes, to embroil the relations between England and her colonies   He, at all
events, was bound to provide that, so far as his own
Department was concerned, the country should be in
a position promptly, and strongly, to enforce by arms a
policy for the adoption of which he himself was so largely
responsible.   And yet, as late as December 1774, he
had deliberately reduced the Navy by four thousand
men, on a total strength of twenty thousand, of whom
a full quarter were Royal Marines.   Eleven months
afterwards he called on Parliament to vote an addition
of twelve thousand men.   The number of seamen was
doubled in a single evening ; and the process of violently
and suddenly withdrawing so vast a multitude from their
homes, their habits, and their avocations, paralysed commerce, and caused wide-reaching and unnecessary suffering to individuals.

The newspapers made known the story with a
copious employment of those nautical terms which
were familiar to a sea-going nation.   Thirty sail of
ships, (it was reported,) were "tumbling in Yarmouth
Roads at single anchor," without anyone on board any
of them except the master, and a few little cabin-boys.
As many more lay in Harwich harbour, losing their
voyage at a time when there was a great demand for
their cargoes in the London markets.   A captain, who
owned his vessel, and whose sailors had been taken

out of her by the press-gang in an Essex haven, paid fifty-six guineas for a crew to work her round to London; whereas, with his own people to help him, it would have been done for as many shillings. The mariners of the Northern counties, formidable in a strike or a Revenue-riot, were not submissive under this more serious invasion of their liberty. Hundreds of prime seamen left their families penniless in the ports of Durham and Northumberland, and ran off, with the project of remaining away until the heat of the Press was abated. But that time was long in arriving; for the maritime conscription grew more active and stringent as the necessities of the country deepened, and her enemies multiplied. Discontent after a while led to open violence. The impressed men, on board a tender in the river between North and South Shields, rose upon the crew, took possession of the ship, and carried her to sea under cannon-fire from her consorts, and from a fort which protected the entrance of the channel. A week or two afterwards a Lieutenant of the Royal Navy organised a raid upon the Colliers which lay in the estuary. A great number of sailors came to the help of the vessel which he first attacked, and mustered on the forecastle to repel boarders. The fight commenced with lumps of coal and billets of wood on the part of the defenders, answered on the other side by a blunderbuss, which first missed fire, and then killed a man at whom it had not been aimed. Newcastle citizens, who had learned by repeated experience the temper and quality of a Quayside mob, felt greatly relieved when they ascertained that Lieutenant Oakes and his party had escaped with their lives.[1]

In and below London the misery was intense; and the resistance of the sufferers, though less determined, entailed a longer list of fatal accidents. Upwards of a thousand seamen were captured in the Thames alone

[1] *Local Records of Northumberland and Durham;* by John Sykes, Newcastle, 1832.

Towards the end of October 1776, twenty armed boats
came up river from Deptford and Woolwich, and took
every man, except the master and mate, from every
ship that they found in the stream.   A Royal officer
was shot with a pistol as he went up the side of a
vessel; and eight merchant-sailors endeavoured to escape by swimming, and were drowned in the attempt.
The West Indian captains, especially, were in pitiable
case.   They had everything ready for weighing anchor.
Their holds were full; they had paid their crews for
the time spent in the river, and for a month of the
voyage in advance; and now every man who slept
before the mast was carried off with his money in his
pocket.   The needs of the Royal Navy had to be met
with a hurry which did not admit of careful selection,
or of a decent regard for individual claims to indulgence
and consideration.   The hatches of the tenders were
battened down upon a mixed crowd of fisher-folk
and merchant-sailors, with sore hearts and undressed
wounds; of townsmen who had never been on board a
ship before; and of old broken mariners who had gone
to sea so often, and for so long, that they had earned a
right to spend the rest of their days where, and how,
they chose.   One press-gang had to answer in the law-
courts for having laid hands on a veteran whose skull
had been fractured in the last French war.   Another
swept off a group of people from a lottery office, while
they were engaged on insuring the numbers which they
had drawn.   "Come, my lads," said the lieutenant, " I
will insure you for good berths on board a ship of war."
A knot of labouring men, who had been buying their
family dinners, were assailed on their way homewards,
and showed fight to some purpose.   One sailor was
knocked down with a leg of mutton, and another with a
bundle of turnips; and, before their party could make
good their retreat, the whole of them had been ducked
by the crowd.   That was a touch of pantomime, in the
midst of many silent and obscure domestic tragedies.
An advertisement appeared to the effect that the bodies

of five impressed men, suffocated in the hold of the
Hunter tender, had been brought on shore to be owned.
It was uncongenial work for bluff, hearty, tars who were
told off for that odious duty. The crime, (so a spirited
journalist reminded his readers,) rested not on the
sailor's bludgeon, nor on the lieutenant's cutlass, but on
the unthinking head of a minister who, through many
years of peace, forgot the future probability of a war,
and left every precaution alone until it was too late to
act without violating humanity.

Enthusiasm for the naval service there was none.
The war was barren of prize money; no glory was to
be obtained out of a campaign against privateers commanded by Yankee skippers who knew very well when
to attack, and when and whither to run, and, moreover,
many a poor fellow, who in days gone by had helped to
beat the French and Spaniards, was in his rude way a
patriot Mariners, who had served the guns under
Hawke and Saunders, had no mind for exchanging shot
and blows with men who fought their ship in English
fashion, and who, when the battle had gone against
them, begged for quarter with an English tongue. The
irritation caused by the harsh and precipitate action of
the Admiralty was general throughout London, and nowhere so acute as within the City bounds. It was a
short journey to Cornhill from Rotherhithe and Green-
wich, opposite the river front of which the Jamaica fleet
lay, and seemed likely to lie until the timbers rotted;
and West Indian captains, and their employers, might
be seen whispering together with long faces under the
colonnades of the Royal Exchange, and across the tables
of the neighbouring coffee-houses The dignity of the
Corporation was offended by the invasion of the press-
gangs, and the City fathers had been touched in a tender point, for the supply of fish was scanty and irregular.
Essex boatmen had transferred themselves and their
nets to Holland; and a naval officer, of more than
common hardihood, braving a storm of malediction
from the conception of which the imagination shrinks,

laid forcible hands on a number of seamen in the very heart of Billingsgate market.

That district lay within the Lord Mayor's jurisdiction; and the situation was still further strained by the impressment of Mr. John Tubbs, a Waterman of the Lord Mayor's Barge.[1] The outraged Magistrate issued an order for the apprehension of all naval officers who carried on their operations inside the limits of the City. Three lieutenants and a mate, belonging to a ship of the line, were arrested, and brought before the Guild-hall Bench. A very eminent Judge attended the examination in order to support the accused officers with his countenance and advice. His Lordship was stiffly rebuked by the sitting Aldermen, who told him that they themselves would never venture to intrude their presence upon him in his own Court on such an errand. The defendants refused to find bail, and were duly committed to the Poultry Counter, where they remained in durance until the Attorney and Solicitor General gave it as their opinion that bail had better be procured. At one moment it seemed as if the forcible enlistment of seamen within the City would be impracticable. The Lord Mayor declined to back the press-warrants; and his example was afterwards followed by Sir Thomas Halifax, his successor in the Chair. But that difficulty was surmounted by the warrants being taken for signature to Alderman Harley, as stout a Tory as ever Sawbridge was a Whig. Harley, who was grand-nephew of the celebrated Earl of Oxford, had a good hereditary title to show for his political opinions, and, as a firm supporter of Lord North, he had oppor-

[1] Rex *versus* Tubbs became a leading case in the King's Bench, where Lord Mansfield took occasion to deliver himself in favour of the legality of pressing for the Royal Navy "A pressed sailor," he pronounced, "is not a slave. No compulsion can be put upon him except to serve his country; and, while doing so, he is entitled to claim all the rights of an Englishman." The readers of Smollett, and even of Captain Marryat, may be permitted to question what those rights were worth to a landsman with a broken head, imprisoned many feet below the water-line in the hold of a frigate which had put to sea for a three years' cruise in distant waters.

tunities placed at his disposal which enabled him to make a mountain of money by the war [1]

There had been a war anterior to 1776, and there have been wars since, when the youth of the City, — abandoning the employments by which they lived, and giving up, in some cases, assured and attractive prospects of commercial advancement, — took arms for the prosecution of a quarrel which they regarded as their country's cause. But the dispute with America excited no enthusiasm in the mercantile community. Whatever martial ambition might exist among respectable civilians was deadened and discouraged by the humiliating possibilities which awaited every volunteer who donned the scarlet coat. It was almost universally believed in military circles that flogging was a valuable preservative of discipline at home, and quite indispensable on active service That last named article of belief has died hard, and it survived the longest in official quarters. It was the task of independent members of Parliament, some of whom are not yet old men, to break it down by argument, and practical experience, on a scale and of a nature which enforces conviction, has now finally settled

[1] The impunity with which press-gangs acted, and the terror that they inspired among humble civilians, are amusingly illustrated by a story from the unpublished Memoirs of Archbishop Markham. Some years after the American war a party of Westminster boys dressed themselves up as men-of-warsmen, — which was not difficult in days when an officer kept watch on board ship in any costume which he found most comfortable. They stationed themselves at the corner of Abingdon Street, and were headed by a stout lad in a pea-jacket and hairy cap, "who had acquired the art of making a cat-call by whistling through his fingers," and who personated the lieutenant. They promptly pounced on the first passer-by, examined him; pronounced him a fit person to serve his Majesty, and then dexterously loosed their hold, and allowed him to run. While they were occupied over their fifth victim, an under-master came by, and the sport ended Dr Vincent thought the affair so serious that he called in the Archbishop, who in his day had been a Head-master of Westminster with whom no scholar ever trifled. "That," said the old man of the world, "was a very smart piece of fun Now do show me the hairy cap '" and the boys got off with a hundred lines of Virgil apiece.

It was said that gold-laced hats were worn by people who could ill afford them, because they had a military look, and were therefore a protection against the attentions of the press-gang.

the controversy. Within the last four years, in South Africa, order and obedience have been effectively maintained, without recourse to corporal punishment, in by far the largest and the most variously constituted force that Great Britain ever put into the field, and kept there over a very long space of time under circumstances exceptionally trying to the spirits and temper of an army. Some of our most distinguished officers, for more than a century past, felt sufficient faith in their countrymen to anticipate a happy result which now is matter of history;[1] but, during the war of the American Revolution, such wise and far-seeing prophets were few   On an April day of 1777 the whole neighbourhood of Whitehall was disturbed by the most dreadful shrieks, proceeding from the Parade-ground behind the Horse-guards and the Treasury   A soldier was receiving the first instalment of a thousand lashes; and a hundred were afterwards inflicted upon a drummer whose heart had failed him during the operation.   When such things were done in St. James's Park, a stockbroker or a clerk, of reputable character and good position, would unavoidably reflect as to what might be his fate when he was on detached service in the backwoods of America, at the mercy of an unfriendly and tyrannical sergeant who possessed the confidence of the regimental officers

[1] "At the same time that the British soldiers were maintaining with such devoted fortitude the glory of England, their camps daily presented the most disgusting and painful scenes.   The halberts were regularly erected along the lines every morning, and the shrieks of the sufferers made a pandemonium, from which the foreigner fled with terror and astonishment at the severity of our military code.   Drunkenness was the vice of the officers and men; but the men paid the penalty, and the officers who sate in judgement in the morning were too often scarcely sober from the last night's debauch.   It will be a consummation of my most anxious wishes, grounded upon my memory of these early scenes of abuse of power, when the system of punishment, such as I have described it, shall be referred to only as a traditional exaggeration."   So wrote General Sir Robert Wilson with reference to the campaign in Flanders of the year 1794.   That was the end of what had been worst   The standard of personal behaviour among officers in Wellington's Peninsular army was high, and punishments, though still very severe, became less frequent when the soldiers could look to their superiors for a worthy example, and for watchful and kindly guidance.

The American war brought into the City a tribe of
interlopers whose presence there was viewed with moral
repugnance by the worthiest portion of the community,
and who inflicted very serious damage upon the material
interests of established traders and financiers Sometimes it was a man of rank and pleasure, and sometimes
an impudent and voluble upstart of doubtful antecedents,
who came eastward through Temple Bar armed with a
contract for rum, or beef, or army-cloth, which replaced
to him, many times over, the three or four thousand
pounds that he had sunk in the purchase of his seat for
a Cornish borough. When the Chancellor of the Exchequer had recourse to one of his frequent borrowings,
he passed over the hereditary bankers whom investors
trusted, and who would have been satisfied with a fair
and reasonable commission for their risk and trouble.
The money was largely raised through the agency of a
great number of members of Parliament, — who, for the
most part, had never lent anything before in their lives,
but had borrowed much, — on terms of scandalous laxity
which had been arranged for the express purpose of
rewarding them for their votes.   Lord North himself
admitted that, on a single loan of twelve millions, upwards of a million had gone in clear profit among the
individuals to whom it had been allotted, and half of
them were politicians who sate behind him in the House
of Commons. "I agree with you," (Lord Abingdon
wrote to Lord Rockingham,) "in thinking the loan to be
a very abominable transaction"   That was how clean-
handed senators viewed the disgraceful proceedings;
but harder things still were said in bank-parlours.   The
spectacle of fine gentlemen, and of some gentlemen who
were anything but fine, masquerading about Thread-
needle Street and Birchin Lane with the air of partners
in Glyn's or Child's, and talking a financial jargon which
they supposed to resemble the conversation of the
capitalists whose gains they intercepted, inspired in
genuine City men a disgust which, (since they were
neither more nor less than human,) pointed and sharp-

ened their disapprobation of the Government policy in America.

That disapprobation was grounded upon large knowledge and long observation. The City had been firmly persuaded that the knot of colonial discontent could never be cut by the sword. The Funds always fell after British defeats, and never very visibly recovered themselves in consequence of a British victory. In August 1774, before the Revolution began, the Three per Cent. Consols stood at 89. A month before the news of Long Island arrived in London they were at 84; a fortnight after that news they were at 82; and that was all the effect produced by a complete rout of the Americans, which was hailed by courtiers at home, and English diplomatists abroad, as a most reassuring, and almost a conclusive, success. By October 1777 Consols had fallen to 78. The tidings of the capture of Burgoyne brought them down to 70. They fell, and fell, until the capitulation of Lord Cornwallis reduced them to 54; and they could hardly have gone lower if they were to retain any value at all. Then Lord North made way for a Ministry pledged to recognise the independence of America, and to abandon the right of taxing her wealth and controlling her commerce; a right which Lord North and his adherents had always insisted to be absolutely essential for maintaining the prosperity of British trade and British manufactures. And yet Consols, when the situation came to be understood, rose six points on the mere prospect of a peaceful settlement with our former colonies; although England was still at war, all the world over, with France, Spain, and Holland. The silent testimony of the Stocks, those authentic witnesses who never boast and never flatter, unanswerably proves that the City of London at no period shared with the Court and the Cabinet in the delusion that the colonies could be subdued by arms.

The state of opinion in London was evident on the surface; but it is more difficult to collect indications of the feeling which prevailed elsewhere. The sentiments, however, which were current in one famous region of industry and enterprise have been recorded by a witness whose evidence on this point is above suspicion. Samuel Curwen, a prominent Massachusetts Loyalist, — who had been a high official in his native province, and who now was an exile in England, — made a tour in the Midland counties, and spent a week at Birmingham Walking there on the Lichfield road, Curwen was invited indoors by a Quaker, and found him "a warm American, as most of the middle classes are through the Kingdom." He passed an agreeable day with a merchant, who had been in America, and who was "her steady and ardent advocate" He stepped into the shop of a gunmaker. The British Ministry, — with foresight which, for the War Office, might almost be called inspiration, — had given the man an order to construct six hundred rifles for the use of General Howe's army . and yet, (said Curwen,) "he is an anti-ministerialist, as is the whole town "[1] If such was the case in a district where Government orders for military supplies had been freely placed, it may well be believed that political discontent and disgust were not less acute in those commercial centres which greatly suffered, and in no way profited, by the existence of hostilities. Yorkshire manufacturers, especially, had no part in the war except to pay increased taxes, to borrow from their banker on terms, that every month grew worse, money that every month they needed more, and to see their warehouses glutted with goods which they were forbidden to sell to those New Englanders, and Pennsylvanians, who had formerly been their very best customers "In the West Riding," wrote John Wesley, "a tenant of Lord Dartmouth was telling me, 'Sir, our tradesmen are breaking all round me, so that I know not what the end will be.' Even in Leeds I had appointed to dine at a merchant's; but, before I came, the bailiffs were in possession of the house. Upon my saying, 'I thought Mr. —— had been in good circum-

[1] Samuel Curwen's *Journal* for August 1776.

stances,' I was answered, ' He *was* so, but the American war has ruined him.' " [1]

That war was marked by a feature unique in English history. Not a few officers of every grade, who were for the most part distinguished by valour and ability, flatly refused to serve against the colonists; and their scruples were respected by their countrymen in general, and by the King and his ministers as well. An example was set in the highest quarters. The sailor and the soldier who stood first in the public esteem were Augustus Keppel, Vice Admiral of the White, and Lieutenant General Sir Jeffrey Amherst. Keppel made it known that he was ready as ever to serve against a European enemy, but that, although professional employment was the dearest object of his life, he would not accept it " in the line of America." After that announcement was made, and to some degree on account of it, he enjoyed a great, and indeed an extravagant, popularity among all ranks of the Navy; and, when a European war broke out, he was promoted, and placed in command of the Channel Fleet. Amherst had absolutely declined to sail for New England in order to lead troops in the field. He withstood the expostulations and entreaties of his Sovereign, who in a personal interview, (as Dr Johnson truly testified,) was as fine a gentleman as the world could see; and who never was more persuasive and impressive than when condescending to request one of his subjects to undertake a public duty as a private favor to himself. The circumstance was not remembered to Amherst's disadvantage. He was retained as Commander-in-Chief of the forces; within the ensuing five years he became a peer, the Colonel of a regiment of Household Cavalry, and a full General in the army; and he died a Field-Marshal

Amherst, although determined not to fight against the colonists, who had fought so well under him, was a poli-

[1] John Wesley to Lord Dartmouth. *Historical Manuscripts Commission;* Fifteenth Report, Appendix, Part I.

tical friend of the existing Administration; and, in the
main, a supporter of their colonial policy. His course
of action naturally enough commended itself to military
men who were opposed to the Government, and who believed that the American question had been grievously
mismanaged. Their views obtained expression in a
statement made by a brother-soldier, whom of all others
they would have chosen for their spokesman. Conway,
like Amherst, terminated his career a Field-Marshal;
but his most glorious and joyous years were those which
he passed as aide-de-camp to the Duke of Cumberland in
Flanders The immediate vicinity of that intrepid prince,
during a battle, was quite hot enough for most people,
but not for Harry Conway. At Fontenoy the young
fellow contrived, on his own account, to get hand to hand
with two French grenadiers; and at Lauffeld he was
within a finger's breadth of being killed in a desperate
scuffle with some French hussars. His courage, however, had seldom been so severely tested as when, in
November 1775, he addressed the House of Commons
on the limits of military obedience. That subject, (he
said,) having been started in Parliament, it might look
like an unworthy shrinking from the question if he did
not say a few words to it. No struggle in the mind of
a military man could be so dreadful as any doubt of this
kind. There was a great difference between a foreign
war, where the whole community was involved, and a
domestic war on points of civil contention, where the
community was divided. In the first case no officer
ought to call in question the justice of his country; but,
in the latter, a military man, before he drew his sword
against his fellow-subjects, ought to ask himself whether
the cause were just or no. Unless his mind was satisfied on that point, all emoluments, — nay, the sacrifice of
what people in his situation held dearest, their honour, —
would be nothing in the scale with his conscience He,
for his part, never could draw his sword in that cause.[1]

---

[1] Debate in the Commons on bringing in the American Prohibitory Bill
Parliamentary History of England, Vol. XVIII., page 998.

Those words were frank and weighty; but for the purposes of history the manner in which they were taken is far more important and significant than the words themselves. The influence of Conway upon politics rose steadily in the course of the coming years, throughout which his view of a soldier's obligations never wavered, and never was concealed. The candour and fairness of his character, (we are told,) drew much respect to him from all thinking and honest men.[1] In February 1782, during his country's dark hour, Conway recommended Parliament to terminate the contest with America, — a course which he had always thought to be the duty of England, and which many, who had long been deaf to duty, were beginning to contemplate as necessary to her interests. His proposition was rejected by a single vote on a division in which nearly four hundred members took part; and a few nights afterwards he induced a larger and a wiser House to condemn any further prosecution of the war by a majority of nineteen. Such a Resolution on such a subject, — carried against all the efforts and influence of a powerful Court, and of a Cabinet which to external appearance was unanimous, — is unprecedented in the annals of our Parliament, and perhaps in those of any national assembly. No more sincere and striking proof could possibly be given of the estimation in which Conway was held by his fellow-senators. They admired him none the less, and trusted him all the more, because, at the outbreak of the war, he had not shrunk from declaring himself on as abstruse a point of conduct as a soldier and a patriot was ever called upon to determine.

The same respectful and considerate treatment was very generally extended to other military and naval men whose personal action was governed by the same motives. Some left the service outright, and re-entered private life, with no diminution to such popularity, or social predominance, as they had hitherto enjoyed.[2] Some re-

[1] Walpole's *Last Journals*, February 22, 1782.
[2] Such an one was Mr. Bosville of Thorpe Hall. That gentleman, after

mained on half-pay until Great Britain was attacked by
European enemies, when they promptly and joyfully
placed their swords once more at the disposal of the
Government.   Others, again, accepted a commission in
the militia ; a post of unusual danger and importance at
a moment when England, stripped bare of regular troops,
had temporarily lost command of the sea in consequence
of the scandalous improvidence of the Board at the head
of which Lord Sandwich sate.   Whatever course they
adopted, their fidelity to principle appeared reasonable,
and even laudable, to their countrymen of the middle
and lower classes ; and in their intercourse with equals
they brought down upon themselves and their families
no penalties whatsoever.   The American war, from the
outset to the finish, was an open question in English
society.   A general or colonel, who had refused to take
a command against the colonists, lived comfortably and
pleasantly with his country neighbours.   The strong
Tory politicians among them might grumble against him
as fanciful or factious ; but much harder things would
have been said about him if he had shot foxes, or given a
piece of ground for the site of a Nonconformist chapel

To the general public of our own day, — as indeed
had always been the case with every well-read Englishman, — the name of Lord Chatham stands for patriot-

---

serving a campaign with Howe, had quitted the army because he would not
act any longer against American Independence   Season after season he
kept open house in town for Fox, and Grey, and Erskine, and Sheridan,
nor for them only ; for one of his constant guests was Lord Rawdon, than
whom the Americans had no more stern and dreaded adversary in arms all
the while that the war had lasted.   Until he grew old, in order to avoid the
daily trouble of entertaining at home, Bosville's board was spread at the
Piazza Coffeehouse , where, when five o'clock came, two dozen men of
fashion frequently sate down to dine well, even though only half a dozen
had been expected   Whether the company was small or large, the host
was king of it, or rather despot ; and a despot of the kind which London
needed then, and needs still   For dinner was served when the hour struck ,
and any one who came late knew that the only thing left for him was to
go away, and dine elsewhere.   The custom of proposing toasts and sentiments after the cloth was drawn, — destructive to conversation, and most
depressing to the convivial happiness of the shy and the inarticulate, —
was abolished at Bosville's table   See the *Life of General Sir Robert
Wilson ;* Volume 1, chapter ii.

ism. For he raised England, in a very few years, from
distress and discredit to a brilliant and unquestioned
pre-eminence; he made our Empire; and he expressed
the national sentiment, which was ever present with
him, in unusually apt and glowing language. Chatham
gave his sons to his country. Great as were the pains
which he bestowed upon the training of the second
brother as an orator and a ruler, it was with equal ardour
that he incited and encouraged the military studies of
his eldest boy. Lord Pitt was sent into the army at
fifteen. The father, who never was entirely happy
unless he had all his family about him, felt the separation keenly;[1] and he was actuated by a sole view to
the young man's usefulness in that profession which he
regarded as not less honourable, and hardly less important, than the calling of a statesman. "My son's
ambition," (so Lord Chatham informed the Governor
of Canada in his stately manner,) is to become a real
officer; and I trust he already affixes to the appellation
all the ideas that go to constitute a true title to the
name." General Carleton learned with infinite satisfaction that the ex-minister, — who possessed so extensive
and accurate a knowledge of the higher ranks on the
British army-list, wished his son to serve an apprenticeship on Carleton's staff, and had purchased him a
pair of colours in the regiment of which Carleton was
the Colonel.

The letter from which that extract is taken was dated
in October 1773. In February 1776 Lady Chatham
wrote to thank the Governor warmly, in her husband's
name, for the favour and attention which Lord Pitt had
received from his chief, in garrison and in the field.
"Feeling all this, Sir," (so she proceeded,) "as Lord
Chatham does, you will tell yourself with what concern
he communicates to you a step that, from his fixed opin-

[1] "The time draws nigh for our dear Pitt joining his regiment at Quebec. What pain to part with him! And what satisfaction to see him go
in so manly a manner, just in the age of pleasures!" Lord Chatham to
Lady Stanhope; March 23, 1774.

ion with regard to the continuance of the unhappy war with our fellow-subjects of America, he has found it necessary to take. It is that of withdrawing his son from such a service." Two years afterwards, when the French war broke out, the family, (and who could blame them?) discovered a bright side to that great public calamity in the reflection that a son and brother could now return to the profession of arms with an easy conscience.[1] Lord Pitt went back to the Service, and was appointed aide-de-camp to the Lieutenant-Governor of Gibraltar. He had not yet left England when Lord Chatham was struck down by death; but he sailed before the funeral, and handed over the post of chief mourner to his brother William. The House of Commons heard, with deep emotion, the noble words in which the dying man was said to have bidden his son honour a father's memory by responding on the instant to his country's call.[2] Lord Pitt was rewarded for his filial behaviour by the privilege of taking his share in that immortal defence of our Mediterranean citadel which did so much to restore the imperilled supremacy, and to salve the wounded pride, of England.

The Earl of Effingham was a regimental officer, in the spring of life,[3] and passionately attached to his vocation. At a moment when there was no fighting to be witnessed west of the Carpathians, he had joined the Russian army as a volunteer, and had gone through a campaign against the Turks[4] with a name for conspicu-

[1] Letter from the younger William Pitt to the Countess of Chatham, March 19, 1778.

[2] Speech of Lord Nugent, May 13, 1778. *Parliamentary History*, Vol XIX, page 1227.

[3] In the Correspondence of the Marquis of Cornwallis, chapter 1, Effingham is styled a Lieutenant General, but, according to Collins's *Peerage*, he was not thirty years old in 1775. A note to the *Parliamentary History* describes him as a captain, and that statement is borne out by the regimental lists preserved in the War Office. It was his father, the second Earl, who was a Lieutenant General.

[4] Lord Effingham's behaviour was specially marked in 1770, when almost the whole of the Turkish fleet was burned in a bay on the coast of Anatolia. It was the Sinope of that war.

ous enterprise and valour. He did not belong to the class of people who are prone to self-questioning, and inclined to crotchets or fanaticisms. A plain, rather rough, country squire, he lived according to the less ideal habits of his period and his order.[1] And yet, when his regiment was told off for America, he threw up his commission, and, though far from a rich man, renounced the prospect of sure and quick advancement. In May 1775 he made his explanation in Parliament. His highest ambition, (so he told the House of Lords,) ever since he had any ambition at all, was to serve his country in a military capacity. If there was on earth an event which he dreaded, it was to see that country so situated as to make his profession incompatible with his obligations as a citizen; and such an event had now arrived. "When the duties," he said, "of a soldier and a citizen become inconsistent, I shall always think myself obliged to sink the character of the soldier in that of the citizen, till such time as those duties shall again, by the malice of our *real* enemies, become united." Effingham sate down as soon as he had made this remarkable confession; but none of his brother peers, who were present, took exception to his speech; nor was he ever subsequently taunted with it in debate, although he was a frequent, a fiery, and a most provocative assailant of the Government. Outside Parliament, not in any way by his own seeking, he at once became celebrated, and vastly popular. Mason, the poet, inquired if ever there was anything, ancient or modern, either in sentiment or language, better than Lord Effingham's speech.[2] Public thanks were voted to him by the Corporations of London and Dublin. The Free Citizens of the Irish metropolis, many of them gentlemen of wealth and standing, and Protestants all, dined together and drank

---

[1] His lady hunted, and rode over five-barred gates. He himself liked his wine; and a summer-house on the estate had been christened Boston Castle, — not as a tribute to the American cause, but because no tea was ever drunk there

[2] Mason to Walpole; June 17, 1775.

toasts to the Glorious and Immortal memory of the great King William, to Lord Chatham; to the brave General Carleton, the Man of too much Humanity for the purpose of a Cruel and Cowardly Minister; and to the Earl of Effingham, who did not forget the Citizen in the Soldier.

Lord Frederic Cavendish, (a name which is the synonym of loyalty,) had been a soldier from his youth onwards. At the outbreak of the Seven Years' War he had made a compact with three other promising officers, — Wolfe, Monckton, and Keppel, — not to marry until France was defeated, and finally brought to terms.[1] He was an aide-de-camp to the Duke of Cumberland in Germany, and during several campaigns he rode at the head of a brigade of infantry in the army of Prince Ferdinand of Brunswick. Already a Lieutenant General of repute when the American disturbances broke out, he still, at the age of five-and-forty, had the best of his career before him; but he allowed it to be known that he would not apply for a command against the colonists. Lord Frederic, however, continued in his profession; and in subsequent years he was made a full General by the Whigs, and a Field-Marshal by the Tories. Before it was ascertained that he declined to take part in the war, something disagreeable was written about him by a Mr. Falconer of Chester, who cannot be ranked as a very noteworthy critic. "The times assist the Americans. They are united by our divisions. Lord Frederic Cavendish is going to this service. If he acts consistently, he should turn to their side, for that family has been the best friends to Faction of every kind, and the most furious enemies to civil order."[2] Burke, on

---

[1] This account of Lord Frederic Cavendish is largely taken from the *Dictionary of National Biography*. The article allotted to Lord Frederic in that work recounts an anecdote about him and the Duc d'Aiguillon, which very pleasantly recalls the chivalrous relations existing, in time of war, between the nobles and gentlemen of France and of England.

[2] Letter by Mr. Thomas Falconer, among the family papers of James Round, Esq, M.P.: *Historical Manuscripts Commission*, Fourteenth Report, Appendix, Part IX.

the other hand, described the Cavendishes as men who were among the ornaments of the country in peace, and to whom the King owed some of the greatest glories of his own, and his predecessor's reign, "in all the various services of the late French war." Great integrity; great tenderness and sensibility of heart, with friendships few but unalterable; perfect disinterestedness; the ancient English reserve and simplicity of manner, — those, according to Edmund Burke, were the marks of a true Cavendish.[1] Such was the opinion held about the Devonshire family by one who assuredly knew them more intimately than ever did Mr. Falconer; and the one judgement may be weighed against the other.

Public attention had recently been strongly and favourably drawn to a man who was the forerunner of a class which, from that time to ours, has played an unostentatious and unrecompensed, but a most commanding, part in the history of moral and social progress. Effingham and Chatham, Conway and Cavendish, were peers and members of Parliament; but Granville Sharp, though not himself a senator, had the originality, the native strength, and the indefatigable enthusiasm of one whose behests, in the long run, senators are irresistibly compelled to obey. He had recently been invited to enter Holy Orders with the promise of a valuable living; but he put aside the offer on the ground that he could not satisfy himself concerning his qualifications for the function of a spiritual teacher.[2] Granville Sharp was one of the founders of the Bible Society; he learned Hebrew in hopes of converting a Jew, and Greek in order to refute a Socinian; and his criticisms upon the sacred texts were recommended to the attention of theological students by a Bishop   If he was not fit to be a clergyman, it is hard to see how the Church of England

---

[1] Letter drafted by Burke in 1771.   Burke's *Character of Lord John Cavendish.*

[2] Letter to the Rev. Granville Wheler, Esq.: *Memoirs of Granville Sharp, Esq.,* by Prince Hoare; Part I., chapter 1. The singular address which the envelope bore is explained in a note at the bottom of the page

could have been manned. Nevertheless when Granville Sharp advanced, as an additional reason for declining to take orders, his belief that he could serve the cause of religion more effectually as a layman, there was much good sense in his decision. He was already deeply committed to a laborious, a rude, and a hazardous undertaking which, though it was inspired by Christianity, could only be forced to a successful conclusion by a free use of carnal weapons. Between 1765 and 1772 he carried on a seven years' war of his own for the establishment and vindication of the doctrine that a slave is liberated by the act of setting his foot upon English ground. He had Lord Mansfield against him; until, by his undaunted pertinacity, he brought to his own opinion jury after jury, and at length the Bench itself. London then, and especially the lower districts on the Thames river, can hardly be said, in the modern sense of the word, to have been policed at all; and Granville Sharp stood in constant peril from the ruffians who were employed to re-capture runaways, or to kidnap negroes and negresses at the instigation of people who had not a tittle of claim to the ownership of their victims His small patrimony was soon eaten up by law-costs, and by the expense of harbouring, clothing, and feeding the poor wretches whom he endeavoured to protect; but he contrived to support existence on his salary as a clerk in the Ordnance Department.

That slender resource failed him of a sudden. On the twenty-eighth of July, 1775, there occurs the following clumsily worded, though not ungrammatical, entry in Granville Sharp's diary: " Board at Westminster. Account in Gazette of the Battle at Charlestown, near Boston, and letters with large demands for ordnance stores, being received, which were ordered to be got with all expedition, I thought it right to declare my objections to the being any way concerned in that unnatural business." The chiefs of the department, both military and civil, behaved in a manner that did them honour; and their treatment of him, (as his biographer remarks,) was a specimen of the respectful kindness which the probity of Mr. Sharp's character attracted even from those who differed from him in opinion.[1] That difference was not very deeply marked in the case of the most conspicuous among Mr. Sharp's official superiors. Sir Jeffrey Amherst, who was at the head of the Ordnance, must have felt it a doubtful point whether he himself was justified in shipping gunpowder to America, when he could not find it with his conscience to go thither for the purpose of firing it off against the colonists. The Commissioners of Ordnance declined to accept Mr. Sharp's resignation. They gave him continuous leave of absence for nearly two years, by instalments of two months, and three months, and six months, at a time; and they would not accede to his urgent request that his salary should meanwhile be apportioned to the payment of the substitutes who did his work, so that the office might incur no additional expense upon his account. But in the end he had his own way, as sooner or later he always had his way about everything. In 1777 his place was declared vacant; and at an age well past forty he was thrown penniless on a world where people, even less unworldly than Granville Sharp, find it difficult to make an income by new and untried methods after once they have turned the corner of life.

By the year 1775 something had been heard of a man who, in the course of a very long and honoured career, did as much in defence of our political freedom as Granville Sharp accomplished for the cause of humanity. John Cartwright, the younger son of a Nottinghamshire squire, entered the Royal Navy in 1758 at a late age for a midshipman. He soon made up for lost time, and attracted such notice by activity and intelligence, joined to a singularly amiable and chivalrous character, that Lord Howe took him on to his ship, the Magnanime, which then was reputed the best school for a rising officer. Cartwright became a prime favourite with his captain, — if such a word can fairly be applied in the

[1] Prince Hoare's *Memoirs of Granville Sharp*, Part I., chapter vi.

case of a chief the degree of whose favour was invariably determined by merit. Howe, who knew every man
in his crew and every corner of his vessel, contrived
special arrangements to ensure that the young fellow
should live with congenial comrades, and that he should
enjoy all possible facilities, which the space and the
routine of a man-of-war would permit, for learning the
theory of his profession.[1]   Cartwright, (as was likely to
happen with Pitt for war minister, and Anson for First
Lord of the Admiralty,) soon had a trial of that profession in its most practical and exciting shape.   At the
battle in Quiberon Bay he had the care of four guns on
the lower deck ; and, out of his twenty-six men, thirteen
were swept down by one discharge.   Lord Howe had
the adversary's flag-ship, and two of her consorts, upon
him at one and the same moment ; and John Cartwright
informed his friends at home that, more than once in
the course of the engagement, he expected little less
than to be diving for French cockles.   When Howe was
selected by Hawke to lead an attack on those ships of
the enemy which had run for safety into the Vilaine
river, Cartwright was one of the three officers who accompanied his Lordship in the boats.   The Magnanime was
kept at sea for the best part of two busy years, until the
crew had to be at the pumps during the whole of every
watch.   At length Howe surrendered the command, and
was succeeded by a very different kind of officer ;[2] and

[1] Until the rules of spotless cleanliness and careful stowage, which were
initiated by Lord St. Vincent and perfected by Lord Nelson, had been established throughout the British navy, a seventy-four gun ship, with her
six hundred men between decks, was neither an abode of comfort, nor the
place for quiet and uninterrupted studies   Dr. Johnson, whose standard
of tidiness was not exacting, often quoted his stay on board a ship of war
in Plymouth Sound as an experience which reconciled him to any, and
all, the drawbacks incidental to life on shore   " When you look down,"
he said, " from the quarter-deck to the space below, you see the utmost
extremity of human misery, such crowding, such filth, such stench."

[2] It would be more profitable, (so Cartwright declared,) to be taken
prisoner for a few months, and to have the advantage of learning to fence
and talk French, than to serve under a captain who lingered about wherever he could get fresh meat and syllabubs, and who missed opportunities
for a fight " the loss of which would make a parson swear."

the single thought of the young lieutenant was henceforward to attain such a proficiency in seamanship as would render him worthy of his luck if ever the day came for him to sail with Howe once more [1]

That day arrived at last ; and a sad day it was for John Cartwright. In February 1776 Lord Howe was appointed to the American station ; and he forthwith invited Cartwright to call at his house in Grafton Street, and earnestly pressed him to embark on board the flag-ship [2] Cartwright, too deeply moved to argue with a patron whom he almost worshipped, intimated that he was unable to accept the offer, and placed in the Admiral's hands a letter which explained the reason of his decision ; and Lord Howe in reply acknowledged, mournfully enough, that opinions in politics, on points of such national moment as the differences subsisting between England and America, should be treated like opinions in religion, wherein everyone was at liberty to regulate his conduct by those ideas which he had adopted upon due reflection and enquiry.[3] Cartwright continued to reside in his native county, respected and loved by young and old. He was known in the hunting-field for a fine horseman, who rode with the courage of a sailor ; and he passed in the Militia for a most just and kind, but a very strict, officer, who made his battalion, which had been much neglected, into an example for discipline and organisation. His value was recognised, and his friendship sought, by the General in command of the district, — the Lord Percy who helped to win the day at Fort Washington, and who saved as much of it as could be saved at Lexington. About a twelvemonth after he had refused to serve against the colonists, Major Cartwright

---

[1] *Life and Correspondence of Major Cartwright* · London, 1826 ; Vol I., pages 8 to 29

[2] Cartwright was well aware of the chance which he was losing. Lord Howe, (so he told his friends,) now commanded more ships than had ever fallen to the lot of one man since the defeat of the Spanish Armada, so that it would be "the fairest field for rapid promotion that could possibly be imagined"

[3] *Life and Correspondence of Major Cartwright* Vol I , pages 72 to 81.

received the freedom of the town of Nottingham; a significant indication of the views prevailing in a community
which had the Commander-in-Chief of the Royal Army
in America for a parliamentary representative.[1]

It has happened again and again that, when a nation
is engaged in serious hostilities, the partisans of peace
have been exposed to humiliating, and sometimes very
unmerciful, treatment from outbreaks of popular violence. But opponents of the American war had in this
respect very little to complain about, if we may judge
by the noise made over some very mild instances of persecution which were loudly advertised, and vociferously
rebuked, by the chorus of Whig journalists. After the
battle of Long Island, (so their story went,) preparations
had been made to illuminate Manchester whenever the
tidings arrived that New York was taken. One of the
citizens put out a notice that he, for his part, had no
intention of joining in the demonstration; and that, if
his windows were broken, informations would be lodged
against the offenders. Thereupon a certain Reverend
Doctor was said to have transmitted a copy of the notice
to one of the Secretaries of State, with the expectation
that "the writer would be immured in Newgate, and that
he himself would be complimented with the first vacant
Bishopric;" neither of which consequences, so far as
history records, came to pass. Again, it was alleged by
the Opposition newspapers that the Jacobites in the town
of Derby, who toasted the Stuarts kneeling, had celebrated the successes of the Royal Army in America
with a banquet where they drank confusion to the Whig

---

[1] Among the officers who objected to serve in America some, as may
well be conceived, failed to express their disinclination in terms which satisfied the taste of a military superior. "For the safety of the Service I
must recommend that Major Norris, of the 27th Regiment, may have leave
to sell. He came to me, and found fault with this most just and necessary
war his Majesty is obliged to make against his rebellious subjects. When
I would have interrupted him, he thundered out a hundred Greek lines
from Homer. He then talked to me out of Plutarch's Lives. In brief,
my Lord, he convinced me that he will be better out of the King's service
than in it." General Irwin to Earl Harcourt, September 1, 1775.

corporation; and the ministerialists of Taunton were accused of having taken a liberty with the Parish Church by ringing the bells in honour of Howe's victory on the Brandywine. When such trumpery occurrences were minutely narrated, and solemnly adduced against the Tories as proofs of insolence and outrage, their political adversaries must have been very hard put to it in order to find a real grievance; and it must have been seldom indeed that any friend of America, in any city of England, was harshly or disrespectfully used by those among his neighbours who belonged to the war party.

The story of a disturbance, which took place on the reception of the news of Lexington, rather tends to suggest that the idler and less responsible section of our population was in sympathy with the colonists. On an evening in August 1775, a party of scapegraces smashed the lamps at Vauxhall; pulled the door of the Rotunda off its hinges; stormed the Throne of Orpheus, and ejected the musicians who occupied it; and chased out of the gardens the whole staff of the establishment, together with all the constables, calling out that they themselves were the Provincials beating the Regulars. That, for some years to come, was the only riot in which civilians were concerned. On other occasions the most effective violators of public order appear to have been subalterns in the army. At Lincoln Lieutenant Macintosh, of the Sixty-ninth Regiment, entered a printshop, took from the window a picture of General Putnam, tore it in pieces, and then paid for it across the counter. Soon afterwards Macintosh came back again, destroyed another picture without giving compensation, and swore that next time he would run his sword through the panes of the shopfront. On the Monday following some other officers, (mistaking for an enemy one who, in effect, if not in intention, was among England's most serviceable allies,) cut the head out of an engraving of General Charles Lee, and threatened that, if the tradesman did not mend his ways, the soldiers should be ordered to pull down his house.

The proceeding was a boyish ebullition of military
loyalty, pardonable in the eyes of any fair man who
himself had worn a uniform when he was one-and-
twenty; but Whig scribes, who saw deep into every mile-
stone on the road from Edinburgh to London, cited it
as a proof that a Scotchman might insult English citizens with impunity. If officers, (it was said,) had behaved with such turbulence and want of breeding in the
good old King's reign, they would have been broke, or,
at the least, would have received a public reprimand at
the head of the regiment; but now, with Lord Bute behind the Throne, no colonel in the army would dare to
censure a lieutenant whose name showed that he came
from Inverness. These enormities, (as the Opposition
journalist styled them,) afforded so many additional indications that the "only path to preferment was by
trampling upon law, and turning into ridicule the rights
and privileges of the people." It undoubtedly was the
right and privilege of a shopkeeper to exhibit the portraits of American generals as popular heroes; but it
was a right which he would have been very cautious
indeed of exercising if any large proportion of his neighbours had been ardent supporters of the war. That
such, however, was the case either in the town of Lincoln, or generally throughout England, is disproved by
facts and considerations the significance of which it is
not easy to deny.

In time of war a political agitation, — especially one
that is aimed against institutions and abuses on the continuance of which the supremacy of the party in power
depends, — is almost certainly doomed to languish and
to fail; and that such an agitation should be too insignificant for serious notice may well be the best thing
which could happen for its promoters. During the great
war with France, towards the close of the eighteenth
century, the bolder advocates of parliamentary reform
were sometimes rabbled by mobs, and sometimes punished in the law-courts with exemplary severity; whereas
twenty years previously, all the while that our armies

were fighting Washington in America, the art of Constitutional agitation at home was brought to a perfection, and pursued with an amount of success, surpassing
anything which had ever been known before.   A combined movement, — directed towards the improvement
of our electoral system, and the extinction of those mani-
fold facilities for corruption by which the Court kept in
awe the Cabinet, and the Cabinet controlled the Parliament, — ran its course with growing velocity; and neither
the Government at Whitehall, nor its adherents throughout the country, endeavoured to repress that movement
either by penal legislation or by lawless violence   There
were open meetings of Freeholders in the shires, and of
Freemen in the cities; County Associations for the redress of grievances; Committees of Correspondence
which maintained uniform and concerted action among
reformers all through the kingdom; and public dinners
with toasts so bravely worded as to ring like the challenge of a trumpet, and so numerous, when drunk in
bumpers, as effectually to drown every vestige of caution
and timidity.   That such methods, without entailing any
disagreeable consequences on those who employed them,
should have been put in practice against a Ministry
which was engaged in the conduct of an important war,
is an indirect, but a most material, proof that the war
itself was disliked by the nation.
- The direct evidence is stronger yet; for at many
County meetings there was a Resolution, at most
banquets a whole string of flowery Sentiments, and
prominent in every Petition and Address an emphatic
paragraph, all of which denoted friendliness towards
America, and exhaled hearty aspirations for an immediate Peace.   At length, in December 1781, the Liverymen of London, in public assembly duly convoked, took
action which has been so forcibly narrated by a contemporary historian that it is well to reproduce his
description, italics and all.   "They besought the King
to remove both his public and *private* counsellors, and
used these stunning and memorable words: '*Your*

armies are captured; the wonted superiority of your navies is annihilated; your dominions are lost.' " These words, (so the writer proceeded,) could have been used to no other king: "for no king had lost so much, without losing all. If James the Second lost his crown, yet the Crown lost no dominions."[1] The Address from the Livery was never presented, but the last had not yet been heard of it, for a week afterwards, in Westminster Hall, a similar petition was proposed by Charles Fox, and adopted by a vast concourse of Westminster electors. The footguards were held in readiness for the protection of Downing Street against a possible incursion of the Opposition mob, and not at all from an apprehension lest the war-party should invade the Hall, and attempt to break the heads of the peace-party. Experience had often shown that there was no ground for anticipating any such contingency. Anti-war meetings always passed off quietly between 1776 and 1782; although there is no reason to suppose that our ancestors were more tolerant, or better-mannered, than their descendants. The Wilkes riots, and the Keppel riots, conclusively demonstrated what Londoners of the period were capable of doing for the promotion of disorder whenever they had a mind that way. There exists one tenable theory, and one only, to account for the tranquillity and security amid which those, who opposed the Government on the question of America, were able to carry forward their political operations. The rational explanation is that the disfavour beneath which, from other causes, the Ministry had long and deservedly laboured, instead of being diminished, was confirmed and aggravated by the war.

[1] *Last Journals;* December 4, 1781.

CHAPTER XXVI

THE TALK OF MEN.   CONTEMPORARY HISTORIANS.
THE PAMPHLETEERS   THE "CALM ADDRESS"

AN Englishman who approved the war was quite willing that Englishmen who disliked it should be at full liberty to express their opinions; but he had no inclination whatever to conceal his own. The printed memoirs of the period are sprinkled thickly with scraps of many conversations; and brief selections from the familiar utterances of famous men have been deliberately reported for the amusement and enlightenment of future ages. From these sources it is possible to catch at least an echo of the bluff jolly talk which flowed round the tables of country houses, while the Gainsboroughs and Romneys, with their colours still fresh, looked down upon the company from the panelling of the walls. The disputants on either side met in a fair field and on equal terms, and handled the fiery topics of the war as unreservedly as their grandsons in the days of Peel argued about the Corn Laws [1] A gentleman in the Western Counties complained that the Dissenters, who in that part of the world were " as thick as mushrooms," not contented with the unmolested enjoyment of their own mode of worship, mixed themselves up with State affairs, and presumed to sit in judgement on the American policy of the Government; but, in spite of his disgust, he could not escape from

[1] How people then talked about America, — or, (what is the next thing to it,) how, in the view of their contemporaries, they seemed to talk, — may be gathered from imaginary conversations written and published, generally with a controversial object, by authors belonging to both political parties. A sample from one of them, with a touch of liveliness and reality about it which renders it well worth reading, is given in the Second Appendix at the end of this volume.

hearing all that the Dissenters had to say.[1] A Loyalist refugee from New England who, for want of something better to occupy him, spent much of his time in public places, described to a friend at Boston the sort of talk which went on around him in London. "America," he wrote, "furnishes matter for dispute in coffee-houses; sometimes warm, but without abuse or ill-nature; and there it ends. It is unfashionable, and even disreputable, to look askew on one another for difference of opinion in political matters. The doctrine of toleration, if not better understood, is, thank God, better practised here than in America "[2]

During the earlier years of the American conflict people wrangled about colonial politics for the pleasure of unburdening their own souls, and of hearing vigorous epithets, and well-worn taunts, sounded forth by their own voices; for they had little expectation of converting an adversary. Starting from directly opposite premises, they entered the lists armed respectively with an entirely different equipment of facts Each man retailed what he found in his favourite newspaper; and the newspaper which was Gospel for the one seemed a magazine of mendacity to the other. Whigs proclaimed their distrust of every statement in the "London Gazette," and their belief in many items of intelligence which they could not find in its pages. Tories as roundly asserted that Congress had bought the entire Opposition press through the agency of Arthur Lee; — a Virginian, (so they described him,) who had been bred a physician, but had turned lawyer, and now was finishing as a rebel.[3] Horace Walpole, with the impartiality of one who accepted nothing for truth but what he read in a private letter, said that it was incredible how both sides lied about the war.[4] The distance

---

[1] Letter from a Gentleman in Somersetshire to a Friend in London ; October 6, 1776

[2] *Journal and Letters of the late Samuel Curwen*, Edited by George Atkinson Ward ; New York, 1845

[3] Letter of 9th August, 1775 ; Round MSS

[4] Walpole to Sir Horace Mann ; August 11, 1776.

from the scene of action, and the uncertainty of communication by sailing vessels, gave unbounded scope
to the audacity of any London penman who seasoned,
and served up, contemporary military history in a
form to suit his reader's palate. And so it came to
pass that, when they were debating the events of the
current campaign, men of contrary parties were seldom
agreed as to the direction in which things were moving; although everybody admitted that they moved very
slowly.[1]   Our ancestors were vehement in assertion, and
not over choice in repartee; but there was a point in
most controversies when discord and contradiction ceased,
and an appeal was made to the ordeal of the wager.
Fifty guineas even, that the war would terminate
before Christmas 1779 without America being independent of the Crown of Great Britain, thirty guineas
to ten that Sir William Howe was not in possession of
Philadelphia by June 1777; twenty-five guineas for
every three months that France remained at peace with
England from the first of March 1779 onwards; and a
bet of fifty guineas, to run for three years, that Lord
North died by the hand of justice before Mr. Hancock,
the President of the Continental Congress; — those are
a few authentic specimens of a characteristic national
practice, the resort to which, at the critical moment in
a dispute, restored the harmony of many a social
evening, and averted the necessity of a hostile meeting at some dismally early hour on the morning of the
morrow.

Many wars have ere this been waged, not by England
only, in pursuit of inadequate and illusory ends, and have
been carried on long after the course of events had made

---

[1] " Don't you begin to think, Madam, that it is pleasanter to read
history than to live it ? Battles are fought, and towns taken, in every
page , but a campaign takes six or seven months to hear, and achieves no
great matter at last.   I dare to say Alexander seemed to the coffee-houses
of Pella a monstrous while about conquering the world.   As to this
American war, I am persuaded it will last till the end of the century "
Walpole to the Countess of Ossory, Strawberry Hill, October 8,
1777.

it manifest that those ends were impossible of attainment. Wars of that class are the despair of historians belonging to the school which would fain account for every great national undertaking by a theory that the people, — instinctively, even if ignorantly and unconsciously, — are impelled by an unerring sense of the national interests. Such wars are commenced in anger, and afterwards continued from obstinacy, or, it may be, from the necessities of self-preservation ; and the actual explosion generally follows close upon some striking and theatrical occurrence which evokes an eruption of moral indignation and international repugnance. In 1793 the execution of Louis the Sixteenth was a signal for the clash of arms; and the spilling of the tea in Boston Harbour had, not less certainly, been the exciting cause of that protracted struggle which finally resulted in the independence of America. It will always be remembered to the credit of Pitt and Grenville that, under the shock of the French Revolution, they laboured gallantly, honestly, and perseveringly to maintain peace between France and England All the while that Burke was preaching a crusade against the wicked Republic with a fury of rhetoric which took the conscience of our country by storm, the Prime Minister, and the Foreign Minister, insisted that the counsels of moderation should be heard, and kept their followers in hand as long as it was possible to hold them.[1] But, throughout our American troubles, the rulers of the British Empire exerted upon public opinion an exasperating, and not a restraining, influence. Even in the business letters which he ad-

[1] "No hour of Pitt's life," (wrote Mr. Green in his *History of the English People*,) "is so great as the hour when he stood, lonely and passionless, before the growth of national passion, and refused to bow to the gathering cry for war "

"I bless God that we had the wit to keep ourselves out of the glorious enterprise of the combined armies, and that we were not tempted by the hope of sharing the spoils in the division of France, nor by the prospect of crushing all democratical principles all over the world at one blow." That was said by Lord Grenville as late as November 1792 , two full years after Burke had thrilled England by his celebrated appeal to Chivalry on behalf of Queen Marie Antoinette.

dressed to Lord North the King could never write about
New Englanders with patience. Lord Dartmouth, indeed, treated the colonists with sympathy, and evinced
a desire to ascertain and understand their own view of
their own case ; but in that regard he was almost alone
in the Cabinet. After the quarrel had become enven-
omed, few members of the Government, whose words
counted for anything, spoke of Americans in Parliament
with respect, or even with common propriety.

The cue was given, and the fashion set, to all partisans
of the Court and the Ministry. Their talk, (so much as
has reached us,) ran in a channel of considerable violence, but of little depth. How far reconciliation was
practicable ; by what steps, and through the employment
of what agents and intermediaries, it might be achieved ;
what was the judgement of contemporary Europe, what
were the schemes and inclinations of foreign governments, and what would be their action if the war was
indefinitely prolonged ; how that war affected the prosperity of our own West Indian islands ; whether America
could be subdued by force ; how long, if reconquered,
she could be kept in subjection, and at what cost ; —
those were speculations altogether too abstract and un-
practical to engage the attention of Lord North's supporters. The staple of their conversation, even in the
case of men who posed as authorities on the colonial
question, consisted in wholesale and vehement abuse of
the disaffected colonists. James Boswell, though a sound
Tory, entertained scruples about the right of Parliament
to tax America. Like a good disciple he begged, and
again begged, Doctor Johnson to clear up his misgiv-
ings, but on each occasion he was handled in such a
fashion as to regret, (which was most unusual with him,)
that he had not been discreet enough to leave burning
topics alone. Once, however, he enjoyed the opportunity of listening to the famous teacher at a moment when
his mind had been attuned to milder and holier thoughts
Johnson was maintaining, in opposition to a handsome
and eloquent Quakeress, that friendship could not strictly

be called a Christian virtue. He urged that, whereas the ancient philosophers dwelt only on the beauty of private friendship, Christianity recommended universal benevolence, and enjoined us to consider all men as our brothers. "Surely, Madam," he said, "your sect must approve of this, for you call all men *friends.*" But that weather was too calm to last. "From this pleasing subject," wrote Boswell, "he made a sudden transition. 'I am willing,' he cried, 'to love all mankind except an American;' and his inflammable corruption bursting into horrid fire, he breathed out threatenings and slaughter, calling them rascals, robbers, pirates, and exclaiming that he would burn and destroy them"[1]

Considering that he was a professed master in the science of ethics, Dr. Johnson's estimate of the American character was not very judicial or discriminating; and still less could it be expected that people, who had never claimed to be philosophers, should mince their words when they were engaged in denouncing the iniquities of the colonists. That mattered little in a discussion with English Whigs, who gave as good as they got, and who were much more concerned to speak their mind against the Cabinet than to defend the Americans But there was a class of men whose feelings were cruelly wounded by the tone of conversation which largely prevailed in London society; men whom it is impossible to name without a tribute of respectful compassion. The town was full of refugees from every colony in America, who had sacrificed all that they possessed to their love for Britain, and their veneration for Britain's King. Their condition, sad in itself, was melancholy indeed by contrast to that which they had known at home. Some of them had been proprietors of vast districts, with powers and prerogatives far exceeding those of an English landowner. Others had held office as Lieutenant-Governors of Provinces, Judges, Councillors, and Commissioners of Revenue. Others, again, had been Presidents of Colleges, or clergymen in charge of rich,

[1] *The Life of Samuel Johnson*, Sept. 23, 1777, April 15, and 18, 1778

and once admiring and affectionate, congregations
Among the five occupants of the Bench in the superior
Court of Massachusetts all save one were Loyalists; and
three of them were driven into banishment. The political faith for which these gentlemen suffered is finely
summarised in the epitaph on Chief Justice Oliver, the
president of their tribunal, which may be seen in St.
Philip's, Birmingham; — a church standing in the very
centre of the city, with an ample space about it, and its
doors hospitably open to the passing stranger.[1] One of
Oliver's colleagues died in Nova Scotia, and another in
England; and at least five members of his family, who
were living in Massachusetts as grown men before the
Revolution broke out, are buried in different corners of
our island. When General De Lancey of New York was
laid in his grave a fellow-refugee said, truly enough, that
there would be scarcely a village in England without
some American dust in it by the time they were all at
rest. And not in England only; for, in the course of
our wars against the French Republic and the French
Empire, many American Loyalists, both of the first and
second generation, breathed their last on the field of
honour in one or another of our country's battles.[2]

[1] The monument is erected to the Honourable Peter Oliver, formerly
His Majesty's Chief Justice of the Province of Massachusetts Bay in New
England; and the inscription runs : " In the year 1776, on a Dissolution
of Government, He left his Native Country, but in all the consequent
calamities his Magnanimity remained unshaken, and, (though the source
of his misfortunes,) nothing could dissolve his Attachment to the British
Government, nor lessen his love and loyalty to his Sovereign "

[2] " Mr Flucker died suddenly in his bed yesterday morning, and it is
the forty-fifth of the refugees from Massachusetts, within my knowledge,
that have died in England. He was Secretary of State for Massachusetts."
Curwen's diary, Feb 17, 1783.

Wellington's Quartermaster General, who was killed at Waterloo, was
a De Lancey of New York Colonel James De Peyster, of the same province, had, as a youth, distinguished himself on the British side during the
war of the American Revolution. In 1793 he led an assault on an almost
impregnable French position at Lincelles in West Flanders, and was shot
dead in the moment of victory. Those were two out of many, for Loyalists
of the upper class were a fighting race throughout all the colonies. Tory
farmers and shopkeepers, and Tory mechanics, in the Northern and Central
provinces, showed much less inclination to take up arms for their opinions.

When Governor Hutchinson of Massachusetts was superseded in June 1774, many leading merchants, and most of the officials, united to present him with an Address approving his political conduct, and wishing him a prosperous future. Among the names attached to the paper was that of Samuel Curwen of Salem, Judge of the Admiralty for the province. Popular pressure was brought upon the subscribers for the purpose of inducing them to withdraw their signatures, and to insert in the newspapers an apology for the action which they had taken. Many yielded; but Curwen thought it best to go elsewhere in search of that security, and those personal rights, which, (to use his own words,) by the laws of God he ought to have enjoyed undisturbed in his native town His wife, not a little to his surprise, disliked a sea voyage more than she feared the Sons of Liberty; and, in his sixtieth year, he sailed alone for England. He solaced his leisure in that country by the composition of a journal which presents, in subdued but distinct colours, a very cheerless picture of the exile's existence.

The misery of such an existence has been sung and spoken in many languages, by famous people of many nations; but it has never been more irksome than to men of our own busy and energetic race Among those men, the New England refugees belonged precisely to the class upon whom the trials and discomforts of banishment pressed the heaviest. In America they had been important personages, successful already, or on a sure and easy road to success, wealthy according to the standard of the community in which they resided; and with every day of their life filled and dignified by serious occupations. But in England they were nobodies, with nothing in the world to do. It is true that the sights of London were there to be admired, if only they had the heart to relish them. They attended as spectators at numerous processions characteristic of the period and the country. They saw their Majesties returning from a Drawing-room in sedan-chairs; the

King in very light cloth, with silver buttons, and the
Queen in lemon-coloured flowered silk on cream-coloured
ground.   They saw the milkmaids and chimney-sweeps
keep May-day in all its ancient splendour, with many
hundred pounds' worth of silver plate disposed amid
an enormous pyramid of foliage and garlands   They
watched five couple of young persons chained together,
walking under the care of tip-staves to Bridewell.   They
visited the British Museum, and examined the Alexan-
drine Manuscript.   Readers of Shakespeare, like all of
their countrymen who read anything, they made an expedition to the Boar's Head tavern in the City for the
sake of Falstaff, and into Hertfordshire in order to
inspect the great Bed of Ware.[1]   They heard blind Sir
John Fielding administer justice at Bow Street.   They
were present when the Reverend Doctor Dodd, at the
Magdalen Hospital, delivered a discourse which set the
whole chapel crying, not much more than a twelvemonth before he preached his own Condemned Sermon
in Newgate gaol   They saw Garrick in tragedy; and
were crushed, and buffeted, and almost stifled, for the
space of two hours at the Pit door of Drury Lane
theatre in a vain attempt to see him in comedy.   They
dined with the ex-Governor of Massachusetts, and met
each other ; and with the ex-Attorney General, and
met each other again.   They sought distraction in the
provinces, and made a round of manufacturing towns,
and cathedrals, and feudal castles, and romantic prospects.   They explored Blenheim, and Old Sarum, and
Stonehenge, and the inn at Upton where Tom Jones
found Sophia Western's muff with the little paper pinned
to it.   But all was to no purpose.   After eighteen months
spent in surveying the wonders and beauties of the
mother country with sad and weary eyes, Judge Curwen
pronounced, as the conclusion of the whole matter, that
his flight to England had been a dreadful and irrepara-
ble mistake.   The tyranny of an unruly rabble, when
endured beneath a man's own roof, with a plentiful purse

[1] *Twelfth Night;* Act IV., Scene 2

and all his friends around him, was, (he confessed,) an enviable fate compared to liberty under the mildest government on earth, when accompanied by poverty, with its horrid train of evils [1]

The American exiles, with very few exceptions, were bitterly poor.[2] Curwen found London "a sad lickpenny," where the vital air could not be breathed unless at great expense. Everything was ruinously dear, — the lodging ; the food ; the wine, without the production of which no business could be transacted, and no visitor honoured , and, above all, the fuel. In January 1776 there came a cold Sunday, when the Thames bore, and the mercury stood at eight degrees below zero. "The fires here," Curwen wrote, "are not to be compared to our large American ones of oak and walnut. Would that I was away !" Numerous applications to the Treasury by Loyalists, who had stronger claims than his, excluded him from the most distant hope of relief. To beg from chance acquaintance was humiliating, "and to starve was stupid ; " and so, — with a mild stroke of sarcasm against Seneca and the long list of moralists, heathen and Christian, who wrote most edifying treatises on the duty of contentment and resignation, but had never known what it was to want a meal, — he went into a cheap and dull retirement at Exeter, where he kept body and soul together on something less than half a guinea a week.[3] John Wentworth, who had been formerly Governor of New Hampshire, resided in Europe all through the Revolution He was received with exceptional favour by the Ministry and by the King ; and yet he esteemed the lot of an exile, at the very best, to

---

[1] Samuel Curwen to the Hon. Judge Sewall; Exeter, Jan. 19, 1777.

[2] One of these exceptions was Charles Steuart, a rich tobacco-merchant of Norfolk in Virginia. Steuart, contrary to all intention of his own, did a memorable service to liberty; for he brought with him from America the negro Somerset, whose name will always recall Lord Mansfield's declaration of the principle that our free soil makes a free man.

[3] Letters to the Revd Isaac Smith, June 6, 1776, to Dr Charles Russell of Antigua, June 10, 1776, and to the Hon. Judge Sewall, Dec. 31, 1776.

be all but intolerable.   When the war was over, he thought himself bound to give the benefit of his experience to those unhappy Loyalists who still lingered on their native soil, stripped of all their property, and exposed to the insults of triumphant and unforgiving adversaries.   However distressing might be their plight, he earnestly recommended no one to seek a refuge in England who could get clams and potatoes in America. " My destination," he added, " is quite uncertain   Like an old flapped hat, thrown off the top of a house, I am tumbling over and over in the air, and God only knows where I shall finally alight and settle." [1]

The affection of the Massachusetts Loyalists for the chief town of their province grew with absence, and only, ceased at death.   A distinguished Nova Scotia statesman, the son of a refugee, has given a pleasant and spirited account of his father's unalterable attachment to the city of his birth, which had cast him out.   In 1775 John Howe, who then was just of age, had served his apprenticeship as a printer, and, like a true young American, was already engaged to be married ; and yet " he left all his household goods and gods behind him, carrying away nothing but his principles, and his pretty girl." [2]   He settled at Halifax and prospered.   Though a true Briton, he made no shame of loving Boston with a filial regard.   While the conflict between England and the revolted colonies was still at its height, John Howe

---

[1] Sabine's *Loyalists*, Vol I., page 322, and Vol II , page 10   In the *American Archives* there is a letter addressed by Thomas Oliver to a friend who had escaped from Boston to Nova Scotia   " Happy am I," (Oliver wrote from London,) " that you did not leave Halifax to encounter the expenses of this extravagant place   Every article of expense is increased fourfold since you knew it.   What the poor people will do, who have steered their course this way, I cannot tell.   I found Mrs. Oliver well, and settled in a snug little house at Brompton, in the neighbourhood of London; but I shall continue here no longer than I am able to find an economical retreat.   I have no time to look about me as yet.   Some cheaper part of England must be the object of my enquiry."

[2] The words are quoted from a speech delivered by the Honourable Joseph Howe in Faneuil Hall, Boston, on the Fourth of July, 1858.   Joseph Howe was Secretary of the Province, and leader of the Liberal party, in Nova Scotia.

did every kindness in his power to American prisoners
of war, if only they were Boston men, and, far into the
nineteenth century, whenever he was in poor health, his
family, as an infallible remedy, shipped the old fellow off
southwards to get a walk on Boston Common. Wherever a banished New Englander wandered, and whatever he saw, his model of excellence, and his standard
for comparison, was always the capital of Massachusetts.
At Exeter, according to Judge Curwen's calculation, the
inhabitants were seven-eighths as numerous as at Boston;
but the city was not so elegantly built, and stood on
much less ground. Birmingham, in its general appearance, looked more like Boston, to his eyes, than any
other place in England. There was something very
pathetic in the feeling with which the exiles regarded
the home where they never again might dwell Awake,
or in dreams, their thoughts were for ever recurring to
old Boston days; they tried to believe that a more or
less distant future would bring those good times back
for themselves and their families, and they industriously
collected every scrap of news which came by letter from
a town where their places had already been filled by
others, and their names were by-words. Assailed by the
fierce and implacable hostility of their own fellow-citizens,
and treated too often with contemptuous indifference in
England, they tasted the force of that verse in the Book
of Proverbs which says: "The brethren of the poor do
hate him. How much more do his friends go far from
him! He pursueth them with words, but they are wanting unto him."

For, in one important particular, a painful disillusion
awaited the exiles at their arrival on our shores. They
had anticipated the enjoyment of much rational and
sympathetic intercourse with the most select and the best
of company. In their own country, — since the troubles
began, and the Stamp Act, and afterwards the Tea-duty,
had been to the fore in every conversation, — they had
been alarmed by the spread of Republicanism, and infinitely disgusted by the manners of some who pro-

mulgated that novel and hated creed.   The father of
Mrs. Grant of Laggan, for instance, had acquired a
large property in Vermont, which he called by the name
of Clarendon, and liked to describe as a Baronial estate.
But social tendencies in New England, (if ever they had
taken that direction,) now altogether ceased to point
towards the formation of an aristocracy   "My father,"
wrote Mrs. Grant, "grew fonder than ever of fishing
and shooting, because birds and fish did not talk of
tyranny and taxes   Sometimes we were refreshed by
the visit of friends who spoke respectfully of our dear
King and dearer country , but they were soon succeeded
by some Obadiah, or Zephaniah, from Hampshire or
Connecticut, who came in without knocking, sate down
without invitation, lighted his pipe without ceremony,
and began a discourse on politics that would have done
honour to Praise God Barebones."[1]   In contrast to all
that seemed vulgar and offensive to them in America,
the emigrants had beguiled themselves with an ideal
picture of the welcome which they would receive from
the refined society of England.   A writer unequalled
in his acquaintance with the surface aspects of the Revolution, and not less observant of the inward causes which
then governed the ebb and flow of political opinion, has
remarked that a prodigious obstacle to the Whig cause
in the colonies was the worldly prestige, "the purple
dignity, the aristocratic flavour," of the Tory side of the
question.[2]   To live familiarly amid such associations, to

[1] In order to escape this infliction, the Lord of the Manor of Clarendon
retreated to his native Scotland in the summer of 1770 ; and, before very
long, every acre that he left behind him in America had been confiscated.

[2] These are the epithets used by Professor Tyler, in the 30th chapter
of his *Literary History*. He there quotes an account by Francis Hopkinson, the Whig humourist, of a lady who did not possess one political
principle, nor had any precise idea of the real cause of the contest between
Great Britain and America , and who yet was a professed and confirmed
Tory, merely from the fascination of sounds   The Imperial Crown, the
Royal Robes, the High Court of Parliament, the Lord Chancellor of England, were names of irresistible influence , while captains and colonels
who were tailors and tavern-keepers, and even the respectable personality
of General Washington the Virginian farmer, provoked her unqualified
disdain.

be at home in such circles, to be recognised as the martyrs of loyalty within the very precincts of the shrine where the object of their worship dwelt, — such privileges would go far to compensate the expatriated Loyalists for all that they had endured and sacrificed.

Their disappointment was in proportion to their expectations. They found the upper class of Great Britain absorbed in its own affairs, and intent upon pleasures most uncongenial to a plain and frugal American on account of the money they cost, the amount of time they consumed, and the scandal which not unfrequently attended them. In 1790 the French emigrants, who sought sanctuary across the British Channel, experienced much comfort and advantage from the fraternity which had long existed between the nobility of France and of England; but in 1775 the knowledge that a stranger came from Boston, — whether of his own accord, or because he could not help it, — was a poor introduction to the good graces of Almack's, of Newmarket, and of Ranelagh. The Bostonian habit of mind, according to the language then in vogue, was marked by "the low cunning of a petty commercial people;" and the mere circumstance that a citizen of the obnoxious town was a Tory, instead of a Whig, did not exempt him from the social consequences of that sweeping criticism. A ghost at a banquet was hardly more out of place than a sober and melancholy New Englander in a St. James's Street Club. George Selwyn, and his like, had little use for a companion who, when people of fashion were mentioned, did not know to what county they belonged, or with what families they were connected, who had never in his life amused himself on a Sunday, and not much on any day of the week, who was easily shocked, and whose purse was slender. The hand of charity, (Judge Curwen said,) was very cold; and the barriers which fenced in the intimacy of the titled and the powerful were all but impenetrable. More than twelve months after he first landed at Dover, the diarist noted, as a very uncommon event, that he had a free conversation with a couple of very affable gentlemen; "the better sort of gentry being too proud or reserved to mix with those whom they did not know, or to indulge in a promiscuous chat." [1]

Loyalist emigrants, who desired to talk American politics with Englishmen from the English point of view, were thrown back upon the casual acquaintances of the coffee-house, the stage-coach, and the inn parlour. Recruiting-officers, commercial travellers, tradesmen on a surburban jaunt, and gentlemen of the turf on the road to a race-meeting, were among those with whom they frequently were reduced to consort. The allusions to their own country, by which on such occasions they were regaled, though not discourteously meant,[2] affected them with more pain than pleasure; for they consisted mainly in sweeping denunciations of vengeance against the New England people, and blatant depreciation of the New England character. More than once an exile confessed that he felt nowhere so much at ease as in the company of quiet middle-class citizens of Birmingham or Bristol who were opponents of the war; for there, at all events, whatever difference of opinion might exist between the guest and his hosts, he was sure of hearing nothing said which grated on his feelings. Over and over again, in public vehicles and in places of general resort, the refugees would gladly have taken their share in a reasonable talk about the equity of demanding that the colonies should contribute towards the expenses of our empire, and the importance to America of retaining her connection with Great Britain; but the dialogue almost always took such a turn that, before half a dozen sentences had been spoken, they were forced by their self-respect as Americans to assume the cudgels against defamers of their nation. Judge Curwen, while journeying from the West

---

[1] June 10, and July 13, 1776.

[2] Curwen was only once subjected to direct and intentional impertinence. "In our way through Long Row we were attacked by the virulent tongue of a vixen, who saluted us by the name of 'damned American rebels.'" — *Curwen's Journal;* Bristol, June 17, 1777.

by way of Tewkesbury, met an officer who allowed himself great liberties respecting America. "I took the
freedom of giving him several severe checks; and my
companion spared not till he was thoroughly silenced
and humbled He said many ungenerous, foolish, and
false things, and I did not forbear telling him so." In
December 1776 a Mr. Lloyd of the Twentieth Regiment, who had just arrived from Canada, treated the
New England Loyalists to a discourse which he no
doubt sincerely intended as a compliment to themselves,
and a tribute to their political views "He speaks,"
said Curwen, "of the Yankees, (as he is pleased to call
them,) as cowards, poltroons, cruel, and possessing
every bad quality the depraved heart can be cursed
with. It is my earnest wish the despised Americans
may convince these conceited islanders, by some knock-
down irrefragable argument, that, without regular standing armies, our continent can furnish brave soldiers and
expert commanders; for then, and not till then, may we
expect generous or fair treatment It piques my pride,
I confess, to hear us called '*our* Colonies, *our* Plantations,'
with such airs as if our property and persons were absolutely theirs, like the villains in the old feudal system." [1]

Those were strange sayings in the mouth of a man
who had broken up his life, and wrecked his happiness,
because he would not side with the colonists in the
attitude which they had adopted towards the mother-
country. The most distressing element in the lot of
the emigrants was that they had always been animated,
and now were tortured, by a double patriotism; for
they were condemned to stand by, idle and powerless,
while the two nations, which they equally loved, were
tearing at each other's vitals. Symptoms of the
conflict between loyalty to Britain, and affection for
America, are visible on every page of Judge Curwen's
Journal, and in every paragraph of his correspondence.
He rejoiced at having justice done to his countrymen
by an English officer of character in Sir Guy Carleton's

[1] *Curwen's Journal*, Sept 11, and Dec. 18, 1776.

army, who testified that Arnold and the Provincials had displayed great bravery in the battle on Lake Champlain, but had been out-matched by superior weight of metal. He expressed himself as not a little mortified when, standing on a height which overlooked Plymouth Harbour, he saw a captured American priva-teer brought round from Dartmouth; nor were his ears a little wounded when they were condemned to hear another such prize sold at open auction. He noted with despair the determination of the King and his advisers to overwhelm and ruin the rebellious colonies. "Would to God," he cried, "that moderate and just views of the real interests of both countries might pos-sess the minds of those who direct the public measures here, and there! The language of the Court, (the papers say,) is, as it ever has been, *Delenda est Carthago* If this be not slander, woe betide my poor country."[1] At last, when Lord North and his colleagues began to reap the fruits of their senseless policy in a harvest of national perils, Curwen's fears for America, though none the less gloomy, became overshadowed by his anxiety about the future of England. In March 1778 he heard "the dreaded sound, War declared against France." Some few days before, he had written to a Birmingham friend that, when he contemplated the decline and fall of great and powerful states, — and the causes of that decline which, in the history of the world, were uniformly the same, — he could not recall to his mind the commanding and secure position of Great Britain four years since, as compared with the present alarming crisis, without horror and trembling. "May my apprehensions," he said, "exist only in imagination! I had rather be a mistaken man than a true prophet"[2]

Those apprehensions about the stability of the British power, which racked the imagination of the banished

---

[1] *Journal* of Dec. 21, 1776, and Feb. 28, 1777. Letter to the Reverend Isaac Smith, Jan 17, 1778.

[2] *Journal* of March 20, and letter of March 16, 1778.

American, were always present to the minds of Englishmen who had watched many wars, who knew the continent of Europe, who cared for their country, and who understood that country's interests. Horace Walpole, in more than one manly and thoughtful passage, reviewed the long correspondence with his old friend at Florence which had begun when his own father was still Prime Minister; had continued while England was "down at Derby. and up at Minden;" and was still in progress now that she had dashed herself, (so he sorrowfully declared,) below the point to which no natural law of gravitation could have thrown her in the course of a century.[1] The middle portion, said Walpole, of that correspondence had been the most agreeable. Its earlier part was the journal of a civil war, when an army of Scottish rebels penetrated almost unopposed into the very centre of the island. Fifteen years afterwards, — when our generals marched, and our fleets sailed, under Chatham's auspices, — it was his proud and pleasant task to recount victory upon victory, and conquest upon conquest, but for the last five years his letters had been the records of a mouldering kingdom. The ministers, indeed, encouraged their countrymen by recalling how England had more than once maintained herself successfully against both France and Spain; but, (said Walpole,) we on former occasions had America as a weight in our scale of the balance, whereas now it was in theirs; and moreover we then possessed a Lord Chatham, who did not seem to have been replaced. "As I have no great faith," he subsequently wrote, "in virtue tempted by power, I expect that the American leaders will not easily part with dictatorships and consulships to retire to their private ploughs. Oh, madness to have squandered away such an empire!"[2]

Predictions of that sort were no new things, and people endeavoured to relieve their uneasiness by reminding each other how there never had been a time

---

[1] Horace Walpole to Sir Horace Mann, Sept. 5, 1779.
[2] Walpole to Mann, May 27, 1776; June 16, 1779

of serious public danger when somebody did not sincerely believe that the country was on the verge of destruction.   Sir John Sinclair, — the prince of busybodies,
— brought Adam Smith the news of Saratoga, and
added, on his own account, that the nation was now
ruined   "There is a great deal of ruin in a nation,"
was the philosopher's quiet reply,[1] and yet Sir John
Sinclair might well have proved to be in the right, if
George the Third had pursued his course to the end,
unchecked.   The prophets of evil, for once in a way,
were the wise men ; and their predictions would undoubtedly have been fulfilled to the letter, had it not
been for a contingency which the most sanguine patriots did not venture confidently to anticipate.   How
long the end would have been in coming no man fortunately now can tell, but, in the long run, the policy
of the Court must have been fatal to the country unless
Parliament had taken the matter into its own hands,
and insisted on composing the quarrel with America.
Parliament, however, during many sessions seemed to
have been effectually bribed into acquiescence ; and the
means at the disposal of the Treasury for gratifying
the cupidity of venal politicians grew in proportion to
the growing expenditure on military and naval operations   Every new expedition to the Carolinas or the
West India seas, and every fresh enemy who came
against us in Europe, increased the mass of profits from
loans, and lotteries, and contracts which was available
for being divided among supporters of the Government
The war fed corruption, and corruption kept on foot
the war, but there was something in the English nature
whereon George the Third and the Bedfords had not
counted ; and two successive Parliaments, which had
both begun very badly, shook themselves free from
the trammels of self-interest and servility, defied their
taskmasters, and saved their country.

   The scholarship at our universities in the earlier days
of George the Third was less severely accurate than it

----

[1] *Life of Adam Smith*, by John Rae , chapter xxii.

became during the first fifty years of the succeeding
century; but many English gentlemen, not only at
college, but in after life, read Latin as they read
French; and every one who pretended to literature had
a fair knowledge of ancient history, and a clear conception with regard to the personal identity, and the
relative authority and merit, of the most famous Greek
authors. It was well understood that the narratives of
Xenophon and Polybius, of Sallust and Suetonius, owed
much of their peculiar excellence to the fact that those
writers had been alive during at least some part of the
periods which they treated; and had been acquainted
with not a few of the warriors and rulers whose actions
they immortalised, or whose mistakes and crimes they
condemned. Despairing English patriots, who correctly
predicted a succession of disasters, but who did not
foresee that the public ruin would ultimately be averted
by a resurrection of national common-sense, looked
around them for an historian who might undertake the
melancholy task of chronicling the misfortunes of England. They sought a Tacitus; and they thought to
have discovered one, ready to their hand, in Doctor
William Robertson, whose " History of Scotland " had
founded his position as an author, and whose " History
of Charles the Fifth " had won him a European name
Robertson had for some years been occupied with the
earlier annals of America, and was steadily approaching
the point where he would come into contact with the
great political question of the hour; for the first instalment of his work, which appeared in 1777, brought him
much more than half-way between Christopher Columbus
and Charles Townshend The hopes excited in the
reading world are indicated by Edmund Burke, in
language on a higher level than is often reached by a
letter of thanks for a presentation copy. " There remains before you a great field I am heartily sorry we
are now supplying you with that kind of dignity and
concern which is purchased to history at the expense of
mankind. I had rather, by far, that Doctor Robertson's

pen were employed only in delineating the humble scenes of political economy, and not the great events of a civil war. However, if our statesmen had read the book of human nature instead of the Journals of the House of Commons, and history instead of Acts of Parliament, we should not by the latter have furnished out so ample a page in the former. . . . Adieu, Sir! Continue to instruct the world, and, — whilst *we* carry on a poor unequal conflict with the passions and prejudices of our day, perhaps with no better weapons than other passions and prejudices of our own, — convey wisdom to future generations."[1]

Robertson's "America" was ransacked greedily by people who hoped to discover in its pages satirical references to current events, and arch strokes against the politicians of their own time. But the admirable historians whom that generation produced, both in Edinburgh and in London, habitually refrained from those contemporary allusions which a French writer has stigmatised as the sidelong leers of history, in contra-distinction to her straightforward and honest glances into the facts of the past. In his account of the settle-ment of the Western Continent, Doctor Robertson had much to say about the projects of Las Casas, and much about James the First and Sir Walter Raleigh; but there was not a phrase which could be twisted into a covert expression of his views on the Declaratory Act or the Boston Port Bill. Sedate and sagacious Scotch divine that he was, he had no intention whatever of diving into a perilous controversy which he was not enough of a partisan even to enjoy. Although he con-sidered the Americans premature in asserting their independence, he none the less was of opinion that the whole matter had been sadly mismanaged by the Cab-inet.[2] It must not be forgotten that Doctor Robertson was the King's Historiographer for Scotland. The

[1] Edmund Burke, Esq., to Doctor Robertson, June 10, 1777
[2] Letter from Doctor Robertson of October 6, 1775, as printed in Section III of his Life by Dugald Stewart.

emolument, indeed, was of no object to him in comparison with the profits of literature; for his "Charles the Fifth" alone had produced a sum of money which amounted to twice the capital value of his official salary. Nor, as he on more than one occasion gave honourable proof, was he afraid of speaking his mind when he conceived reticence to be unworthy of his station and his character. But the post of Historiographer had been revived, with the King's consent and at the King's cost, as a particular compliment to Robertson himself; and he was not disposed to requite his Majesty's favour by recording, for the information of all time, the improvidence and incapacity of his Majesty's ministers.

Robertson had a stronger reason yet for circumspection and caution in his reluctance to begin telling a story whose catastrophe was still hidden in the unknown future. His professional pride as an historian forbade him to put forward theories, and deliver judgements, which the issue might show to be erroneous, and even ridiculous. In whatever manner, (so he wrote in the preface to the first volume of his History,) the unhappy contest might terminate, a new order of things must arise in North America, and American affairs would assume quite another aspect. He would therefore "wait, with the solicitude of a good citizen, until the ferment subsided, and regular government was again established." When those days arrived Robertson must expect to be over sixty; and an extensive history, commenced at that time of life, is too often not so much a tribute to Clio as an excuse to Charon The Latin saying, which warns the artist that life is brief, came forcibly home to one who had so continuously and conscientiously practised the very longest among all the arts

Robertson apart, of the triumvirate of noted British historians Gibbon and David Hume remained; but Hume did not remain long. He died on the twenty-fifth of August, 1776, and met his fate with a cheerful serenity which deeply scandalised some excellent persons who had pleased themselves by conceiving a very different picture of the sceptic's death-bed [1]   But, though without any uneasiness as to what might befall himself, he passed away in the conviction that immense dangers overhung the country.   A stronger Tory than George the Third, Hume had not allowed his views and prejudices concerning home politics to blind his insight into colonial questions.   The most caustic remarks about the folly of alienating the Americans, and the impossibility of subduing them, came from the pen, not of any Whig or Wilkite, but of David Hume; and Hume was a Jacobite who would have been heartily pleased if the King had hanged Wilkes, had shot down the Liverymen and their apprentices by hundreds, and then, after making a terrible example of London, had announced his intention of reigning ever afterwards in Stuart fashion.[2]   The autumn before his death Hume was requested to draw up an Address to the Crown from the county of Renfrew; but he declined, on the ground that he was an American in principle, and wished that the colonists should be let alone to govern, or misgovern, themselves as they thought proper.   If, (such was the form that his suggestion took,) the inhabitants of the county felt it indispensably necessary to interpose in public affairs, they should advise the King to punish those insolent rascals in London and Middlesex who had set at nought his authority, and should dutifully inform him that Lord North, though an estimable gentleman, had no head for great military operations.

[1] Any mention of the calmness and equanimity with which Hume departed this life never failed to arouse in Doctor Johnson very opposite emotions.   Adam Smith had borne testimony to the tranquillity of his friend's closing hours; and Johnson could not forgive him.   Sir Walter Scott's account of the interview at Glasgow between the two philosophers, in spite of the serious nature of the topic, is a gem of comedy   Note to Croker's edition of Boswell's *Tour to the Hebrides*, under the date of the 29th October, 1773

[2] Hume prayed that he might see the scoundrelly mob vanquished, and a third of London in ruins.   "I think," he wrote, "I am not too old to despair of being witness to all these blessings "   Hume to Sir Gilbert Elliot , 22nd June, 1768.

"These," (he said,) "are objects worthy of the respectable county of Renfrew, not mauling the poor unfortunate Americans in the other hemisphere."[1]

Gibbon, indeed, was still in his prime; but he did not even contemplate the notion of exchanging the colossal literary undertaking, to which he looked for the establishment of his fame and the improvement of his modest fortune, for such a hypothetical theme as the decline and fall of England. He had no inclination to leave untold the defeat of Attila at Châlons, and the siege of Constantinople by Mahomet the Second, in order to expend his gorgeous rhetoric over the battle at Monmouth Court House, or the investment and evacuation of Boston. His political opponents, who likewise were his constant and familiar associates, professed to discover a less respectable motive for his unwillingness to transfer his historical researches into another field.

> " King George, in a fright
>   Lest Gibbon should write
>   The story of England's disgrace,
>   Thought no way so sure
>   His pen to secure
>   As to give the historian a place."

The little poem, whereof that is the first stanza, has been attributed to Charles Fox, and most certainly it emanated from Brooks's Club; an institution which contained a group of witty and scholarly men of the world who, — as the graceful, flowing verse of the

---

[1] Letter to Baron Mure; Oct 27, 1775 Hume was closely connected with John Crawford, the friend of Charles Fox and the Member for Renfrewshire It was Crawford who induced young Lord Tavistock to read Hume's History, which the Duke of Bedford, a careful Whig parent, had forbidden his son and heir to open.

A very few months before his death Hume confided to his most intimate friend his belief that England was on the verge of decline, and pronounced himself unable to give any reason for the complete absence of administrative genius, civil and military, which marked the period. *John Home's Diary of his Journey to London in company with David Hume;* April 30, 1776.

Rolliad very soon made manifest, — literally thought in rhyme. Brooks's had an exceedingly strong case against Gibbon. In the first stages of the American Revolution he was a staunch, though a silent, adherent of the Ministry; but he consorted mainly with the Opposition, among whom he found that which, to his excellent taste, was the best company in London.[1] He belonged to the club as of right; for, great man of letters though Gibbon was, he never ceased to be a recognised personage in the world of fashion. He wrote his letters at Brooks's; he supped there, or at Almack's, after the House of Commons was up for the night; and he freely accepted the condition on which alone it was possible to enjoy good Whig society, inasmuch as he listened tolerantly, — and, (as time progressed,) even complacently, — to orthodox Whig views. "Charles Fox," he wrote, "is now at my elbow, declaiming on the impossibility of keeping America, since a victorious army has been unable to maintain any extent of posts in the single province of Jersey "[2]

Gibbon, — to whom usually, at this period of their acquaintance, Fox was "Charles," and nothing more distant or ceremonious, — loved the young statesman, and never tired of hearing him discourse. The historian, however, did not need any one to teach him the deductions which his own bright and powerful intellect drew from a contemplation of the political facts. Gibbon's familiar epistles already frankly indicated that he had begun to pass through the mental process which, sooner or later, was traversed by almost every sensible man in the country whose perceptions were not distorted by the promptings of self-interest. Even before Saratoga he had serious qualms. In August 1777 he

[1] "This moment Beauclerk, Lord Ossory, Sheridan, Garrick, Burke, Charles Fox, and Lord Camden, (no bad set, you will perhaps say,) have left me." Gibbon to J B Holroyd, Esq ; Saturday night, 14th March, 1778 "I have been hard at work since dinner," (he wrote elsewhere,) "and am just setting out for Lady Payne's Assembly; after which I will perhaps sup with Charles, etcetera, at Almack's "

[2] Almack's , Wednesday evening, March 5, 1777.

spoke of himself as having found it much easier to defend the justice, than the policy, of the ministerial measures, and, — in a phrase worthy to stand among the weightiest that he ever printed, — he admitted that there were certain cases where whatever was repugnant to sound policy ceased to be just. In the following December, Gibbon had got to the point of saying that, however the Government might resolve, he could scarcely give his consent to exhaust still further the finest country in the world by the prosecution of a war whence no reasonable man entertained any hope of success, in February 1778 he stated it as his opinion that Lord North did not deserve pardon for the past, applause for the present, nor confidence for the future; and on one critical occasion he passed from word to action, and voted with Fox in a division bearing on the conduct of the war.[1] None the less, in the summer of the next year, he became a Lord Commissioner of Trade and Plantations. He joined a Board where, according to Edmund Burke, eight members of Parliament received salaries of a thousand pounds a year apiece for doing nothing except mischief, and not very much even of that;[2] and thenceforward, as by contract bound, he acted with the ministers His story curiously illustrated the artificial and mechanical character of the support which enabled the Court to prolong the American war in opposition to the genuine wish of the people. Eleven

---

[1] On February the 2nd, 1778, Gibbon was in a minority of 165 to 259 on Fox's motion, "That no more of the Old Corps be sent out of the Kingdom "

[2] Burke's *Speech on presenting to the House of Commons a Plan for the better Security of the Independence of Parliament, and the Economical Reformation of the Civil and other Establishments.* The passage relating to the Board of Trade and Plantations, — in itself a treasury of wit and wisdom, — covered a twelfth part of that vast oration, and must have taken twenty minutes to deliver. "I can never forget the delight with which that diffusive and ingenious orator was heard by all sides of the House, and even by those whose existence he proscribed The Lords of Trade blushed at their own insignificance." That good-humoured confession is from a note in the most comprehensive of Gibbon's numerous Autobiographies

days before accepting office, Gibbon, in Brooks's Club, had informed as many of the members as stood within hearing that there could be no salvation for the country until the heads of six of the principal persons in the Administration were laid upon the table That truculent sentence was carefully entered by Charles Fox in his copy of the "Decline and Fall," with the addition of some biting comments. Two years afterwards an execution took place at Fox's house, and all the volumes in his library were sold by auction; — whether he had acquired them on credit at a shop, or, (which was the case here,) as a present from the author Poor Charles's autograph enhanced the value of the History. "Such," wrote Walpole, "was the avidity of bidders for the smallest production of so wonderful a genius that, by the addition of this little record, the book sold for three guineas." [1]

In default of these great authors whose names are still known, and whose works are still read, expectation was for a while concentrated upon a writer who then lived in a halo of celebrity which is now dim almost to extinction. Mrs. Catherine Macaulay, the sister of Lord Mayor Sawbridge, had for many years past been giving to the press a History of England from the Accession of the Stuart Family. Each successive volume was hailed by able, learned, and even cynical, men, (if only they were Whigs,) with admiration and delight quite incomprehensible to modern students. Mason pronounced Mrs. Macaulay's book the one history of England which he had thought it worth his while to purchase, and confessed his national pride to be gratified when he learned that, although her husband's name was Scotch, she herself had been born of English parents. Gray ranked her above every previous author

---

[1] *Last Journals*, June 20, 1781. Anthony Storer, writing to Lord Carlisle, gave a somewhat different account of the matter. "Charles's books, which were seized, were sold this week. Gibbon's book, which contained the manuscript note by Charles, was smuggled from the sale , for, though Charles wished to have sold it, yet it never was put up. He bought in most of his books for almost nothing."

who had attempted the same subject, and thereby gave her the preference over Clarendon, Hume, and Burnet ; [1] and Horace Walpole endorsed Gray's estimate in the most unqualified language. George, Lord Lyttelton, the historian of Henry the Second, said that she was a prodigy, — solemnly and sincerely, as he said everything, — and exhorted mankind to erect statues in her honour. Portraits of Mrs. Macaulay, in fancy characters, and by engravers of note, were on every print-seller's counter ; and an artist came over from America expressly in order to model her and Lord Chatham in wax She was one of the sights which foreigners were carried to see in London ; and she met with flattering attentions in Paris, where England was so much in fashion that current English reputations were taken unreservedly, and sometimes even rapturously, on trust. Among the more audacious thinkers in the society of the French capital enthusiasm was ecstatic with regard to a lady who was a republican by conviction, and the severity of whose strictures upon a State clergy were not prompted by the narrowness or fanaticism of a religious sectary.[2]

Overrated by some clever judges, and adulated by many foolish people in exceedingly foolish ways, Catherine Macaulay was at the height of her repute when the American controversy was developed into a war. In one month of 1776 three set panegyrics on her talents and deserts appeared in the columns of a single London newspaper.[3] Readers were keenly excited by her promise of a " History of England from the Revolu-

[1] So did not Lord Macaulay. An industrious, but not very discerning, critic had remarked that Bishop Burnet's *History of His Own Times* was of a class with the works of Oldmixon, Kennett, and Macaulay. That lady's distinguished namesake wrote thus on the margin of the passage " Nonsense ' Who reads Oldmixon now ? Who reads Kennett ? Who reads Kate Macaulay ? Who does not read Burnet ? "

[2] " What could persuade the writer that Mrs Macaulay was a Dissenter ? I believe her blood was not *polluted* with the smallest *taint* of that kind " Extract from a letter, as given in *Nichols's Literary Anecdotes ;* Vol. IX., page 689.

[3] The opening of a Birthday Address, (by a poet who was not afraid of repeating an adjective which pleased his fancy,) exemplifies the taste of

tion to the Present Time, in a series of Letters to the Reverend Doctor Wilson, the Rector of St. Stephen's, Walbrook;" for Mrs. Macaulay had not emancipated herself from the delusion that sprightliness could be infused into a dull book by arranging its contents in the form of epistolary correspondence. "Sir Robert Walpole, my friend, was well acquainted with the blindness of the nation to every circumstance which regarded their true interest." That is a specimen sentence from Mrs. Macaulay; and it is difficult to imagine how such a style of composition could be tolerated by Horace Walpole, whose own youthful narrative of the scenes in Parliament, which led up to his father's fall, palpitates with life as do the political letters of Cicero.

The literary form, into which Mrs. Macaulay had thrown her History, proved in the sequel fatal to her reputation as an author. The Doctor Wilson, for whose edification the book professed to be written, was no ordinary, or parsimonious, admirer. He had made over to Mrs. Macaulay his house at Bath, with the furniture and library; he placed her statue, adorned with the attributes of the Muse of History, inside the altar-rails of his church, and he built a vault where her remains should rest when her spirit had joined the immortals.[1]

the age, and the high-flown language which it was customary to use when complimenting Mrs. Macaulay. She was born in April, and she then resided at Alfred House, — a name that suggested the motive of the poem.

> " Just patriot King! Sage founder of our laws,
> Whose life was spent in virtue's glorious cause :
> If aught on earth, blest saint, be worth thy care,
> Oh! deign this day's solemnity to share,
> (Sacred to friendship and to festive mirth,)
> The day that gave the fair Macaulay birth ;
> Whose learned page, impartial, dares explain
> Each vice, or virtue, of each different reign,
> Which tends to violate thy sacred plan,
> Or perfect what thy sacred laws began.
>
> Blest month! Tho' sacred to the Cyprian Dame
> This day, at least, let sage Minerva claim,
> (Sacred to friendship and to social mirth,)
> The day which gave her loved Macaulay birth !

[1] *Nichols's Literary Anecdotes*, Vol VIII., page 458.

The first volume of the Continuation of her History was published in 1778. Before that year ended Mrs. Macaulay took to herself a second husband, who was very much less than half her own age, and who was not Doctor Wilson. The statue was at once removed, the house reclaimed, and the vault sold. The clergyman and the lady paraded their mutual grievances before a disenchanted world; and that world, as its custom is, revenged its own infatuation upon the idol whom it had unduly worshipped. The complimentary odes, in which her praises had once been sung, gave place to satirical parodies reflecting on a Certain Female Patriot; the new book was recognised to be detestably bad; and it was the last of the series. A sense of humour could not be counted among Mrs Macaulay's gifts, but she perceived the absurdity of continuing, through a long succession of volumes, to pour forth exhaustive disquisitions on the Stamp Act, and minute examinations of the New England Charters, interspersed with affectionate epithets addressed to an elderly gentleman between whom and herself there notoriously existed an irreconcileable quarrel.

No worthy record of that eventful time can be found in any contemporary book which was deliberately compiled as a history; but the age nevertheless gave birth to a vast mass of political literature, written for the purpose of the moment, some portion of which will never be allowed to die. There is a stirring and decisive chapter in the story of ancient Greece which a good scholar makes shift to pick out, and piece together, for himself from the orations of Æschines and Demosthenes, and so,—between the day that George the Third instituted the system of Personal Government, down to the day when the American war, (the chief, and almost the solitary, fruit and product of that system,) ended in public disaster and national repentance,—the most brilliant and authentic account of the period may be drawn from Edmund Burke's published speeches and controversial treatises. Apart from, and above, their unique

literary merit, those performances are notable as show-
ing how the gravity of a statesman, and the sense of
responsibility which marks a genuine patriot, can co-exist
with an unflinching courage in the choice and the handling of topics.   That courage, in Burke's case, had been
exercised with impunity throughout the most perilous of
times.   Multitudinous and formidable were the assailants
whose attacks, from the in-coming of Lord Bute to the
out-going of the Duke of Grafton, were directed against
the King, and those King's Friends who made office
a purgatory for every King's Minister whom the King
did not love; but all their effusions together were less
damaging in their effect on the minds of impartial men than
the "Thoughts on the Cause of the Present Discontents,"
the last ten pages of the "Observations on a late State
of the Nation," and one very brief paragraph of courtly
and almost reverential irony in that marvel of point and
compression which is entitled a "Short Account of a
Short Administration."[1]

Other, and less redoubtable, critics of the Government,
— as well as the very craftsmen who printed, and the
tradesmen who sold, their writings, — were punished
with the utmost rigour of the law, and harassed by the
arbitrary vindictiveness of Parliament; but neither the
Attorney-General, nor the Sergeant-at-Arms, ever med-
dled with Burke or his publishers.   It was the strongest
possible testimonial, on the part of his adversaries, to
his character and his standing in the country.   The
agents of the Government would no more have ventured
to prosecute Edmund Burke for libel than they would
have dared to arrest Lord Chatham on a charge of treason
as he passed out of the House of Lords after delivering

[1] "In the prosecution of their measures they were traversed by an Opposition of a new and singular character; an Opposition of placemen and
pensioners.   They were supported by the confidence of the nation; and,
having held their offices under many difficulties and discouragements, they
left them at the express command, as they had accepted them at the
earnest request, of their Royal Master"   So mildly did Burke refer to the
usage which Lord Rockingham and his colleagues encountered from
the monarch whom they so faithfully served

one of his diatribes against the influence of the Crown.
Burke enjoyed immunity himself, and extended the
shield of his protection over his humbler associates in
the business of giving his opinions to the reading world,
during the miserable years when the persecution of the
Press was at its height. All the more, after the American difficulty had become serious, — when the power of
the Executive was on the decline, and the Censorship had
lost its terrors, — the great Whig publicist, if his taste
and self-respect had permitted, might safely have pursued the Court and the Cabinet with an unbounded
licence of invective. But he wisely preferred to set
forth his opinions with the same measured and dignified
force of argument and illustration as he had displayed
when the Middlesex Election was the question of the
day. He could not, indeed, write better than he had
written already; but close reasoning, supported by a
solid array of facts and figures, has nowhere been presented in a shape more attractive and persuasive than in
Burke's "Letter to the Sheriffs of Bristol," and in the
authorised report of his "Speech on moving the Resolutions for Conciliation with America."

A literary work of rare merit seldom stands alone,
and in most cases proceeds from the pen of one who
does best what many around him are attempting to do
well. Burke's masterpieces were produced at a time
when the political essay was widely practised, and held
in great account. The historian, who is destined to relate the events of our own generation, will be under an
obligation to read leading articles by the furlong and the
mile, for, during the past half-century, the leading article
has frequently dictated the action of the State, has inspired or terrorised its rulers, and has kept them up to
the mark, or below it, until their allotted task has, for
good or evil, been accomplished. But between 1774 and
1783 the leading article, strictly so called, was yet in the
future. The news in newspapers, already ample in
quantity, year by year improved in accuracy, but the
editorial comments on public affairs were confined to

paragraphs of five or six, to a dozen, lines, allusive rather than explanatory in their character, and for the most part of a humorous and satirical tendency. Serious instruction and exhortation were conveyed to the world in the pamphlets of well-known men who acknowledged their authorship; and, (within the columns of daily and weekly journals,) by means of long, elaborate, and often extremely able letters, signed by some adopted name, for the periodical reappearance of which a large circle of readers eagerly looked Charles Fox, who was conversant with every legitimate method of influencing opinion, has clearly drawn the distinction between the signed letter and the newspaper paragraph. Grave problems in foreign and domestic politics must, (he said,) first be treated in some earnest and plain way, and must be much explained to the public before any paragraphs alluding to them could be understood by one in a thousand.[1] These responsible, or semi-responsible, personal manifestoes, (for a writer who styled himself Atticus or Publicola was expected to be rational in his arguments, and constitutional in his views, almost as much as one who called himself by his Christian name, and his surname, in full,) had never been so numerous, or attained so high an average level of excellence, as during the American war. Junius, indeed, whoever Junius was, had not published a single sentence of print since Philip Francis sailed for India A conspicuous niche was vacant, which no single successor or imitator had been reckoned worthy to fill; but the lists of controversy were thronged by a perfect phalanx of well-informed and fervid partisans, who, under a variety of Greek and Roman pseudonyms, in-

---

[1] "I cannot think as you do of the insignificancy of newspapers, though I think that others overrate their importance. I am clear, too, that paragraphs alone will not do. Subjects of importance should be first gravely treated in letters or pamphlets or, (best of all perhaps,) in a series of letters; and afterwards the paragraphs do very well as an accompaniment It is not till a subject has been so much discussed as to become threadbare that *paragraphs*, which consist principally in allusions, can be generally understood." Fox to Fitzpatrick; St. Ann's Hill, Sunday, November, (or December,) 1785.

sisted on the madness of the policy which Parliament
had adopted, and held up to reprobation the ministerial
and military blunders which prevented that policy from
being crowned with even a transitory success

As opposed to all this spontaneous ardour, and unfet-
tered intellectual activity, there was very little independent talent on the side of the ministers.   It was their
own fault   In Parliament, and in literature, they had
bought up everything that was for sale, and they found
themselves in the position of a general when he has
overpaid his mercenaries, and cannot get volunteers who
are disposed to fight for him, and willing to subject
themselves to the necessary discipline.   Doctor Tucker,
the Dean of Gloucester, was a declared adversary of the
Rockingham party.   His pamphlets had a large circulation; but he took a line of his own which sorely em-
barrassed the Government.   A disinterested man, he
possessed a cultured and original mind, with a singularly
accurate perception of the direction in which the world
was moving.   When his gaze swept a sufficiently wide
horizon, he gave proofs of a foresight which is the wonder of those who have learned by frequent disappoint-
ments what their own political prophecies are usually
worth.[1]   He was, however, woefully deficient in tact,
and his ignorance of the motives which guided the
action of contemporary public men, and parliamentary
parties, was hopeless and complete.   He appears sincerely to have believed that the opponents of the Court,
whom he called the Modern Republicans, were in point
of fact Jacobites who admired Doctor Price as their
predecessors in the reign of Queen Anne had admired
Doctor Sacheverell   Doctor Price wrote much and well
in favour of reconciliation with America, and Dean
Tucker was never so happy as when belabouring him

---

[1] "I have observed," (Dean Tucker wrote,) "that measures evidently
right will prevail at last.   Therefore I make not the least Doubt that a
Separation from the Northern Colonies, — and also another right measure,
viz, a complete Union and Incorporation with Ireland, — (however unpopular either of them will now appear,) will both take place within half
a century."

and Edmund Burke on account of their partiality for
the New England colonists, whom the Dean himself
cordially abominated.   But his blows seldom got home
upon either of his antagonists; and the cudgel with
which he laid about him dealt back-strokes that hit a
ministerial, and occasionally even a Royal, head.

Here, (argued the Doctor,) is a discontented and
riotous population, three thousand miles away across the
ocean, who do not like us, and do not want us.   We
may flatter them, and cajole them, and try to appease
them by making one concession and surrender after
another; and then, when we have eaten a mountain of
humble-pie compounded for us by the philosophers and
orators of the Opposition, the Americans will perhaps
graciously consent to pretend that they will abide a
while longer in their allegiance to the British Crown.
But, as they increase in strength and numbers, an army
of fifty thousand, and before long a hundred thousand,
English-born soldiers, (and none others can be trusted,)
will scarcely be sufficient to keep their turbulent spirits
in awe, and prevent them from breaking forth into
insurrection at every favourable opportunity.   And how
could such an insurrection be quelled?   What British
officer, civil or military, would be so foolhardy as to
order the troops to fire on a New England mob, with
the assured prospect that, if any of the bullets carried
straight, he would be tried for his life on a charge
of murder before a New England jury?[1]   Mr. Burke,
(said Tucker,) would deserve much better of his country
if, — in place of giving the colonists fair words in print,
and speaking respectfully and affectionately about them
when he was addressing the House of Commons, — he
would bid them cut themselves loose from Great Britain,
and thenceforward go their own ways, to their inevitable
loss and ruin   That was Dean Tucker's logical position, and that was his advice in the year 1774.   He undoubtedly made Burke very angry; but Lord North and
the King would sometimes have been quite as thankful

[1] Dean Tucker's Fourth Tract; 1775

if their reverend ally had only been pleased to leave the Cabinet undefended.

The destitution to which ministers were reduced for want of advocates obliged them to accept assistance from a very questionable quarter. John Shebbeare had now during nearly two generations been a scandal to letters. His coarseness and effrontery in the give and take of private society have been faithfully portrayed by Fanny Burney, a judge of manners as indulgent and as uncensorious as was compatible with native refinement and feminine delicacy.[1] Shebbeare made his livelihood by defamation and scurrility. His first literary effort was a lampoon on the surgeon from whom he had received a medical education; and his last was entitled "The Polecat Detected;" which was a libel, and not, (as might have been supposed,) an autobiography. During the reign of George the Second, Shebbeare had been severely, — and, indeed, arbitrarily and most improperly, — punished for a fierce attack upon the House of Hanover. He now enjoyed a pension of two hundred pounds a year; and he was aware of the conditions on which, for such as he, the payment of his quarter's stipend depended. Throughout the American war he vilified the group of great statesmen, whom George the Third persisted in regarding as adversaries, with the same ill-bred vehemence which he had formerly directed against that line of kings who were the rivals and supplanters of the Stuarts. Shebbeare was the man whose name Thomas Townshend, in the House of Commons, had coupled with that of Samuel Johnson, on the ground that they both had once been Jacobites, and both now were pensioners; and Townshend's ill-natured remark had called forth from Charles Fox an eloquent and indignant

---

[1] On the 20th February, 1774, Miss Burney and some of her friends, one of whom was a very young girl, were unfortunate enough to find themselves guests in the same drawing-room as Shebbeare "He absolutely ruined our evening, for he is the most morose, rude, gross, and ill-mannered man I ever was in company with" Much of his conversation, as reported by Miss Burney with her transparent fidelity, was incredibly brutal; and still worse passages were crossed out in the manuscript.

protest which, to his dying day, Johnson gratefully recollected.

There were members of the Government who had long been anxious to enlist Doctor Johnson's literary skill, and personal authority, on behalf of the Government measures. In this case there was no compulsion. The King entertained a true regard for his eminent subject, and felt a lively satisfaction at the thought that his own generosity had enabled a great author, — who had long known want, and sorrow, and the slavery of set tasks and uncongenial labours, — to spend the rest of his days in conversation, and travel, and the desultory and fragmentary reading which he so dearly loved. It was Johnson himself who conceived that his duty towards his Royal Master required him to do a good turn for those ministers who possessed the Royal favour; and he intimated his willingness to assist the Cabinet with his pen. The subject of each successive pamphlet was suggested to him by great men in office; but the opinions which he enunciated were unmistakably his own. Indeed, Johnson was so strong a partisan that the censors of Downing Street interfered with him only to tone down his declarations of policy, and to blunt the edge of his satire. One cutting and contemptuous epigram in his " Thoughts on the late Transactions Respecting the Falkland Islands " so scared Lord North that the sale of the first edition was stopped after only a few copies had got abroad.[1] In the spring of 1775 Johnson brought out his " Taxation no Tyranny," which, as the title implied, went down to the root of the quarrel between Great Britain and America. It was revised and curtailed by the ministerial critics,

---

[1] The words which did not please Lord North related to George Grenville, and originally stood thus " Let him not, however, be depreciated in his grave. He had powers not universally possessed. Could he have enforced payment of the Manilla ransom, he could have counted it." In the second edition the sentence ran : " He had powers not universally possessed ; and, if he sometimes erred, he was likewise sometimes in the right; " which is true of every public man that ever lived, and does not require a Samuel Johnson to say it.

who struck out of the text one passage as unnecessarily insulting and alarming to the colonists [1] Johnson's sturdy good-humour was proof against a trial which would have touched the vanity of a more susceptible author. If, (he said,) an architect had planned a building of five stories, and the man who employed him ordered him to build only three, it was the employer, and not the architect, who must decide.

The utmost severity of expurgation would have failed to convert " Taxation no Tyranny " into a felicitous performance. Admirable, and thrice admirable, disquisitions on State affairs have been published by famous literary men who descended for a while into the arena of political controversy. Such were Swift's " Examiners ; " and Addison's " Freeholders ; " and, (better still, and nearer to our own times,) Sydney Smith's " Plymley Letters " on the Catholic Claims Nor was any more ably composed, and entirely readable, State paper ever issued than that Memoir, in the French language, in which Gibbon, at the request of ministers, towards the commencement of 1778 submitted the case of England, as against France, to the judgement of Europe. But Johnson was not even potentially a statesman. He had never thought deeply, or wisely, on politics ; and his everyday conversation abundantly proved him to be peculiarly ill adapted for arriving at a just conclusion upon the American question. He was incapable of maintaining a rational and considerate attitude towards any great body of men with whose opinions he disagreed. His vociferous declamations against the Americans were annoying and oppressive to the companions with whom he lived. He might be heard, (they complained,) across the Atlantic. The study which he bestowed upon the commercial in-

---

[1] " He told me," wrote Boswell, " that they had struck out one passage which was to the effect 'That the colonists could with no solidity argue, from their not having been taxed while in their infancy, that they should not now be taxed. We do not put a calf into the plough. We wait till he is an ox ' "

terests, which so profoundly affected the relations
between the mother-country and her colonies, had been
very superficial.   He once comforted a friend, who was
anxious about the effect of the war upon trade, by assuring him that, if we had no commerce at all, we could
live very well upon the produce of our own island.   On
the connection between taxation and parliamentary representation, which his treatise was ostensibly written to
discuss, he argued like a man who had not the most elementary conception of, or sympathy with, the principle
of self-government.   He was fond of saying that a
gentleman of landed property did well to evict all his
tenants who would not vote for the candidate whom he
supported.   If he himself, (so the great moralist once
put it,) were a man of large estate, he would drive every
rascal, whom he did not like, out of the country, as soon
as ever an election came.

When "Taxation no Tyranny" appeared in print,
most of Johnson's admirers perused the piece with
regret, and with something of apprehension   They
began to fear that, as a writer, he had seen his best
days; and they never recovered their confidence in his
powers until, some years later on, his "Lives of the
Poets" were given to a charmed and astonished world.
There he was on his own ground.   There he revelled
in the consciousness of supreme capability.   He cast
aside, at that late moment, the elaborate and florid
diction of his early and middle period   During the
half of every day, and of every night, since the well-
directed bounty of the State had made him his own
master, he had been discoursing on every conceivable
topic to all who were privileged to listen; and he had
insensibly acquired the habit of writing as he talked.
He now had an ideal subject for a biographer endowed
with his vigorous common-sense, his vast and insatiable
interest in the common things of life, and his acute perception of the rules which ought to govern conduct.
We may well doubt whether so delightful and instructive a book as Johnson's "Poets," on a large scale and

of serious purpose, was ever commenced and finished in the two years that precede, and the two that follow, the age of seventy.[1]

Johnson's pamphlet, by indirect means, obtained a startling notoriety His bolts fell innocuous; but his thunder awoke an echo which was heard far and wide. Of all people then living, — of all, perhaps, who ever lived, — no one had so profound an acquaintance with the state of opinion at home, and in America, as John Wesley. He knew Scotland well, and England as a man must know it who preached eight hundred sermons annually, in all corners of the island; who, fine or rain, travelled his twelve-score miles a week on horseback, or in public vehicles, which for him was a more perilous mode of conveyance,[2] and who lodged, — an easily contented, an affable, and a communicative guest, — with the farmer, the tradesman, and the cottager. Soon and late, he more than fifty times crossed the Irish Channel. He had passed nearly two years in America, and he had learned by personal experience how long it took to get there; a fact ill understood by those ministers who had misgoverned our remote colonies in peace, and who now were attempting to reconquer them by war. Wesley relates, in the first pages of his incomparable "Journal," how he and his comrades took ship at Gravesend on the fourteenth of October, 1735; and how, on the following fifth of February, God brought them all safe into the Savannah river. The voyage was long enough for him to learn German, and

---

[1] Carlyle completed his *Frederic the Great* when close on seventy ; but he had been working at it fourteen years.

[2] Wesley had reached old age when the American war began ; and thenceforward he more frequently rode in a post-chaise, or a mail-coach. It is worth a reader's while to count the number of his carriage accidents, if only as an occasion for going through the last volume of the *Journal* once again. Sometimes he made a safe journey, as from Coventry in July 1770. "I took coach for London. I was nobly attended Behind the coach were ten convicted felons, loudly blaspheming, and rattling their chains. By my side sat a man with a loaded blunderbuss, and another upon the coach."

increase threefold the number of communicants who
attended his ministrations on board. Ever since that
time he had been kept minutely informed of what was
passing in America by disciples for whom it was a
privilege to correspond with him, and a sacred duty to
write him the truth.

As recently as the year 1770, — when New England
was already in a state of dangerous effervescence, and
the military occupation of Boston had actually commenced, — John Wesley stated in print that he did not
defend the measures which had been taken with regard
to America ; and that he doubted whether any man
could defend them either on the foot of law, equity, or
prudence.[1] So he openly told the world ; and in secret
he dealt very faithfully indeed with the advisers of the
Crown. He addressed to them a series of most impressive letters, in which the exalted diction of an old Scriptural prophet added force and dignity to the solid
arguments of a sagacious and patriotic Englishman.
He warned them plainly that the Americans were an
oppressed people, asking for nothing more than their
legal rights ; who were not frightened, and would not
be easily conquered. As fighting men, (he said in so
many words,) they were enthusiasts of liberty, contending for hearth and altar, wife and children, against an
army of paid soldiers "none of whom cared a straw for
the cause wherein they were engaged, and most of
whom strongly disapproved of it." And he had gone
so far as to implore the Prime Minister, for God's sake
and for the King's sake, not to permit his sovereign to
walk in the ways of Rehoboam, of Philip the Second of
Spain, and of Charles the First of England.

That was John Wesley's view, as conveyed to Lord
North on the fifteenth of June, 1775 Before the sum-
mer was over there appeared a quarto sheet of four
pages, professing itself to be " A Calm Address to our
American Colonies by the Reverend John Wesley, M.A."
It was sold for a penny, and was bought by forty

[1] Wesley's *Free Thoughts on the Present State of Public Affairs.*

thousand purchasers, who were amazed at finding it
nothing more nor less than an abbreviated version of
"Taxation no Tyranny," published without any reference to the original whence it was derived The little
piece was redolent of Johnson's prejudices, and so full
of violent and random assertions that no room was left
for those temperate expostulations which the title promised. Wesley assured the colonists, — and it must have
been news to Samuel Adams and to John Dickinson, —
that the discontent in America was not of native origin.
It had been produced, (he declared,) by the books and
pamphlets of wicked and artful writers resident in England, whose object was to overset the British Constitution ; and, considering that the chief among those writers
was Edmund Burke, to whom every tittle of the British
Constitution was as the Law to a Pharisee or the Koran
to a good Mahommedan, there was something exqui-
sitely ludicrous in such a statement. The nearest ap-
proach to an argument in Wesley's tract was an appeal
to the people of New England, whom, with less than
his customary shrewdness, he appears to have esteemed
a very simple-minded folk. "You say that you inherit
all the rights which your ancestors had of enjoying all
the privileges of Englishmen. You are the descendants
of men who either had no votes, or resigned them by
emigration. You have therefore exactly what your ancestors left you; not a vote in making laws nor in
choosing legislators, but the happiness of being protected by laws, and the duty of obeying them." It would
be difficult to compress into so few words any theory
of citizenship less satisfying to the political aspirations
of Americans, either past or present

Wesley's change of attitude bordered on the gro-
tesque, and to some of his followers was perfectly be-
wildering. At the general election of the previous year
he had advised Bristol Methodists to vote for the candidates who were in favour of conciliation with America ;
and he had urged his friends to procure and study a pamphlet called "An Argument in Defence of the Exclusive

Right claimed by the Colonies to tax themselves." That circumstance Wesley had forgotten; as a man of his years, and his enormous and multifarious occupations, might be excused forgetting anything. Rudely accused of insincerity, he examined his memory, and admitted that he had read the pamphlet in question, and had agreed with its conclusions. In answer to the charge that he had recommended it to the attention of others, he quietly replied: "I believe I did: but I am now of another mind." Wesley's candour failed to disarm his opponents. The "Calm Address" aroused a tempest of controversy; and during several publishing seasons the great preacher was exposed to hailstorms of wild calumny, and unsavoury abuse. He was furiously denounced as a wolf in sheep's clothing; a Jesuit and a Jacobite unmasked;[1] a chaplain in ordinary to the Furies; and a Minister Extraordinary to Bellona, the Goddess of War.

John Wesley contemplated this explosion of passion with mild surprise, in which his adversaries detected a touch of irony; for his intention, (he said,) had been to pour water, instead of oil, upon the flame, and to contribute his mite towards quenching the conflagration which over-ran the land. He reminded his younger coadjutors that Christian ministers should be peacemakers, loving and tender to all, and not addicted to either party. So anxious was he, according to his own account, to avoid the possibility of offence, that, when invited to preach about a matter which savoured of politics, he took the precaution of writing down his sermon beforehand, but, all the same, those opponents of the Ministry who chanced to be present were told from the pulpit that they had screamed for liberty till they were utterly distracted, and their intellects quite confounded. At a later moment in the war Wesley bethought himself of

---

[1] It was not the first time that Wesley had been called a Jesuit. He once was preaching at Dublin to a large assemblage. "One of them, after listening some time, cried out, shaking his head: 'Ay: he is a Jesuit, that's plain' To which a Popish Priest, who happened to be near, replied aloud: 'No; he is not. I would to God he was!'" *Journal* for May 15, 1748

issuing a "Calm Address" to the inhabitants of England, who by that time needed to be soothed and pacified almost as much as the inhabitants of the colonies. But the effect produced, by this his second message of peace, upon contending factions was weakened by an announcement that he himself would no more continue in fellowship with Methodists, who hated the King and Lord North, than with Sabbath-breakers, or thieves, or drunkards, or common swearers, — or with another class of heinous sinners whom he described by an uncompromising epithet which modern delicacy has banished from ordinary use.[1]

Wesley was taunted by the Whig satirists for having borrowed from Johnson without acknowledgement; but no objection was raised by Johnson himself, who had some ground for serious annoyance. The shorter piece, which, by its vast sale, had superseded the pamphlet whereof it was an abridgement, brought into strong relief the worst defects of the original composition; for the "Calm Address," (to employ an old simile,) was to "Taxation no Tyranny" as a bad hash is to a bad joint. So soon as any mention of plagiarism arose, Wesley hastened to place on record that his own publication was but a reproduction in little of Doctor Johnson's more elaborate work. His whole view of the American question, (he confessed,) had been fundamentally altered by a single perusal of that masterly and irresistible treatise Such a conversion, instantaneous as any that Wesley wrought during the sixty-four years of his ministry, was a practical compliment which no author could resist. Johnson warmly assured him that, to have won over a mind like his, outweighed a multitude of ordinary suffrages, and compared himself to the philosopher who, when he saw the rest of his audience slinking away from a lecture, refused to quit the chair as long as Plato stayed [2]

---

[1] *The Life and Times of the Reverend John Wesley*, by the Reverend L. Tyerman, Vol III , sections headed 1775 and 1777.

[2] Johnson to Wesley , Feb. 6, 1776

The reception of Wesley's effort to instruct and convince his fellow-countrymen affords a notable proof that
virtue and disinterestedness, public esteem and vener-
able age, will fail to avert the roughest of treatment
from all who venture upon an incursion into politics.
Gibbon, in the course of this very year, declared that the
ministerial majority in the House of Commons, — when
the month of May was half through, and the end of the
Session in sight, — would not hear even the Archangel
Gabriel on the subject of America ; and Wesley's experience showed that angry partisans, on the Whig side
of the controversy, had neither consideration nor charity
for one who, if ever man did, deserved to be called a
saint. A score of lampoons charged him with being
actuated by self-interest ; and that accusation was repeated by a man of the world, who was as little competent to interpret the thoughts of John Wesley as Festus
and Gallio were to understand St. Paul. The artful patri-
arch of the Methodists, (so Horace Walpole wrote,) had
produced the " Calm Address " in order to court his
patron, Lord Dartmouth; since he probably hoped either
for a deanery or a bishopric. Wesley refuted the imputation in phrases which most certainly were very unlike
those of a courtier. He had published the tract, (he
said,) not to please any man, high or low ; for he knew
mankind too well. He knew that they, who love you
for your political service, love you less than their dinner,
and they, who hate you, hate you worse than the Devil.
The true and sufficient explanation of Wesley's action is
not far to seek. He was a Tory, just as much as Doctor
Parr, and Doctor Richard Watson, were Whigs , and
most Englishmen will stretch a point in order to support
their party when its fortunes are depressed, and its
future dark and dubious. Wesley was much concerned
by the aspect of politics. The ministers, (as he was not
afraid to tell them, and that right bluntly,) were very
generally detested by the nation , and the personal unpopularity of George the Third made his devoted subject
seriously unhappy and profoundly apprehensive. Wes-

ley was firmly convinced that the throne, and even the royal life, would be in danger if any fresh disasters occurred abroad, and if the ferment at home grew hotter. At such a crisis he was instinctively and irresistibly drawn to rally in defence of his party and his Sovereign; and, (as men in those circumstances will,) he brought himself round to approve a policy which, in public and in private, he had been accustomed severely to condemn.

CHAPTER XXVII

THE COLONIAL CHURCHES.   THE BISHOP QUESTION IN
AMERICA.   THE CLERGY IN THE REVOLUTION.   THE
FINAL SETTLEMENT

THE colonial difficulty, like our own Civil War, arose
ostensibly and immediately from a question of taxation ;
but in 1775, as in 1642, the contending parties were inspired and stimulated by religious, at least as much as
by fiscal, considerations.   That truth was perceived by
some contemporary spectators of the American contest,
and it is almost universally recognised by those who, in
our own day, have applied themselves to a comprehensive and unbiassed study of the past.   Vital religion
was, indeed, a less absorbing motive in the eighteenth,
than in the seventeenth, century.   Men were occupied
with more varied, more mundane, and perhaps more
selfish, interests in the later period than in the earlier.
They talked less habitually in Scriptural language, and
dwelt less exclusively upon the niceties of doctrine.   The
society in which George Washington lived was not pervaded and swayed by theology like the England of
Charles the First and Oliver Cromwell ; but the religious
lessons to be drawn from the history of the American
Revolution are of greater practical importance to ourselves, and those lessons were taught with startling
vividness, and most uncompromising completeness   The
thirteen provinces, while still British colonies, had exhibited a picture, or rather a panorama, displaying, — in
deeply contrasted colours, and on a scale large enough
for philosophical observation, — all conceivable forms
and varieties of ecclesiastical institutions.   The result
of separation from the mother-country was to sweep

away every vestige of Church privilege, and to secure absolute and uniform religious equality the whole Union over

The Church of England had, from the very first, been established as a State Church in Virginia and in both the Carolinas; and the Dutch Reformed Church occupied the same advantageous position in the Province of New York. Those stern sectarians of the Northern colonies, who had escaped across the seas from the tyranny of others, indulged themselves in a rigid and authoritative system of ecclesiastical government erected on the basis of Congregationalism. No mere creature or pensioner of the State, the Church was the State itself in nearly every community of New England; but not in all. Roger Williams, a graduate of Pembroke College at Cambridge, was an English Puritan of the highest type. He emigrated to Boston in 1631, because he could not live both honestly and safely within the sweep of an archbishop's crozier, and from Boston he passed southward to Rhode Island in pursuit of the full religious liberty which was denied to him under the theocratical Constitution of Massachusetts. He induced the colonists among whom he fixed his home to adopt a Resolution of infinite moment, and notable originality. "It is much in our hearts," (so they declared,) "to hold forth a lively experiment that a most flourishing civil State may stand, and best be maintained, with a full liberty of religious concernments." [1] That utterance, — the direct reverse of all previous, and then existing, European belief and practice, whether in Roman Catholic or in Protestant countries, — was the first announcement

[1] Petition from the people of Rhode Island to Charles the Second That King, to the horror of some of his high Officers of State, insisted that the prayer of the petition should be granted.

At this point in this chapter I desire, once for all, to express my obligations to the *History of the Rise of Religious Liberty in America* by Mr. Sandford H. Cobb. That admirable book was of all the greater service to me because, before its publication, I had already taken a strong interest in the questions of which it treats; with reference to which I had collected a large amount of material from many, and very diverse, quarters.

of a principle which the United States of America have long ere this accepted in its entirety, and have solemnly embodied in their Constitution. The example of Rhode Island was followed by the founders of other colonies, especially such as held those forms of belief which had been most hotly persecuted in England No State Church was set up in Maryland, where the Proprietary family was of the Roman Catholic persuasion. Pennsylvania and Delaware,—at first together, and, after a while, apart,—carried on their civil administration divorced from an ecclesiastical establishment, and Georgia, youngest of the thirteen colonies, began life under the same conditions Foreigners, who visited America, saw much that astonished and delighted them; but the feature which struck them as the most pleasant and novel was the aspect of social existence in the non-denominational provinces. In Philadelphia, (said Comte de Ségur,) it was not the architecture, and the monuments, that most excited curiosity and commanded respect. The whole city was a noble temple raised to Tolerance, in which Catholics and Presbyterians, Calvinists and Lutherans, Anabaptists, Methodists, and Quakers worshipped after their own fashion, and consorted one with another in peace and amity.[1]

Those ecclesiastical arrangements under which the American colonies started upon their career were not long permitted to continue undisturbed. From a very early period statesmen in London were on the watch to impose an Anglican Establishment upon one or another of those colonies which were as yet without one, and to render existence everywhere as uncomfortable as possible to all except professed Episcopalians. The opportunity of the Government at home came whenever the administrator on the spot was a man of decided clerical leanings, or, (which was quite as much to the purpose,) of a combative and masterful nature; for it by no means

---

[1] *Mémoires par M. Le Comte de Ségur, de l'Académie Française, Pair de France;* Paris, 1825, Vol. I., page 362. De Ségur's first sight of Philadelphia was in 1782.

was the case that a Royal Governor, or a Secretary of State either, who displayed the most abounding zeal for the aggrandisement of the Church was necessarily one who lived in the closest obedience to her rules of private conduct. Anglicanism was after a while established in Maryland; and Roman Catholics were excluded from office, and forbidden the exercise of their religion, on that very soil which had been expressly granted and colonised as a much-needed sanctuary for the members of their faith. Georgia was divided into eight parishes with stipends for Anglican clergy; — although Anglican laymen were so sparse and few that, ten years afterwards, only two Episcopal congregations could be gathered together anywhere in the province   Lord Cornbury vested himself with ecclesiastical authority over the whole of New Jersey, and ordained the due performance of the Anglican ritual "as by law established," at a time when the colony did not possess a single church of the English Communion. The Episcopalian party was numerically very feeble in the province of New York, and the authorities did not venture to apply for a Statute enacting, in so many words, the supremacy of the English Church; but they ousted the Dutch Church, and replaced it by an Establishment which undertook to provide each city and county with "a good and sufficient Protestant Minister."[1]   Interpreting this definition in a sense which it most assuredly would not convey to the ear of a modern High Churchman, the Cabinet in Downing Street, and the Royal Governor and his council in New York, thenceforward wrote, spoke, and acted as if the Church of England had been duly and legally enthroned in the colony

---

[1] Only six years before the Act was passed, a Governor of New York reported on the religious condition of that colony in vigorous, and not very official, language. "Here bee not many of the Church of England; few Roman Catholics; abundance of Quaker preachers, — men, and women especially; singing Quakers; ranting Quakers; Sabbatarians; Anti-Sabbatarians; some Anabaptists, some Independents, some Jews. In short, of all opinions there are some, and the most part of none at all. The most prevailing opinion is that of the Dutch Calvinists."

The early history of all those American communities, in which any form of religion whatsoever had been
established by law, bore deep imprints of a fierce and
narrow bigotry.   Nothing else could be expected from
men who had been nurtured in the old-world theory
that it was the sacred duty of rulers to choose a religion
for the people, and to extirpate heresy.   No one except
a Congregationalist could be a freeman of Massachusetts.   No Roman Catholic was suffered to abide within
the borders of the colony.   Baptists were fined, flogged,
and imprisoned; and some of the early Quaker fanatics,
both men and women, who courted death and bonds
with persistent importunity, were barbarously martyred.
King Charles the Second earnestly and repeatedly endeavoured to secure liberty of religion for members
of that English Church of which he himself was the
Head, and was encountered by the Independents of
Massachusetts with a respectful but inflexible refusal
They reminded His Majesty that they were voluntary
exiles from their dear native country because they could
not read the Word of God as warranting the use of the
Common Prayer Book; and to have the same set up in
America, (so their quaint phraseology ran,) "would dis-
turb their peace in their present enjoyments."   Bad
things were done in those old days, and cruel-minded
sermons were preached and applauded; but, as time
went on, the tendency of opinion throughout New
England was in the direction first of toleration, and
then of religious equality.   Generations grew up in an
atmosphere of responsible self-government, and widely
diffused popular education.   The sons of the men who
had sent Quakers to execution already condemned the
deed; and Boston has been repenting of it ever since,
in prose and verse, with an emphasis and unanimity of
remorse the like of which has been known in no other
community.   Clerical opinion lagged somewhat in the
rear; but the clergy of the Northern colonies could
not afford to be left far behind laymen in the march
of humanity.   They were not priests, invested with

sacerdotal attributes and authority; but teachers, whose influence depended upon their ability to convince the intellect, and hold the confidence, of their hearers. As early as 1691 the full right of citizenship, and the free exercise of public worship, had been extended to all Christians, with the exception of Roman Catholics; and, forty years later on, it was enacted that the taxes for religious objects, which had been collected from Episcopalian householders, should be handed over to their own Episcopalian minister, if there was one within five miles whose services they attended. That was the Five Mile Act of Massachusetts and Connecticut. The English law which bore the same name was an ordinance forbidding a Nonconformist clergyman to show his face within five miles of any corporate city or borough. In 1775, when the American Revolution broke out, that Act still remained in our Statute-book; nor had it yet become a dead letter.[1]

Any progress, which was made towards religious liberty in those colonies where Anglicanism had been established, owed less than nothing to the clergy of the official Church, or to Royal Governors who had the supposed interests of that Church in their keeping In the province of New York, under the rule of Lord Cornbury, places of worship, and religious endowments, — sometimes by chicanery, and sometimes by arbitrary violence, — were wrested from Presbyterians or Independents, and handed over to Episcopalians. Nearly half-way through the eighteenth century, in the same province, Moravian missionaries, the most innocent and guileless of mankind, were proscribed and persecuted on the pretext that they were Popish emissaries with designs against His Majesty's Government And even as late as 1768, — when the country was ablaze with the agitation against the tea-duty, — the Virginian clergy contrived to get three Baptists into gaol for the crime of having re-

---

[1] The Kentish Justices put the Five Mile Act in force against Wesleyan preachers thirty years after Methodism had become a living power in England.

fused to discontinue preaching.[1] There have been periods
in the history of nations when intolerance has been dignified by the intense religious conviction, and the pure,
ascetic, morals of a dominant priesthood; but such was
not the case in the Southern colonies, and least of all in
Virginia. The desirable gifts and graces were often
sadly lacking in clergymen who had been exported from
England to serve the parishes in that province. "As to
other commodities, so of this, the worst are sent us; and
we had few, that we could boast of, since the persecution
in Cromwell's tyranny drove divers worthy men hither."
That was written by a Royal Governor in the reign of
Charles the Second; and a very perceptible change for
the better never took place in the character of the Virginian incumbents until the Church, disestablished and disen-
dowed, was at last thrown back upon her own resources.

There was no bishop, within a distance of three thousand miles, to encourage and promote the worthy, or to
admonish and chastise the reprobate, and the Anglican
clergy of the Southern plantations, without a director
above them, were not a law to themselves. Abandoned
to their own guidance and discretion in parishes sometimes as large as an English county, they frequently
succumbed to the temptations prevalent in a loosely,
and, (so far as slavery was concerned,) a viciously organised society. In one respect they were singularly
unfortunate. The boon companions with whom they
consorted, the Presbyterian neighbours who had to pay
their stipends without attending their ministrations, and
the church-goers who listened to their ill-read prayers
and short and slovenly discourses,[2] belonged to a race

[1] In one case Patrick Henry "offered his services to defend the poor
preachers, and tradition has it that he rode fifty miles to do so. In his
speech he so dwelt upon the folly and wickedness of attempting to punish
a man for preaching the gospel of the Son of God, that he overwhelmed
the court, and secured the immediate discharge of his client." In 1770 two
other Baptists were thrown into Chesterfield County gaol, and there "they
did much execution by preaching through the grates of their windows."
History of Religious Liberty; chapter iv., section 1.

[2] Josiah Quincy,—accustomed as he was to New England sermons
closely reasoned, and divided into many heads,—during a visit to the

largely endowed with caustic humour. It would be easy to compile, and perhaps not difficult to read, a chapter full of racy anecdotes and pungent sayings which bear upon these ancient clerical scandals, but the truth about the Southern clergy may with greater propriety be left to the sorrowing testimony of the best among their own number. Reports sent to the Bishop of London by his Commissaries in America, — who were carefully selected for that office on account of their talents and virtues, but who had no powers to restrain or punish their erring brethren, — tell a most deplorable story from first to last. Their statements were confirmed, and their conclusions summed up, by a favourably disposed and sympathetic spectator who watched the Episcopal Establishment from without. James Pemberton, a member of the Society of Friends, — an excellent man, and a very strong Loyalist, — wrote in 1766 that the vast increase of Presbyterians in America was due to the neglect of the rulers of the Church of England, who, to the dishonour of their profession, had little regard for the morals of the persons that they appointed to the office of clergyman.[1]

This relaxation of ecclesiastical discipline was not the only, nor the greatest, evil inflicted upon the Church of England in America by the want of resident bishops. No native-born colonist could be ordained without incurring the indefinite delays, and unspeakable discomforts, of a sea journey replete with perils which would be incredible to our generation if the record of them did not rest upon incontrovertible evidence. Of three

South in 1774 heard "a young coxcomb preach flippantly for seventeen and a half minutes" in a Charleston pulpit.

[1] The letter is quoted by President Isaac Sharpless, in his *History of Quaker Government in Pennsylvania*. An account of the Bishop's Commissaries, and their Reports, may be found in a paper by Mr Edward Eggleston, in the *Century Magazine* for May 1888 Mr. Sandford Cobb, in the second section of his sixth chapter, relates how the letters written by good American clergymen to the Society for the Propagation of the Gospel, and to the Bishop of London, abounded in references to the bad lives of many among their colleagues, and to the terribly disastrous influence on the repute and efficacy of the Church.

candidates for ordination, sent to Europe from Hebron in Connecticut, one perished on the return voyage; a second died on ship-board; while the third was taken by a hostile vessel, and spent the rest of his life in a French prison. Doctor Johnson, a citizen of the same province, a man of saintly life who had left the Independents to become an Episcopalian minister, lost a son who had sailed for England on the same errand. This, (said the bereaved father,) was the seventh precious life which had been sacrificed; most of them the flower of their country.[1] Such was indeed the case; for American youths who, in the face of immense disadvantages and discouragements, dedicated themselves to the service of the Church of England, were mostly respectable, and sometimes eminent, in character and attainments. But the difficulties of communication between the colonies and the mother-country were, in the majority of cases, prohibitive. The Church in the Southern colonies was mainly supplied from across the ocean; and clerical emigrants, who found their way to those regions, were very generally the failures of English universities, or Scotch and Irish adventurers who sought an escape from the despised and miserable lot of the usher in an eighteenth-century academy. The daily life in a tobacco-parish contained no element of that missionary work which has an attraction for men of high and enthusiastic spirit; from a very early date it had been well ascertained by Oxford and Cambridge Bachelors of Arts that a curate in England had more considerable worldly prospects than a Virginian rector and archdeacon;[2] and those prospects, far from improving, grew poorer as time advanced, and as the esteem and affection of the Provincials became estranged from their established clergy.

That clergy was remunerated in kind, and not in

---

[1] At a later period, according to Doctor Johnson, ten had been lost, out of fifty-four who had gone for ordination.

[2] Letter from Morgan Godwyn to Governor Berkeley, written about the year 1670.

money. Maryland gave an incumbent forty pounds of tobacco for every tithe-payer in the Parish, whether Churchman or Dissenter, white or coloured; and the terms were handsome enough to secure the pick of the clerical market[1] In Virginia the stipends represented a fixed and unvarying quantity, by weight, of the manufactured leaf; and those stipends, for long periods together, were wretched pittances In a bad year even the "sweet-scented parishes," where the minister's salary was calculated on a high-priced and exceptionally fragrant tobacco, yielded only about a hundred pounds sterling; and the parishioners sometimes refused to induct a clergyman unless he would consent to take one salary for serving two parishes In 1758, when the price of the staple had greatly risen, and a church-living had become a reasonable maintenance for an incumbent and his family, the House of Burgesses passed a law fixing the cash equivalent of debts payable in tobacco at one-third of their true and honest commercial value. This piece of legislation, while it did not injuriously affect a single lay creditor, struck two-thirds from the emoluments of every clergyman in the province, and that was the sole object with which it had been devised. The law was invalid, for the King in Council withheld his sanction; but the Virginian vestries at once proceeded to act upon it as though it were a part of the Constitution. The controversy was brought into Court; and a test case was tried, involving a claim on the part of a Rector for many hundred pounds of unpaid salary. The point of law was given in his favour; for no tribunal in the universe could have decided otherwise A jury was summoned to arbitrate on the amount that was due to the plaintiff; and Patrick Henry appeared on behalf of the vestrymen. He rose to his feet an obscure country lawyer, and sat down after a speech which made him

---

[1] One Maryland parish was said to be worth a thousand pounds sterling a year. In 1757 Edmund Burke praised the clergy of the colony as "the most decent, and the best, in North America."

the most celebrated of American orators. Amid a tornado of popular effervescence and exhilaration the jury assessed the damages at one penny, and the clergy had no choice but to accept that outrageous verdict as the death-blow to their cause.

It was a shabby policy, and a shuffling step in the direction of religious equality, unworthy of the reputation for chivalry and generosity which had attached itself to the Old Dominion. None the less was that scene in Hanover Court House a striking and significant contrast to some former chapters in the ecclesiastical history of Virginia. The first set of emigrants, in 1606, made careful provision for the dignity and comfort of those Episcopalian ministers who accompanied them from home. In imitation of the example, and in obedience to the specific behests, of Archbishop Laud, the authorities of the colony harried and persecuted the Puritans, and, — with perverted but indomitable courage, — continued to persecute them long after Naseby and Marston Moor had made Puritanism triumphant and all-powerful in the mother-country Under the Commonwealth those English gentry and clergy, who had suffered for Church and King, found a hospitable asylum in Virginia; and, after the Restoration, the House of Burgesses at Williamsburg vied with the Cavalier Parliament at Westminster in the severities which it inflicted upon sectaries and recusants. The Tobacco Act of 1758, — as compared with the penal statutes framed in defence of Anglicanism by the Virginian Assembly in 1661 and 1662, — affords an accurate measure of the sweeping change wrought by a century's experience of a State establishment in the feelings and inclinations of a community which once was the most Church-loving of all our colonies.[1]

The Episcopalian clergy in the Northern provinces, and more especially in Connecticut, were sincerely

[1] Instances of the signal power and popularity enjoyed in Virginia by the Church of England, during the first three-quarters of the seventeenth century, are given in the Third Appendix at the end of this volume

religious, unimpeachable in character, and of high intellectual quality. Their material circumstances were prosperous; and their social position ranked as among the very best in the land. As far back as the year 1727 both of the great colonies in which Congregationalism was the State religion, — holding out an example of equity, and right feeling, to all other established and endowed churches, — had allotted to the Episcopalian minister that portion of the tithe which was contributed by members of his own flock. The Statute went by a name unmelodious to the ears of a susceptible Anglican; for it was called "An Act for the Ease of such as soberly Dissent," but everything about it, except the title, was much to the taste, and exceedingly to the profit, of the Episcopalian Church, which included among its adherents many of the largest tithe-payers. To the Church of England, (wrote Judge Jones,) belonged the Governor, the Lieutenant-Governor, a majority of His Majesty's Council, many members of the General Assembly, and all the officers of Government, with a numerous train of rich and affluent merchants and land-owners. That was the condition of things in New York; nor was it otherwise in New England The Episcopalian clergy of Massachusetts had lived as youths in close comradeship with those, who later on in life became their leading parishioners, in the refined and rather aristocratic atmosphere of Harvard College; where, before the Revolution, the place of a student in the class was determined, not by his own proficiency in learning, but by the rank of his father, and the importance of his family. The clergy of Connecticut were mostly educated at Yale; and in both colonies the candidates for Anglican orders had used their academical opportunities with profit. Sound divines, fair scholars, and thoughtful preachers, they became conspicuous for propriety of behaviour among a society where people were in the habit of judging themselves and their neighbours by a very strict and precise standard. Such ministers as Doctor Edward

Bass, afterwards the first Bishop of Massachusetts, or
John Tyler and Roger Viets of Connecticut, would have
done honour to any Church in the world during the
best period of its corporate existence.[1]

While the Episcopalian clergy of Virginia were discredited and disliked, those in the Northern colonies
were respected, but feared; for the attitude of English
Churchmen, towards all Americans who did not belong
to their body, was in a marked degree ominous and
menacing. Jurisdiction over the Colonial Church rested
with the Bishop of London for the time being; and the
charge was a disagreeable and embarrassing supplement
to his home duties. "Sure I am," wrote one holder of
that lofty function, "that the care is improperly lodged.
For a Bishop to live at one end of the world, and his
Church at the other, must make the office very uncomfortable to the Bishop, and in a great measure useless
to the people."[2] The majority of that people, however,
would have derived small comfort or assistance from
the presence of a Father of the Church within the
borders of their colony. In 1771 a Bishop of London
told a Secretary of State, plainly and roundly, that he
could not think of accepting a position as trustee of a
local institution in America if his colleagues in that
office were what he was pleased to style " Dissenters."[3]
Those Dissenters numbered considerably over ninety
per cent. of the population resident in the province.
Among them were the Congregationalists, who belonged
to a Church that had been established by law, which in
Massachusetts the Church of England was not; but
the bench of bishops arbitrarily assumed, and openly

---

[1] Judge Jones speaks of Yale College as remarkable for its republican
principles, its intolerance in religion, and its utter aversion to Bishops
and Kings. Nevertheless Mr. Tyler, and Mr. Viets, had taken degrees
there, as well as others among the Loyalist clergy of Connecticut. The
Church of England in that colony was practically founded in 1722 by six
Congregationalists who all became Episcopalians together; and one of
their number was the President of Yale himself.

[2] The Bishop of London to Doctor Doddridge, in the year 1751.

[3] Ric. London to Lord Dartmouth; Fulham, July 9, 1771.

maintained, that any State Church, besides their own, was an imposture and a nullity, and that the levying of tithes by such a Church was a flagrant act of spoliation. A famous prelate complained bitterly from the pulpit that Episcopalians in New England were rated for the support of what the Independents, — who were, (so he frankly admitted,) the greater part of that people, — called, though without any right, the Established Church.[1] In the year 1725 the Congregational clergy had asked leave to hold a Synod in order to consult about measures for confirming and quickening the faith of the Gospel in the province of Massachusetts Bay. When the expression of their desire reached London, the Cabinet, indoctrinated by London's bishop, angrily rejected the proposal on the ground that it would form "a bad precedent for Dissenters." At that time the capital of Massachusetts contained a solitary English church, which was as much a Nonconformist place of worship as Doctor Doddridge's chapel at Northampton, or Doctor Lardner's lecture-hall in the Old Jewry. "In the English view," (it has been aptly said,) "the allowance of one Episcopal church in Boston turned the Established Church of Massachusetts into a congregation of Dissenters."[2]

The Episcopal Church, at home and abroad, owed much to a man whose inspiriting influence, and rare practical talent, have earned him a place among the

---

[1] Sermon preached by Bishop Secker before the Propagation Society in the Parish Church of St. Mary-le-Bow, February 20, 1740-1

[2] *History of Religious Liberty*, chapter v., section 11. A powerful letter, written by John Adams in 1815, gives an interesting account of the state of religion throughout America anterior to 1775, and explains its intimate relation to the events of the Revolution. With regard to Massachusetts he notices "the spirit, the temper, the views, designs, intrigues, and arbitrary exertions of power displayed by the Church of England at that time towards the Dissenters, as they were contemptuously called, though in reality the Churchmen were the real Dissenters. . . . The truth is that the Congregationalists, the Presbyterians, the Anabaptists, the Methodists, or even the Quakers or Moravians, were each of them as numerous as the Churchmen , several of them immensely more numerous , and all of them together more than fifteen to one."

great religious organisers of the world. Towards the beginning of the eighteenth century Doctor Thomas Bray, — shocked and saddened by the stories of spiritual destitution, and clerical inefficiency, which arrived from across the ocean, — declined the offer of valuable benefices in England, sold all the goods that he possessed there, and sailed for America invested with the thankless office of Commissary to the Bishop of London in Maryland. Bray's services to the Church of his devotion extended far beyond the boundaries of the colony to which he was accredited; for he conceived the idea, and designed and constructed the machinery, of the Society for Promoting Christian Knowledge, and the Society for the Propagation of the Gospel in Foreign Parts. Those sagacious and earnest men, who guided the counsels and disbursed the resources of the last-named Association, laboured successfully to infuse vigour and purity into the Episcopalian Churches of America.[1] The rise and spread of Anglicanism in Connecticut was due to their inspiration. Their missionaries, — chosen with care and on the spot, — exhibited an example which awakened the conscience, and stirred the zeal, of the better-intentioned among the parish clergy of the Southern provinces, and shamed the undeserving into decency of conduct, and their agents were the first to undertake, in any systematic way, the religious and the secular instruction of negro slaves. But this excellent corporation, under another aspect, was not blameless. Some of their clerical emissaries refused to work with, and not unfrequently or unwillingly worked against, those other religious denominations which already covered so large a field in the American colonies; and, above all, the annual meeting of the Society in London was an occasion

---

[1] A letter to the Propagation Society, despatched in 1705, deplores the hostility evinced towards the English Church by the Puritans of Massachusetts. "They fail not to improve every little thing against us. But, (I bless God for it,) the Society have robbed them of their best argument, which was the ill lives of our clergy that came into these parts And, the truth is, I have not seen many good men but of the Society's sending."

when Christianity did not habitually display a gracious and inviting countenance The central event of these periodical gatherings consisted in a sermon from a bishop, who too often consumed much of his time, and almost all of his fervour and unction, in contending that no Gospel ought to be propagated except that which was taught by Anglican divines Sometimes the preacher broadly and bluntly animadverted upon the doctrinal tenets and political tendencies of those whom, before that audience, he boldly and safely characterised as "the American Nonconformists;" but these direct attacks were less irritating, and incomparably less alarming, to New England public opinion than were the studied reticences of abler and more artful orators. A favourite method with the preacher of the Anniversary Discourse was to represent the whole American community, outside the circuit of the Anglican Church, as unbroken ground for religious propagandism and missionary enterprise; to describe the settlers as having relapsed into a condition of heathendom ever since they had deserted the ritual of their forefathers; and coldly, calmly, and deliberately to ignore the ecclesiastical existence of those Presbyterians, Independents, and Baptists who constituted the vast majority of the colonial population

Such a sermon, never forgotten or pardoned by those against whom its implied censures were aimed, was delivered by Secker, then Bishop of Oxford, in the year 1742 A notable passage in that discourse solemnly lamented that many of the early emigrants to America carried but little of Christianity abroad with them, while a great part of the rest had suffered it to wear out gradually, until in some provinces there were scarce any footsteps of it left beyond the mere name. In those districts no religious assembly was held, the Lord's day was distinguished from the remainder of the week only by more unbridled indulgence in vice and dissipation, and the Sacrament of Baptism had not been administered for near twenty years, nor that of the Lord's Supper for fifty. Such, (ejaculated the bishop,) was the state of things in more of our colonies than one; and, "where it was a little better, it was lamentably bad" The sermon was published in America, and read, — with what feelings and faces it is not hard to imagine, — by the Deacon and the Elders in many a strictly ordered New Hampshire and Massachusetts parish. The same line of unwarranted assertion, and uncharitable insinuation, was adopted by the Bishop of Gloucester in 1766, and by the Bishop of Llandaff in 1767. That was a time when the friendship between America and Great Britain had already, from other causes, been so seriously disturbed that a true patriot, (not to say a good Christian,) should have been scrupulously watchful to guard and moderate his utterances

Regularly as the year came round, the leaders of the principal Churches in America protested, before Heaven and man, against the injustice of denouncing their nation as, in the main, a depraved and unbelieving people. Doctor Chauncey of Boston eloquently complained that the colonists were accused of having abandoned their native religion together with their parent soil, and of living without remembrance or knowledge of God, without any Divine worship, in dissolute wickedness and the most brutal profligacy of manners. They had sometimes, (wrote the Doctor,) been blamed for having too much religion; but never, except by English prelates, for having no religion at all.[1] Men recalled to each other's memory how Archbishop Laud, in a well-known phrase, had declared that he "could find no religion" in

---

[1] "A letter to a Friend, containing Remarks on certain Passages in a Sermon, preached by the Right Rev^d. John Bishop of Llandaff, before the Incorporated Society for the Propagation of the Gospel in Foreign Parts, at the Anniversary Meeting in the Parish Church of St. Mary le Bow, London, Feb. 20, 1767, in which the highest Reproach is undeservedly cast upon the American Colonies By Charles Chauncey, D D, Pastor of the First Church of Christ in Boston." As also "A Letter to the Right Reverend Father in God, John Lord Bishop of Llandaff, occasioned by some Passages in his Lordship's Sermon, in which the American Colonies are loaded with great and undeserved Reproach; by William Livingston of New York"

Scotland, — at a period in history when, in the country which had produced John Knox and Andrew Melville, it was difficult for an unprejudiced observer to find anything else.   Hardly less disdainful, on the eve of the Revolution in America, was the behaviour of English bishops towards every Church on that continent save and except their own   They were actuated, (so Congregationalists and Presbyterians sincerely believed,) by Laud's spirit; and, if ever they had the power and the opportunity, they would be only too eager to revive Laud's policy.

These mutual jealousies and suspicions had long ago been concentrated over the question of planting a bishop in America.   The suggestion was heartily favoured by Churchmen in every colony abroad, and in the palace of every diocese in England.   Archbishop Tenison, and Sir John Trelawney the Bishop of Winchester, had left a thousand pounds apiece towards the foundation and equipment of a Transatlantic see.   Secker bequeathed a like sum ;   and a substantial legacy was devised by a Lady of great family, who yet was "incomparably more eminent for her Virtues than her Quality."   In the year 1697 a worthy Virginian divine exclaimed that, on the day when a Bishop landed in America, he would say, with Saint Bernard in his Epistle, that the finger of God was in it.   Commissary Bray of Maryland, and Commissary Blair of Virginia, — who were the mainstay and ornament of the Anglican Church in their respective provinces, — had been instant with the Government at home to take steps for making Episcopacy in America a living reality ;   and their clerical colleagues and successors were universally of the same mind.   The cry was swelled by the voices of lay partisans, some of whom did not know the difference between Presbyterians and Congregationalists, but who abominated both sects equally on account of the length of their sermons, the soberness of their manners, and the severity of their morals.   In that way of thinking was Alexander

Macrabie, the brother-in-law and correspondent of Philip Francis. "Oh! Do let us have a bishop!" (Macrabie wrote in 1769). "Our clergy are quarrelling like dog and bear; and I fear the Presbytery get the better." "The Presbyterians," he said elsewhere, "should not be allowed to become too great. They are of republican principles. The Bostonians are Presbyterians."[1]

Anglicans, — good men, or less good, alike, — were for the appointment of a bishop; but that proposal was keenly resented by the mass of the American people. The colonists had no desire to oppress or starve the English Church within their borders, as the adoption of the Five Mile Act by Massachusetts and Connecticut unanswerably proved. Nor had they in principle any objection to a bishop as the adviser, the overseer, and the spiritual guide of his own clergy; but they would have none of him in the character of a State functionary. Reading the future by the past, all the great Evangelical organisations of America regarded the Anglican Church as an aggressive power. Within no very distant memory, Episcopalians had annexed New York and New Jersey, Georgia and Maryland. In those colonies where Congregationalism was established they received, without any sign of gratitude, their share of all the taxes imposed for purposes of religion; but in Virginia and the Carolinas they kept the whole of those taxes for themselves. While religious persecution was dying out elsewhere, Baptists were still being punished for preaching in a colony where the English Church held sway. In the public assemblies of that Church, and in its printed literature, nine out of ten Americans were classified as schismatics; and it was impossible to contemplate without uneasiness a state of things under which the strategical operations of Anglicanism in

[1] This gentleman, — who apparently was ignorant that the Established Church in Boston was Congregationalist, — hated Presbyterians because they had made one of his friends do public penance for gross profligacy; "and the fellow," said Macrabie, "was worth upwards of ten thousand pounds!"

America would be directed by a bishop, quartered on the scene of action, possessing the ear of the Royal Governors, and backed by all the power and authority of Great Britain whenever a Ministry with Anglican proclivities was installed at Downing Street. There would be an end thenceforward to comfortable and friendly relations between neighbours and kinsmen who professed different creeds. Each colony would be divided into two hostile camps; and all other religious bodies would have to be perpetually on the watch against the assaults and inroads of a Church which could never keep herself contented and tranquil until her own faith became recognised as the State religion. In their opposition to the introduction of a bishop, the American people may be said to have anticipated the Monroe doctrine, and to have applied it to ecclesiastical affairs. John Adams,—looking back to the early Revolutionary period across a space of fifty years,—pronounced it to be a fact, as certain as any in the history of North America, that the apprehension of Episcopacy, as much as any other cause, aroused the attention, not only of the inquiring mind, but of the common people, and urged them to "close thinking on the constitutional authority of Parliament over the colonies." [1]

Dislike and dread of Episcopacy intensified American opposition to the fiscal policy of Parliament; and the Non-Importation Agreement, in the all but unanimous view of its promoters, held good against bishops as well as against all other British products. When the Stamp Act, and afterwards the tea-duty, had inflamed New England,—and when London was in a roar with rioting for Wilkes and Liberty,—the Cabinet would have been pleased if religious differences in the colonies had been permitted to sleep The bishops, (Franklin

---

[1] Ex-President Adams to Doctor Jedediah Morse; Quincy, December 2, 1815 The letter is one of a series of seven, which together form a most interesting and instructive historical retrospect, perfectly marvellous as coming from the pen of a man of eighty. It may well be doubted whether there is any other known instance of intellectual vigour preserved, unimpaired and unmodified, to such an advanced age

wrote,) were very desirous of effecting the enlargement
of the Church of England in America, by sending one
of their number thither; but the Government was pru-
dently deaf to their solicitations.[1]   While, however,
the King and his ministers possessed the means of
keeping live diocesans in order, they had no hold on
the dead, and it was from the grave that their troubles
came   Secker died in July 1768, after having been
Primate of All England for ten years; and a twelvemonth subsequently there appeared "A Letter written
January 9, 1750, by the Right Reverend Thomas
Secker, Lord Bishop of Oxford, concerning Bishops in
America; Printed for J. and F Rivington at the Bible
and the Crown in Saint Paul's Churchyard." Whatever the publication of that letter may have done for
the Bible, it was a very bad stroke indeed for the Crown.
It was understood that, soon after he was settled at
Lambeth, the Archbishop had written in his own hand
directions for printing and circulating the document as
his posthumous message to the world.   His proposals
were extremely moderate, equitable in intention, and
put forward in guarded language;[2] but they at once
excited in the colonies an acute and violent controversy,
in which the memory of the departed prelate was not
spared.   The situation was aggravated by the clumsy
wording of a Memorial which the English clergy of
New York and New Jersey addressed to the Govern-

[1] Benjamin Franklin to John Ross; London, May 14, 1768   In July
of the same year Mr Hollis wrote from England, "There is great reason
to believe that the scheme for bishoping America has been dropped, most
wisely, by the civil ministers here for some months"

[2] Archbishop Secker was quite sincere, if sometimes rather unhandy,
in his desire to conciliate the prevalent religious opinion of America. He
was an ardent Protestant, who acknowledged Protestants of all sects and
churches as his allies, and who lived with prominent Nonconformists, (such
as Doddridge and Chandler, Leland, Lardner, and Watts,) on terms of genial
civility, and, in some cases, of steady friendship   Thomas Hollis of Dorset-
shire, the antiquary and virtuoso, — who was an admiring and confidential
correspondent of Jonathan Mayhew, and a lifelong enemy to sacerdotal
claims, — gave Secker, as a testimony of esteem, "a head of Socrates
engraved on green jasper, and set in gold as a seal, which cost Mr Hollis
six guineas."

ment in London, praying for a bishop, but disclaiming
all wish that he should exercise any jurisdiction over
" Dissenters, or abridge the ample Toleration " which
those Dissenters at present enjoyed. That a denomination, whose members were in a very small minority,
should tell the other fourteen-fifteenths of the population that they might continue to be tolerated, was
regarded as a piece of gratuitous presumption by Presbyterians and Congregationalists. A humiliating and
precarious dole of immunity from actual persecution
was not the sort of religious liberty in quest of which
their forefathers had crossed the ocean.

Edmund Burke, who knew his subject, warned the
House of Commons that the adversaries of Episco-
palianism in America were not a feeble folk   The prevalent religion, (he said,) in our Northern colonies was
a refinement on the principle of Resistance ; under a
variety of denominations it agreed in nothing but in a
communion of the spirit of liberty ; it was the Dissi-
dence of Dissent, and the Protestantism of the Protestant
religion.   Those words were very finely, and most
appropriately, chosen.   All along the Western frontier
lived Irish Presbyterians of Scottish descent ; skilful and
truculent Indian fighters ; men of warlike traditions,
and with very long memories indeed.   Their great-grand-
fathers had borne the brunt of the struggle against
James the Second and Tyrconnell at Londonderry
and Enniskillen ; and, when the peril was over, they
had, as their reward, been driven from their Ulster
homes in scores of thousands by that savage and inquisitorial Test Act which the bishops of the Established
Church, who disliked Nonconformists at least as much
as they feared Roman Catholics, had insisted on obtain-
ing from the Irish Parliament.   The central colonies
held many Huguenot families, whose ancestors, the
salt and leaven of the French nation, had escaped into
exile from the senile bigotry and inhumanity of Louis the
Fourteenth , and the Revocation of the Edict of Nantes,
(although great Court ladies had something to say

towards it,) was mainly attributed to Episcopal inspiration.[1] Far more numerous than Huguenots or Irish
Presbyterians, and to the full as well provided with
reasons for an hereditary distrust of bishops,[2] were the
sons of the old English Puritans; most of whom, in
creed, in temper, and in the usages of their daily life,
might still be accounted as Puritans themselves. Their
spokesman and fugleman in ecclesiastical polemics had
till very lately been Jonathan Mayhew, minister of the
West Church in Boston; a noble preacher and writer,
whose earnestness of purpose, and lofty sweep of
thought, kept in subordination, (but not always,) his
flashing and scorching wit, and vivified his abundant
stores of learning.

Mayhew was no longer alive; for that sharp sword
early wore through the scabbard; but public opinion in
New England was more than ever imbued, and public
action dictated, by his audacious spirit. The denunciations of Episcopacy and arbitrary government, which
he had thundered forth from his pulpit, were still the
favourite reading of a serious-minded and angry people;
and his influence may be traced in Whig sermons and
pamphlets during the whole period that elapsed, from
the closing of Boston Port, to the firing of the volley
on Lexington Common. In a celebrated discourse of
the year 1763 he had bidden his congregation to reflect
upon all that their forefathers suffered from bishops.

[1] "Of seven men, who acted as presiding officer over the deliberations
of Congress during the Revolutionary period, three were of Huguenot
parentage . Laurens, Boudinot, and Jay." *The Homes of American
Statesmen,* by Elbert Hubbard; New York and London, 1898

[2] Many of the American Puritans, or most of them, had not been
Nonconformists at home. John Winthrop, the first and best of Massachusetts Governors, wrote thus in a farewell letter when his ship was
about to sail "Take notice that the principals and body of our company
esteem it our honour to call the Church of England, from whence wee
rise, our deare mother, and cannot part from our native country, where
she specially resideth, without much sadness of heart, and many tears in
our eyes." Those were the sort of people hundreds of thousands of whom
more than now, but for Laud and his coadjutors, would be in the Church
of England to-day.

Would "the mitred, lordly successors of the fishermen of Galilee," (he asked,) "never let us rest in peace, except where all the weary are at rest? Was it not enough that they had persecuted us out of the Old World? Would they now pursue us into the New, compassing sea and land to make us proselytes? What other sanctuary from their oppressions would be left us, if once these colonies were added to their domain? Where was the Columbus to explore for us another America, and pilot us to its shores, before we are consumed by the flames, or deluged in a flood, of Episcopacy?" Mayhew traced the origin of his political and his ecclesiastical creed to the prose works of John Milton; nor was the surge of his eloquence, or the furious, and sometimes turbid, current of his invective, unworthy of the source from which his doctrine had been drawn. The vehemence of language employed by such men at such epochs, — surprising, and even shocking, to a cool and impartial posterity, — has a prime historical value as illustrating the inner mind of those among their contemporaries and fellow-citizens who listened to such high-pitched and scathing rhetoric with unreserved conviction and enthusiastic approval.[1]

The stormy aspect of politics did not intimidate the Anglican clergy of the colonies into letting their demand for a bishop drop. Doctor John Vardill of New York wrote to Lord Dartmouth that the equity and utility of such a measure seemed no longer doubtful, and that the only question now was whether an imme-

[1] Another of Mayhew's sermons, (which John Adams placed on a level of satire and irony with the productions of Swift and Franklin,) was the Discourse concerning Unlimited Submission, preached on the Sunday immediately after the Thirtieth of January, 1750. Mayhew there laid it down as his opinion that the commemoration of the death of Charles the First would have at least one good result, if it should "prove a standing memento that Britons will not be slaves, and a warning to all corrupt councillors and ministers not to go too far in advising arbitrary despotic measures." The time came when such a memento had its uses; but it was not needed while old George the Second was King, and still less when Chatham became his minister.

diate appointment would be seasonable.[1]   His letter
was dated the First of September, 1774; the precise
day when General Gage seized the powder of the
Massachusetts militia, and when the freeholders of the
province marched into Cambridge many thousand strong
in order to show the Royal Governor that he had better
not try their patience again, as there was a very scanty
supply of it remaining.   And then, after no long interval, the fateful moment arrived when

> " The war of tongue and pen
> Learns with what deadly purpose it was fraught,
> And, helpless in the fiery passion caught,
> Shakes all the pillared State with shock of men."

An historian of rare philosophical insight, and unsur-
passed range of reading over all the period which he
treats, has analysed the nature of the moral convulsion
which was produced in the national mind of America
by the outbreak of hostilities between King George's
troops and the minute-men.   "As the news," (so the
passage runs,) "travelled from man to man, on white
lips, up and down the country, all at once on each
group of listeners there seemed to come a spiritual
revolution;" an instantaneous conviction that henceforward all questions of stamps, and paints, and glass,
and tea, — all fine-drawn constitutional arguments about
the Right of Representation and the Right of Petition,
— were already things of a dead past   Americans
found themselves confronted of a sudden by terribly
grave, and in no sense metaphysical, problems relating
to their necks and fortunes, the inviolability of their
homes, and the security of their families.[2]   Every one,
from that moment onward, would have to fight for
whatever, as a private man, he held dearest; and the

---

[1] Before the end of the year Doctor Vardill embarked for England,
"wrote some poetical satires on the Whigs," and eventually closed his
career in a Lincolnshire Rectory.   That was a normal biography for an
Episcopalian clergyman of the American Revolution

[2] Professor Tyler's *Literary History;* Vol. I., chapter xix., section iii.

clergy of the great Evangelical Churches throughout the continent believed that something was at stake which they valued more highly than all their material possessions together. There was not a single instance in history, (said one of them,) in which civil liberty was lost, and religious liberty preserved entire, so that, if the colonists accepted political subjugation, they would at the same time deliver their conscience into bondage. Such was the view of Doctor John Witherspoon, the President of Princeton College, whose library the Hessians ransacked; and that persuasion was almost universally entertained by Presbyterian, Baptist, and Congregational ministers. At the first call to arms they flung themselves into the cause of the Revolution, zealously, uncompromisingly, and with most visible, and even decisive, consequences. In America, (according to one Loyalist writer,) as in the Great Rebellion of England, much execution was done by sermons. "What effect," said another, "must it have had upon the audience to hear the same sentiments and principles, which they had before read in a newspaper, delivered on Sundays from the sacred desk, with a religious awe, and the most solemn appeals to heaven, from lips which they had been taught from their cradles to believe could utter nothing but eternal truths!"

So long as the war endured there was no lack of stated and special occasions for bringing clerical influence to bear. Full advantage was taken of Fast-days, Thanksgiving-days, Election-days, and the anniversaries of battles and of other momentous events which had occurred during the progress of the struggle.[1] In perilous emergencies prayers were ordered throughout the Confederacy for deliverance from the hand of the enemy, for a plentiful harvest which would enable those, who gathered in the crops at home, to supply the needs of their brethren in the army; and,—always and above all,—for genuine and heart-felt repentance of those sins that had brought down God's wrath upon the commu-

[1] Tyler's *History*, Vol. II., chapter xxxv., section 1.

nity. From time to time some Church Synod would
address to its congregations a Pastoral Letter setting
forth, and enforcing, the whole duty of man in time of
war and civil dissension   The Societies were admon-
ished and adjured to maintain the union between the
colonies; to respect Congress, and those delegates who
had been freely chosen by the people; to observe a
spirit of candour, charity, and mutual esteem towards
members of other religious denominations; to discourage profligacy and extravagance , to defend public
order; and, (as in many places legal proceedings had
been unavoidably suspended,) to see that just debts
were promptly and honestly paid.   Whatever other
advice the letter might contain, it began and ended with
a reminder that no man could be a true servant of the
nation, whose private conduct was not regulated by the
Divine law; or a good soldier, unless he fought and
conquered what was evil in himself.[1]

The sincerity of these exhortations was attested by
a general movement for the reformation of manners,
even where they had not been very bad before.   In the
Southern and Central colonies theatrical entertainments
had long enjoyed a popularity which scandalised the
Pennsylvanian Quakers, whom enterprising managers
vainly essayed to conciliate by advertising their come-
dies and tragedies as a series of Moral Dialogues in
five parts.   The Northern provinces, as a rule, kept the
drama rigidly outside their confines; but New England
had her own dissipations.   The company at a funeral
was served with meat and drink; though with a great
deal less of the latter than in Virginia and the Carolinas
Seven hundred, a thousand, and so many as three

---

[1] The *American Archives* give a fine specimen of such a document in
a Pastoral Letter from the Synod of New York and Philadelphia to the
Congregations under their care, to be delivered from the Pulpit on the 20th
of July, 1775. The outbreak of a war, (it is there said,) should be regarded
as " the proper time for pressing all of every rank to consider the things
that belong to their eternal peace.   There is nothing more awful to think
of than that those, whose trade is war, should be despisers of the name of
the Lord of Hosts."

thousand, pairs of gloves had been distributed on such occasions; and the worth of the mourning-rings and silken scarves, which fell to the share of a leading Boston clergyman, constituted a valuable augmentation of his yearly income. Volleys were fired over the graves of distinguished citizens, to the consumption, in one case, of a barrel and a half of powder. But, on and after the nineteenth of April, 1775, all the procurable saltpetre was husbanded for a more urgent purpose, and before that date the First Continental Congress had already pledged every patriot to refrain from expensive articles of adornment at burials, and to shun and discountenance horse-racing, and all kinds of gaming, cock-fighting, exhibitions of shows, plays, and other diversions. If the prohibition of theatrical performances had been enacted by law, (it has been acutely said,) a loophole might have been discovered in the Statute; "but the manager, who should have disregarded the expressed wish of Congress at this time, would have looked the lightning in the face. The actors sailed for the West Indies; to return Northward, like migratory birds of song, when storms should have blown over." [1]

The corporate and collective action of the American clergy was a mighty force in politics; but the influence of the individual minister must be accounted as more important still. That influence, though dependent on the esteem and personal regard felt towards him by his neighbours, was almost absolute in spiritual matters, and not seldom extended over every department of daily life. In the farmhouses which lay within a long walk, or leisurely drive, of his residence, the pastor was a welcome guest whenever the shadow of his great hat

[1] Article on *Social Life in the Colonies*, by the Rev[d]. Edward Eggleston, 1884. During the outburst of feeling against the Stamp Act in 1765, the New York mob, ascetic beyond its wont, pulled down a theatre

The New England Puritans felt and acted like their forefathers when in much the same stress of peril. In 1642, three weeks before Edgehill, the Houses voted that public sports did not agree well with public calamities; and that while sad causes, and set times of humiliation, continued, stage-plays should cease and be forborne.

darkened the threshold. There he would sit, sipping the decoction of sassafras which did duty for tea in a strict patriotic household ; asking affectionately after the son who was serving with his regiment ; smiling gravely at the portrait of King George as it hung head downwards on the wall; reading out, with vigorous comments, the latest news from Congress, and from the Canadian border ; and dropping some uncomplimentary epithet with reference to any Cabinet minister whose name came up in the conversation, save and except the good Lord Dartmouth His more remote parishioners lived in the light of his countenance at least on one day in every week, and all that day long. When the Sunday came, they flocked into the chief settlement of the Township from forest-clearings and upland hamlets, and spent the interval between the Services before the great fire-place in the minister's kitchen, or in the Sabbath-houses and noon-houses which dotted the village green These humble caravanseries provided a stable at the back of the building, and a roughly furnished parlour where the families from a distance ate their cold viands, and in quieter times talked over the sermon, or listened to the reading aloud of an edifying book;[1] but during the Revolution there was, in one notable respect, no restraint upon their talk; inasmuch as it was clearly understood, by all concerned, that the war ranked as a Sunday topic.

Inside the church, fervent, and perpetually varied, prayers for the temporal welfare of the nation, and for the protection of those friends and kinsmen who were under arms in the fore-front of peril, excited warmer emotions than are ordinarily evoked by the weekly repetition of the words set down in the Episcopalian Liturgy for use in time of War and Tumults. Allusions to those public hopes and fears, that filled every heart, kept the sermon alive from the giving out of the text to the valedictory sentence, which was often very long in

[1] Article on *Church and Meeting-house before the Revolution* by the Rev[d]. Edward Eggleston, D.D., April 1887.

coming [1] A preacher, who fell short of what was expected of him as a good citizen, soon received a hint that
his people were displeased and disappointed , [2] but there
were few of their profession who needed spurring ; and,
if any of them hung back for a while, their hesitation
disappeared as soon as muskets had been discharged
in anger.   That clergyman who, on the afternoon of
Lexington, at the head of his parishioners attacked
and captured a provision convoy in the rear of Lord
Percy's column, had been refused the use of a Whig
pulpit because he was suspected of being lukewarm in
the colonial cause ; but his Toryism lasted no longer
than the moment when the red-coats passed in front of
his window on their march to Concord.   There stood
lately, and perhaps now stands, a quaint stone and
brick meeting-house at Rocky Spring in the Cumberland Valley, where, at a certain point in a discourse,
the Presbyterian congregation of Scottish-Irishmen rose
to their feet, and declared their readiness to march at
once to the aid of General Washington.   One of the
mothers, who grudged her son as food for powder at so
short a notice, then and there protested in homely and
cutting phrases ; — a remonstrance to which the preacher
replied by marching with his people as their captain ;
and a very good captain he made. [3]

The ministers, however, who abode in their parsonages
did much more for the Revolution than if they had gone

[1] "Wee have a strong weakness in that, when wee are speaking, wee
know not how to conclude. Wee make many ends before wee make an
end." So wrote, in 1641, the Reverend Nathaniel Ward, author of *The
Simple Cobbler of Aggawam in America* , and the confession still held
good in the fourth generation of New England preachers

[2] Shortly after the battle of Bunker's Hill John Adams wrote to his
wife, inquiring whether a certain clergyman preached against oppression,
and bidding her tell him that the clergy in Philadelphia thundered and
lightened every Sabbath. "They pray for Boston and the Massachusetts.
They thank God most explicitly and fervently for our remarkable successes
They pray for the American army."

[3] "Quit talking, Mr. Craighead," (she said,) "and gang yersel' to the
war. You are always preaching to the boys about it, but I dinna think
ye'd be very likely to gang yersel'. Just go and try it !" Article on the
Country Church in America by William B Bigelow , November 1897.

off in a body to the war.   A new Government, — with a
volunteer army, and a loosely organised political constitution, - - was immeasurably strengthened by the circumstance that at least one person of good education, and
long-established authority, who was at the same time a
keen and indefatigable champion of the popular party,
was planted in every town, and in most of the larger
villages.   The clergy made it their business to see that
staunch patriots, and shrewd men of affairs, were returned to Congress ; that war taxes were generously
voted, and conscientiously paid; that the ranks of the
local Company were replenished with recruits ; and that
whoever had once enlisted should stay with the colours
until his time was up.   A farming lad who tired of cam-
paigning, and was tempted to return home without leave,
knew well that, — even if his sweet-heart forgave him,
and his father was secretly glad to have him back for
the hay-harvest, — he should never dare to face the minister   From first to last, in each district throughout the
continent, there was a leader and adviser always at hand
to encourage those who were more timorous, and less constant, than himself ; whether amid the doubts and mis-
givings of the crucial period when men were first taking
sides, or in the terror and anxiety consequent upon the
early disasters of the Republic, or throughout that fit of
utter weariness which settled down upon the public mind
during the later stages of the lingering struggle.   There
was no exaggeration whatever in the report made to
Lord Dartmouth by his principal American correspondent.   Religion, (this gentleman wrote,) had operated as
much as any other cause to the general distraction ; and
his Lordship would be greatly mistaken unless he regarded the conflict as mainly a religious war.[1]

The Episcopalian clergy of America were not so universally Tory as the Presbyterian and Congregational

---

[1] Ambrose Serle to Lord Dartmouth ; New York, November 1776.
"Your Lordship," (Mr. Serle wrote shortly afterwards,) "can scarcely
conceive what Fury the discourses of some preachers have created in this
country."

ministers were Whig;[1] but those of them, who stood
for the Crown, formed a large majority among their
brethren; and they were very hot partisans indeed   For
the most part they confidently believed that the hour
had come, late in time, when Archbishop Laud's plan
for securing Church government in the colonies might
be successfully adopted.   That prelate, in 1638, had
proposed to send a Bishop across the ocean, and to support him "with some forces to compel, if he could not
otherwise persuade, obedience."   Early in the war a
missionary of the Propagation Society, who had recently
left New York, reported at the Annual Meeting in London that the rebellion would undoubtedly be crushed,
and that then would be the time to take steps for
increasing the Church in America by granting it an
Episcopacy; but after the battle of Trenton, and the
collapse of Howe's campaign, the prospect of that consummation was removed into a less near future   There
was, however, one portion of the American population
already at the absolute disposal of the British Government; and, in their treatment of those unlucky people,
the royal authorities prematurely showed their hand.
The commander of a garrison town where many officers
·of the Revolutionary army, who had been taken in battles, were living on parole, announced himself as having
been informed that the rebel prisoners had held private
meetings for the purpose of performing Divine Service
agreeably to their religious principles.   Such meetings,
(he told them,) would no longer be allowed, but seats
would be provided at the Parish Church, where it was
expected that they would observe the utmost decency.
One of the most esteemed among the prisoners replied
in an address not deficient in dignity and pathos; but
the policy was maintained, and the Americans who had
been captured at Long Island and Fort Washington
were given the choice of abstaining from all attendance

[1] In Garden's *Anecdotes* it is alleged that no fewer than five-and-twenty
clergymen of the Carolinian Established Church were in favour of the
Revolution; but the statement requires confirmation.

on public worship, or of taking part in prayers for the slaughter and discomfiture of their own friends and comrades.[1]

While the Episcopalian Church reigned supreme in all districts over which the Royal standard floated, outside the British lines it nowhere remained dominant, and in many places it very soon became a persecuted body. The Anglican Establishment in the Southern Plantations went down beneath the first gust of the tornado. Ecclesiastical endowments and privileges were extinguished as automatically, instantly, and irrevocably as Feudal dues and services disappeared throughout rural France so soon as the peasants learned that the Bastille had fallen. Moreover, in July 1775, the Virginian Convention ordained certain alterations in the Communion service, and in the fifteenth, and the three following sentences, of the Litany. All mention of the King and the Royal Family was to be expunged from the Prayer-book; and the blessings of Heaven were thenceforward to be invoked on behalf "of the Magistrates of this Commonwealth." It was as drastic a test as the command laid upon primitive Christians to burn frankincense on Jupiter's altar; and it was encountered with almost as much courage and devotion.

Soon after Washington assumed command in New York, he sent word to Doctor Inglis, then Assistant Rector of the Trinity Church in that city, that he

---

[1] It was an action, (so the remonstrance ran,) "totally unworthy of the Christian character, and even short of Heathen tenderness and forbearance. For we read in Scripture that Paul, then a prisoner in Rome, dwelt for two years in his own hired house, and relieved all that came unto him, preaching the Kingdom of God, and teaching those things which concern the Lord Jesus Christ, with all confidence; *no man forbidding him.* This only was our desire; and this we think was our duty. . . . Can it be expected that we could, with the least sincerity, join in prayer for the daily destruction of our brethren? Rather than join in such hypocritical petitions, and perhaps be insulted with sermons calculated to affront us, we have resolved to refuse our attendance on Divine worship, and at our own dwellings silently to spend our returning Sabbaths, in the best manner we can, by reading and meditation, until it shall please the Almighty to restore us again to peace, and to our afflicted families and friends."

would be glad to have the prayers for the King and the Royal Family omitted. The American General was sincerely desirous to be present at the services of his own Church ; but a person of even less ingrained veracity than George Washington would have scrupled to join in supplications for the victory of a monarch against whom he had set in line of battle twenty thousand soldiers, carrying pouches filled with bullets which had been cast from the metal of His Majesty's statue. Doctor Inglis, at the time, took no notice of the General's message, and not long afterwards told him plainly, and to his face, that, with an armed force at his disposal, he could, of course, shut up churches, but that it was beyond his power to make clergymen depart from their duty. The Reverend Jacob Bailey was summoned before a Provincial Committee of Safety, to explain why he refused to read the Declaration of Independence in public. Bailey, — who was an itinerant missionary, married, and with a young family, — replied that he had formerly taken an oath of allegiance to George the Second, and held himself bound thereby not to renounce, but to pray for, George the Third. During the first six months of 1775 the Reverend Jonathan Boucher, of Annapolis in Maryland, always preached with a pair of loaded pistols lying on the cushion in front of him ; and indeed, with no aid from fire-arms, he was well known to be more than a match for any single member of his congregation.[1] But, though valiant, he was not foolhardy ; and the day came when he solemnly and sadly told his people from the pulpit that they would see his face there no more, but that, as long as he lived, he should cry, with Zadok the priest and Nathan the prophet, "God save the King"

---

[1] Some cowardly fellows set a burly ruffian of a blacksmith upon Mr. Boucher The rector at once knocked down his assailant ; but took neither pride nor pleasure in the achievement. He somewhat plaintively and shamefacedly described himself as having acquired, in all that region, greater honour by his act of prowess than would have been accorded to him there if he had possessed the brain of Isaac Newton

That was Jonathan Boucher's farewell sermon at Annapolis. With more or less outrage and insult the stalwart Loyalists among the English clergy were driven from their churches.[1] One or two admirable men, disarming rancour by meekness, remained at their posts, and did as much of their duty, as the Sons of Liberty permitted, with fidelity and rare discretion. The Reverend John Wiswald, of Falmouth in Maine, continued to serve his parish until one of King George's post-captains burned down the little town, and the English church with it. The Reverend John Sayre, of Fairfield in Connecticut, was sadly harried and oppressed by the Whigs of the vicinity; but his patient manliness at length shamed them into forbearance. During several years he continued to officiate on Sundays, reading the Bible and the Homilies, but none of the Prayer-book; because, since he was forbidden to use the Liturgy in its entirety, he could not find it with his conscience to mutilate it. Half-way through the war Governor Tryon, on one of his customary raids, set fire to the town of Fairfield. The flames spread to the English church and the parsonage; the Communion plate was destroyed, as well as a valuable little library given by the Society for the Propagation of the Gospel; and Mr. Sayre was left with "a wife, and eight children, destitute of food, house, and raiment."[2]

Such experiences, in the end, proved too strong even for the most zealous and long-suffering of mankind.

---

[1] There were parishes where the assertion of the popular will was made decently and in order, but to the full as efficaciously as in those where the extreme of violence was employed In August, 1774, the Curate of St. Michael's, in Charleston, preached a political discourse "Every silly clown," he said, "and every illiterate mechanic, will take upon him to censure the conduct of his Prince or Governor, and will contribute, as much as in him lies, to create and foment misunderstandings which come at last to schisms in the Church, and sedition and rebellion in the State." The Vestry of St. Michael's took official cognisance of the sermon, and dismissed the Curate.

[2] Letter addressed by the Reverend John Sayre, towards the close of 1779, to the Society for the Propagation of the Gospel.

Episcopalian churches were silent and deserted;[1] and the wisest and best of the Loyalist Episcopalian clergy took their departure from a country where they were no longer useful. English Churchmen, both at home and in the colonies, readily and spontaneously acknowledged their obligation to those honourable and resolute men. Boucher, soon after his arrival in England, became Vicar of Epsom,[2] and his preaching was much admired; Doctor Inglis passed over to Nova Scotia, where he was eventually appointed the first Colonial Bishop in the British dominions in any part of the world; and Jacob Bailey obtained a Rectory in the same province.[3] Some keen clerical politicians, unable to tear themselves from the tumultuous joys and emotions of the strife, stayed behind at New York, or on the islands in the Bay, for they could not with impunity take up their residence beyond the beat of the British drums. Haunting regimental mess-rooms; collecting and dispensing scraps of Tory gossip; writing those satires and lampoons which were the staple political literature of the period, now that serious constitutional argument had been drowned in the roar of battle; and celebrating the most recent military success over a haunch of venison and a dozen of madeira,—they led a desultory and demoralising life, not altogether becoming to their cloth. Each man of them employed, in the furtherance of the Royal cause, such gifts and accomplishments as he individually possessed,—from the Virginian parson of the old school who, with a bowl of grog in his hand, drank victory to the British arms,[4] up

---

[1] Out of very near a hundred Virginian incumbents, only twenty-eight remained in their parishes, and saw the war through.

[2] Sabine's *Loyalists;* Vol. I., page 240.

[3] Mr. Bailey's unbounded charity and hospitality, all through his life, kept him poor in pelf, though he was very rich in children. One of his sons got a commission in the British line, and was killed at Chippewa in 1814, fighting with his regiment against the army of the United States.

[4] This incident took place at "the Ordinary of Mr. John Tankersly." The Reverend Thomas Jackson, of Virginia, was in consequence denounced by the Charlotte County Committee as an enemy to his country.

to Jonathan Odell, the clergyman-poet, who had been expelled by the New Jersey Whigs from his Rectory at Burlington. That fiery partisan, in imitation of another famous exile, composed an imaginary picture of the Regions of Torment, with immense elaboration and at inordinate length, and peopled it with prominent Congressmen and with Generals of the Continental Army. But, as a consequence of the changes which the lapse of time has wrought in the creed and the taste of the world, certain literary possibilities have passed away, perhaps for ever; and even the genius of Dante, which bore little resemblance to that of Jonathan Odell, would almost certainly have failed over an attempt to produce an eighteenth-century Inferno.[1]

The political action of the Anglican clergy was seriously, and sometimes very painfully, embarrassing to those lay members of their body who had adopted the opposite view of the great question. Such men were very numerous. Among the first five Presidents of the United States, including all who may fairly be classed as contemporaries of the Revolution, no fewer than three were Episcopalians; and a better Churchman,— or, at all events, a better man who ranked himself as a Churchman,—than George Washington it would have been hard indeed to discover. When at home on the bank of the Potomac, he had always gone of a Sunday morning to what would have been called a distant church by any one

---

When the officers, who had been made prisoners at Fort Washington, were confined in Long Island, they were invited to the country-house of a rich New York merchant. "After dinner," wrote one of them, "the son of our entertainer, a boy about seven or eight years of age, came into the room, and his father, putting a glass of wine into his hand, asked him what he drank. 'Church and King'' pronounced the little fellow in an audible voice. Perhaps it was designed as a delicate mode of assuring us that the civility we received was not to be regarded in any degree as a toleration of our principles." It is a pretty story, and indicates how completely the political and religious questions were identified in the American mind.

[1] The last five paragraphs have been chiefly written by the aid of Sabine's *Loyalists*, Tyler's *Literary History*, Garden's *Anecdotes*, and the *American Archives*.

except a Virginian equestrian ; and he spent Sunday afternoons, alone and unapproachable, in his library. In war he found time for daily prayer and meditation, (as, by no wish of his, the absence of privacy, which is a feature in camp life, revealed to those who were immediately about him ;) he attended public worship himself, and by every available means he encouraged the practice of religion in his soldiers, to whom he habitually stood in a kind of fatherly relation   There are many pages in his Orderly Books which indicate a determination that the multitude of young fellows, who were entrusted to his charge, should have all possible facilities for being as well-behaved as in their native villages.[1]   It therefore was the more noticeable that he ceased to be a regular Communicant as long as the war lasted.   Washington always had his reasons for what he did, or left undone, but he seldom gave them ; and his motive for abstaining from the Sacrament was not a subject on which he would be inclined to break his ordinary rule of reticence. On one occasion during his campaigns he is known to have taken the Communion under circumstances which throw some light upon his inward convictions.   While the army was quartered at Morristown, the Presbyterians of the place were about to hold their half-yearly administration.   Washington paid a visit to their minister, and enquired whether it accorded with the canon of his Church to admit Communicants of another denomination. "Most certainly," the clergyman answered.   "Ours is not the Presbyterian table, General, but the Lord's table." "I am glad of it," said Washington   "That is as it ought to be   Though a member of the Church of Eng-

---

[1] The troops were excused fatigue-duty in order that they might not miss church.   If public worship was interrupted on a Sunday by the call to arms, a service was held on a convenient day in the ensuing week.   The chaplains were exhorted to urge the soldiers that they ought to live and act like Christian men in times of distress and danger, and after every great victory, and more particularly at the final proclamation of Peace, the Commander-in-Chief earnestly recommended that the army should universally attend the rendering of thanks to Almighty God "with seriousness of deportment, and gratitude of heart "

land, I have no exclusive partialities " And accordingly on the next Sunday he took his place among the Communicants.

Washington loved his own Church the best, and had no mind to leave it; but he was not hostile to any faith which was sincerely held, and which exerted a restraining and correcting influence upon human conduct. "I am disposed," (he once told Lafayette,) "to indulge the professors of Christianity with that road to Heaven which to them shall seem the most direct, plainest, easiest, and least liable to exception." His feeling on this matter was accurately expressed in the instructions which he wrote out for Benedict Arnold, when that officer led an armed force of fierce and stern New England Protestants against the Roman Catholic settlements in Canada. The whole paper was a lesson in the statesmanship which is founded on respect and consideration for others, and still remains well worth reading[1] In after years, as President of the United States, Washington enjoyed frequent opportunities for impressing his own sentiments and policy, in all that related to religion, upon the attention of his compatriots. The Churches of America were never tired of framing and presenting Addresses which assured him of their confidence, veneration, and sympathy; and he as invariably replied by congratulating them that in their happy country worship was free, and that men of every creed were eligible to every post of honour and authority.[2]

Washington's views were shared by most Virginians of his class and epoch. On the twelfth of June, 1776,

---

[1] Section fourteen of the Instructions to Colonel Benedict Arnold of September 1775. *The Writings of George Washington*, Vol. III , page 89

[2] " We have abundant reason to rejoice," (so, in January 1793, the President told the Members of the New Church of Baltimore,) " that every person may here worship God according to the dictates of his own heart In this enlightened age, and in this land of equal liberty, it is our boast that a man's religious tenets will not forfeit the protection of the laws, nor deprive him of the right of attaining, and of holding, the highest offices that are known in the United States."

the Convention at Williamsburg, with no dissenting voice, adopted their celebrated Declaration of Rights, of which the Sixteenth Article asserted the doctrine of Religious Liberty with eloquence and precision The original draft contained a pronouncement in favour of Toleration; but that equivocal word was expunged at the instance of James Madison, afterwards the fourth President of the United States Toleration, (Madison argued,) belonged to a community where there was an established church, and where a limited freedom of worship was conceded by grace, and not of right. At the very moment when that Sixteenth Article was under discussion before the Convention, the Virginian Baptists, — whose preachers, up to a quite recent date, had been in and out of prison as criminals, — were carrying round for signature a petition praying that they might "be allowed to worship God in their own way, without interruption." So suddenly had the air in the Old Dominion been cleared and purified by the explosion of gunpowder; and so decisively had the public mind judged and condemned the existing system of ecclesiastical predominance, even before there had been time to abrogate it by law. The Virginian Convention could only proceed by Resolution, but half-way through 1776 it ceased to sit, and the first State Legislature was duly elected and assembled under the terms of the new Constitution. An Act was at once passed relieving Dissenters from Church-taxes; and another Statute suspended the payment of salaries to the Established clergy. That provisional arrangement was confirmed and perpetuated by a succession of enactments, which finally culminated in a famous law, the model of its kind, entitled "An Act for establishing Religious Freedom in the State of Virginia."

Virginia's example was more or less speedily followed by all the provinces. When the Revolution began, missionaries of the Propagation Society, in certain counties of Delaware, told all, who wished to listen, that the political agitation against the Royal Government had been deliberately planned by Presbyterians with the object of getting their own religion established ; that it originated in New England; and that it was fostered and abetted by the Presbyterians in every colony.[1] The event triumphantly refuted that idle and gratuitous calumny. Whatever questionable maxim might thereafter come to be adopted by Americans in their secular politics, the sons of the Puritans had not fought the war in order that religious endowments and privileges might be spoil for the victors. The Church of England was disestablished in the Southern Plantations not from greed or malice, but on principle ; and the predominant Churches in the North applied that principle consistently, unsparingly, and honestly to themselves. So great a sacrifice was not made everywhere at once, nor without searching of heart, nor, (in some instances,) without keen regret; but within the second generation after the Declaration of Independence the last vestige of connection between Church and State had ceased to exist in every province of the Union. Long before that period arrived, the collective will of the American people had been announced in language which there was no mistaking. The Federal Constitution was the work of statesmen among whom there were some very brilliant and profuse orators, but they did not seek to display their gifts in the treatment of a theme which can dispense with the aid of rhetoric. They thought it enough to enact, first, that no Religious Test should ever be required as a qualification to any office, or public trust, under the United States; and, then, that Congress should make no law respecting an Establishment of Religion, or prohibiting the free exercise thereof. Those were few and simple words ; but they covered the whole ground of the most universal, and the most vital, of all controversies. Thus it came about that America, (as one of her historians proudly notes,) from the very commencement of her national life ordained throughout the land full liberty of mind, conscience, and worship, and explicitly forbade any unwar-

---

[1] John Adams to Thomas McKean; Philadelphia, 15 November, 1815.

ranted intrusion of human authority into realms where the Divine sovereignty should alone hold sway.[1]

Americans are firmly persuaded that a great service was rendered to the cause of true religion when all their Churches were directed into the paths of independence, self-reliance, and perfect equality before the law. That belief has been shared by a deeply read and widely observant writer who was not an American. De Tocqueville said that he knew of no nation in the whole world where religion retained a stronger influence than in the United States; for, by regulating domestic life, it regulated the Commonwealth, and was the most important among the institutions of the country. The truth of that remark may be disputable; or, at least, it has been disputed; but it is an historical fact that religious equality made for peace and mutual charity between Church and Church in the United States all through the first century of their federal existence During that extended period, (whatever may be the case now, or hereafter,) matters of religion were entirely removed from the political arena, and were arranged, — with no opposition, and very little adverse comment, on the part of the outside public, — by the governing powers of that sect or denomination which on each occasion was specially and solely concerned.

Earliest and foremost among the ecclesiastical problems which were quietly, and permanently, solved was the long-vexed question of American bishops. With characteristic energy and boldness John Wesley was the first in a field where all were now at liberty to tread. The American Methodists had increased, during the ten years of the Revolutionary struggle, from two thousand to fifteen thousand; and their preachers were counted by scores and hundreds. Hardly any of those preachers, however, were clergymen; for during the war it was too dangerous, and for such humble people it had always been too expensive, to go in quest of ordination across the Atlantic Fit candidates, indeed, were not wanting in England who would promise to sail

---

[1] Mr. Sandford Cobb's *History of Religious Liberty;* pages 5 and 509

for the Western Continent after having been admitted
to orders; but the English bishops did not care to combat the spiritual desolation of America, which in their
sermons they were accustomed to deplore, by the aid of
any such auxiliaries. Wesley himself entreated Doctor
Lowth, the Bishop of London, to ordain one of these
Methodist preachers; but his application was refused.
"Your Lordship observes," (so Wesley wrote back,)
"that there are three ministers in that country already.
True, my Lord : but what are three to watch over the
souls in that extensive country? Will your Lordship
permit me to speak freely?" And then, without waiting for that permission, Wesley proceeded to remonstrate
with the bishop for approving candidates who possessed
a smattering of the classics, and who had mastered a
few trite points in the science of divinity, while he never
enquired whether they loved God or the world, and
whether they had any real desire to save their own
souls, and the souls of others. "But your Lordship
did see good to ordain, and send to America, other
persons who knew something of Greek and Latin, but
knew no more of saving souls than of catching whales."

John Wesley was not the man to accept a rebuff,
which at the same time was an almost fatal blow to the
cause whereon the labours of his life had been spent.
If his ecclesiastical superiors would not come to the rescue, he was himself, in the last resort, prepared with a
remedy So far back as the year 1761 he had emitted
an opinion that a belief in the exclusive validity of
Episcopal ordination was an entire mistake He called
himself, in so many words, a High Churchman ; but he
was far from orthodox on the doctrine of the Apostolic
Succession. Perhaps he thought that the chain of con-
tinuity had been already severed; perhaps he doubted
whether it was worth preserving intact; and he accordingly resolved to look around, on his own account, for
some one endowed with the qualifications required of a
bishop in the First Epistle to Timothy He found what
he wanted in Doctor Thomas Coke. That able and

devoted, though not unambitious, divine had once been a Gentleman Commoner at Oxford, and subsequently held a benefice in the West of England. There he had sought out John Wesley, and confided to him a doubt whether clergymen were justified in limiting their administrations to a single congregation. "Go out, Brother!" answered Wesley. "Go out and preach the gospel to all the world!" The time had now arrived when a notable effect was given to this solemn injunction. In the autumn of 1784, at Bristol, in a private room, Wesley laid his hands upon the head of his friend, and set him apart as an overseer of the Methodist Churches in America, with a commission to ordain proper persons to the ministry. With Thomas Coke was associated Francis Asbury, who had been the pioneer of Methodism in America; a man who did not seek, and who had led a life which was above, worldly praise. Wesley called his two delegates by the name of superintendents; but they exercised Episcopal functions, and they speedily assumed the Episcopal title; for in May 1787 they addressed to the President of the United States a Memorial commencing with the words, "We the Bishops of the Methodist Episcopal Church."[1]

Coke and Asbury soon had colleagues in their dignified office, and many colleagues; for their Church increased in numbers, wealth, and repute with extraordinary rapidity The Roman Catholics in the States were erelong provided with Bishops, and Archbishops, and, (in the fullness of time,) a Cardinal; but no ecclesiastical body gained so much by the establishment of Religious Liberty and Equality as the Church which had been entitled the Church of England so long as the English connection lasted.[2] Up to the Revolution the members of that body had been Episcopalians without

---

[1] Tyerman's *Life and Times of John Wesley;* Vol. III., pages 214, and 433 to 437. Pages 249 and 250 contain a sketch of Francis Asbury's career, a record which is the more valuable because that high-minded, and, (in this respect especially,) exemplary man forbade any biography of himself to be published, — an order which was not disobeyed

[2] Dean Tucker of Gloucester had foretold that result thirteen years

a bishop, to their own infinite loss and inconvenience; and the obstinate determination of all the other Churches to keep them in that condition of disadvantage, though not without excuse, had fostered very uncharitable and unchristian feelings in the religious world of America. After the Revolution, however, the grievance under which the Episcopalians had so long suffered was removed with the willing assent of all, and the hearty and helpful concurrence of some who had figured among the most eminent and formidable opponents of the British Government. John Adams, as the first American Envoy at the Court of St. James's, was both active and discreet in his efforts to promote the consecration of American bishops in London. Benjamin Franklin, though himself no great church-goer, had all through life been very ready to give advice upon religious matters, and sometimes to volunteer it in quarters where it was not acceptable. He had been the prime mover in equipping Philadelphia with a non-sectarian meeting-house, for the use of any preacher of any persuasion. Sectarian places of worship he seldom entered; (for he complained that the minister aimed at making his hearers good Presbyterians and Congregationalists rather than good citizens,) but he taught his neighbours how to fit their steeples with lightning-conductors, and there was no end to the conspicuously unselfish trouble which he took in helping them to warm the inside of their churches. His interest in other people's religion once carried him so far that he assisted a Noble Lord of his acquaintance to abridge the Anglican Liturgy; but that was almost the only unsuccessful venture of his enterprising career, inasmuch as very few copies were sold, and the bulk became waste paper.[1]

before it happened. A very curious passage from his pen is printed in the Fourth Appendix at the end of this volume.

[1] Letter from Franklin printed in the *Memoirs of Granville Sharp, Esq.;* Part II., chapter vi. Franklin attributed the failure of the book to his noble collaborator, who had abridged the Prayers very badly. He himself had undertaken only the Catechism, and the reading and singing Psalms. Franklin had suffered, very early in life, for his zeal in endeav-

Franklin had always desired to see the controversy about American bishops settled upon equitable and reasonable terms; he was ashamed of the evil-speaking and ill-temper which the dispute provoked;[1] and, when the war had terminated, he did all he could to assist the Episcopalians in the accomplishment of their wishes. On their behalf he knocked at many doors. He inquired of the Pope's Nuncio at Paris whether candidates might be ordained as Protestant clergymen by the Roman Catholic bishop in America; but to get such a prayer granted was beyond even Franklin's powers of persuasion[2] He then advised that recourse should be had to Frederic Augustus Hervey, the Lord Bishop of Derry in Ireland, whom he described, most assuredly in no exaggerated terms, as "a man of liberal sentiments." He suggested an application to the ecclesiastical authorities in Sweden and Denmark; and, if all else failed, he recommended American Episcopalians, after the example of the primitive Christian Church in Scotland, to elect and induct a bishop for themselves. A hundred years from that date, (Franklin said,) it would seem inconceivable that men, qualified by their learning and piety to pray for and instruct their fellows, should not have been permitted so to do until they had made a voyage of six thousand miles out and home, in order to ask leave of a cross old gentleman at Canterbury.[3]

It was fortunate for the American Episcopalians that

ouring to curtail religious ceremonies; for, after the manner of most reformers, he began young, and began on his father. Old Mr. Franklin was packing a barrel of beef in the cellar; and Benjamin suggested that time would be saved in the future by asking a blessing, once for all, over the whole barrel.

[1] Franklin wrote to his sister from England on this subject in February 1769. "Your squabbles about a bishop," he said, "I wish to see speedily ended . . . I do not conceive that bishops residing in America would either be of such advantage to Episcopalians, or such disadvantage to anti-Episcopalians, as either seem to imagine Each party abuses the other The profane and infidel believe both sides, and enjoy the fray"

[2] "The thing is impossible," said the Nuncio, "unless the gentlemen become Catholics."

[3] Franklin to Messrs. Weems and Gant, Passy, 18 July, 1784.

their cause had been espoused by a more suitable champion than Benjamin Franklin For a good many years
past their unhappy condition had appealed to a man
whose sympathy was never a barren or idle emotion.
Granville Sharp possessed rare qualifications for the
office of a mediator between the mother-country and
her former colonies.   His upright character, and earnest piety, secured for him the confidence of every sincere and devout member of the Church of England;
and the most vindictive Whigs of Massachusetts or Virginia could not forget that, in the crisis of the recent
struggle, he had accepted poverty rather than consent
to raise his hand against the American cause.   Standing between the two parties, and revered by both,
Granville Sharp adjured the Congregationalists and
Presbyterians of the United States not to grudge their
Episcopalian fellow-citizens a boon which was their undoubted right, and essential to their welfare; he stirred
the conscience of those among the English bishops who
had grown lukewarm towards the Church in America
ever since they had been forced to abandon the hope
of seeing it established, and regnant, throughout that
country; and he quickened the pace of the British Parliament which, after its fashion, preferred to move by
easy stages.   Our laws forbade the ordination of any
candidate, who found himself unable to take the Oath
of Allegiance to the King; and in May 1784 an Act
was passed, dispensing with this obligation in the case
of priests and deacons who were not the King's subjects.
No clergyman, however, who declined to swear could
be consecrated as a bishop; and accordingly it was obvious that in the United States bishops there could be
none.   An aspirant for orders must still cross the
Atlantic, or remain a layman; and the Church in
America, although in no worse, nevertheless was as yet
in no better, position than in the old days before the
Revolution.

The existing conditions were intolerable, and the prospect of improvement small.   Lord Chancellor Thurlow,

the most potent force in Pitt's Cabinet on questions which touched the Church and involved the law, held that concession had gone too far already, and set his face stiffly against all further progress. But a still stronger, and a much better, man than Thurlow at this critical moment made his appearance on the scene. This was Doctor Seabury, who, under the name of a Westchester Farmer, wrote with so much wit and fire against the American Revolution during its earlier stages; and who, in the interval between two fierce battles, had preached in General Howe's camp on the duty of fearing God and honouring the King. In the course of the war, Seabury had been ruthlessly used by political opponents who were his implacable personal enemies. He had been despoiled of almost everything else that belonged to him, but he had retained, and increased, the respectful admiration with which he was regarded by good men of all parties among his compatriots. In the spring of 1783, (so we are told,) a little company of the clergy, — men as noble as ever manned a forlorn hope, or went down to ruin for a sacred idea, — assembled in a lonely Connecticut parsonage, solemnly designated Samuel Seabury as the first bishop of the American Episcopal Church, and requested him to go to England for consecration.[1]

To England he went; and there he was told by the Archbishop of Canterbury that the object which the Church in Connecticut sought was greatly to be desired, but that the difficulties were insuperable. "If your Grace," replied Seabury, "will not grant me consecration, I know where to obtain it." He left the room abruptly, and started forthwith for Aberdeen; and he was there admitted as a bishop by three non-juring prelates of the Scottish Episcopal Church[2] Shortly afterwards the King of Denmark ordered Mr. John Adams to be informed that the Danish bishops were prepared to ordain any American of proper qualities, and good

---

[1] Tyler's *Literary History*, Vol. I., chapter xv., section vii.
[2] *Memoirs of Granville Sharp*, Part II, chapters vi. and vii.

character, who would subscribe the Articles of the Church of England. His Majesty, moreover, intimated his willingness to set up a bishopric in one of the West Indian Islands which belonged to Denmark, so that the candidates for orders might find facilities within a comparatively short distance from their native shores. This announcement brought matters to an issue.[1] The knowledge that, in more than one quarter, there was competition for the future good graces of the Church in the United States produced an immediate effect on the British Cabinet, and on the Episcopal Bench in the House of Lords In the Spring Session of 1786 a Statute was passed which allowed the Oath of Allegiance to be omitted at the Consecration of Bishops who were citizens of foreign countries;[2] and, in February 1787, Granville Sharp enjoyed the well-deserved satisfaction of conducting two American clergymen to Lambeth for consecration. Before the close of the nineteenth century there were eighty bishops, in communion with the Church of England, on that soil where not a single one had been able to show his face until the establishment of National Independence deadened the memories, and soothed the apprehensions, which the Episcopal title formerly excited in an American's mind. A bishop, from that time forwards, was regarded as the freely chosen administrator and rector of a self-governing religious body; and no longer as the emissary of a militant State Church beyond the seas, which was abetted in all its invasions and encroachments by those Royal governors who wielded the authority of the Crown.

---

[1] John Adams had been in correspondence with the Danish Government with reference to the ordination of an American student of divinity, named Mason Weems. When a favourable answer came from Copenhagen, it was communicated to Mr Weems ; "and," wrote Adams, "it soon procured him a more polite reception from the English clergy. Indeed, it laid the foundation of not only Mr. Weems's ordination, but of the whole system of Episcopacy in the United States."

[2] "An Act to empower the Archbishop of Canterbury, or the Archbishop of York, for the time being, to consecrate to the Office of a Bishop persons being Subjects or Citizens of Countries out of His Majesty's Dominions "

APPENDICES

APPENDIX I

See page 140

Extracts from Lieutenant-Colonel Markham's Journal

" On January first, 1777, an express arrived to me at Spank-
town, containing orders to march immediately to join General
Matthew who commands at Brunswick, and to leave only an
officer and thirty men to protect my baggage during my
absence. As it was late before the order arrived, it was two
o'clock in the afternoon before I began my march. At this
time there was a general thaw, and cold raw wind with sleet
and rain. It was a very dark night, and we were up to our
knees in mire; crossing waters of mill-dams; every now and
then walking over sheets of ice, officers and men continually
tumbling. I myself had I know not how many falls, every
moment expecting to be attacked by the rebels. I never was
more fatigued. At last I could scarcely move. General
Matthew sent an officer to meet me, to show me his quarters,
to which I was just able to crawl. The General asked me if
we were not in want of some refreshment. I then plainly
told him we had neither food nor liquor, and he very politely
told me we should be supplied with both. He pressed me to
sup with him, which I declined, as I wanted rest more than
anything else. Exhausted as I was, though my spirits were
still good, I crawled back to my quarters, where the General
sent me a large piece of roast beef, one ditto boiled, a roast
goose, and a dozen bottles of Madeira, port, and rum This
was a prodigious relief to us. I got to bed about twelve
o'clock, but too tired to sleep. At about one o'clock the
General called upon me to tell me he had just received orders
to march instantly to Brunswick, and for this purpose I was

to form a battalion as soon as possible, and cross the bridge over the river, drawing up on the other side, to cover the bridge, while the cannon, stores, and baggage, were crossed over. At about six in the morning we got to Brunswick, the road being as bad as that over which we had before marched. I was now as much dead as alive, however my spirits did not fail me. We occupied the first houses at the end of the town, where the enemy was expected to attack, without taking off our accoutrements until eight in the morning."

.   .   .   .

"My company lost a waggon loaded with baggage, by neglecting to protect it, and suffering the Yankee driver, (who, I suppose through fright, drove it off,) to fall into the hands of the rebels. They had small parties skulking about us. My Lieutenant has lost all his baggage by this unlucky hit. I am the more concerned for his loss, as he is only a soldier of fortune, and therefore can ill afford it. I felt, I think, what I should do if I was rich. His loss is, I believe, about 120*l.* Did the King know it, I am sure he is too good to let him be a sufferer. The only posts we now possess in the Jerseys are Paulus Hook, Perth Amboy, Bonnum Town, the Raritan landing-place, and Brunswick. Happy had it been if at first we had fixed upon no other posts in this province ! Before, our line was ninety miles long, which we had to defend, and our small number of scattered troops formed too weak a chain This post of Perth Amboy is far from being a good one, should Washington attack us. There is no market here ; and all we have to trust to is the King's allowance of provisions The rebels here spread themselves all over the country, so that we cannot go beyond our sentries with any degree of safety."

APPENDIX II

See page 220

The correspondent of a London newspaper, in January 1776, represents himself as having dined at the house of a worthy gentleman in the West of England who, "for the sake of good neighbourhood, endeavoured to make his table a neutral ground for such of his friends as could calmly communicate over a turkey and chine, and a cheerful glass, without drawing daggers for Whig and Tory." A personage, who is identified as the *First Member of Parliament,* regretted that more attention had not been paid, either in the passing Session, or in the last, to the Petition from the merchants and planters of our Sugar Islands.

Second Member: "Pshaw! I know nothing of this Session, as it began in the hunting season, but I remember very well what we thought of their petition last year. We determined to give them a hearing for form's sake, but not till we had settled how the business would go."

Third Member: "Aye, aye It signifies nothing what they says upon the matter. I am sure, (and I shall never alter my mind,) we were right. These Americans must be conquered, and must be taxed too. Why should we pay for they? They have cost us a world of trouble, and never brought us anything but vexation."

Bristol Gentleman "But how do you reconcile it to equity to tax people who have no representatives among you?"

Third Member: "Representatives? Why, hasn't we passed Resolutions that we does represent them? And hasn't the Declaratory Act settled the right, and power, and all that? What dost talk of equity for? Ha'nt we sent over the fleet and the army to settle everything? We represents 'em all, every one of 'em, be sure."

First Member: "I protest, I cannot help fairly acknowledging that I do not represent them; for I was not elected, nor returned, by any of them. I cannot conceive how our friend here, that does not so much as know what part of the world they are in, should fancy himself their Representative"

Third Member: Pooh! I knows well enough in the main. We was fools for taking 'em from the French and Spanish, all along of that old fellow Pitt; and I with all my heart wish they had them, and Hanover too, back again."

Bristol Gentleman: "Have you ever delivered your sentiments in the House, Sir, on this subject?"

Second Member: "No, damme, he never speaks further than aye or no He's wiser than some folks in that. I spouted away once or twice; but it did not signify much, though my Lord North spoke to me very kindly upon it."

Third Member: "Aye, aye, you spout away finely; but I believe I gets as much for my silence as you does for your speechifying The main thing is to know which is the right side of the question, and that I'm never out in. If I was Lord North, as soon as I had told 'em my mind, I'd make old Perriwig pop the question directly; and then I'm sure and sartin we might go to dinner every day at four o'clock, and have the rest of the evening to ourselves, instead of sitting to hear nonsense till midnight"

The peculiarities of this West-country senator's colloquial style seem natural to those who remember that, only one generation back, Squire Western was the greatest Commoner in Somersetshire, and most certainly might have been member for his County, if he had cared to sit.

APPENDIX III

See page 276

The Church of England in Virginia

Mr. Sanford Cobb, in his *History of Religious Liberty*, draws out a long and unbroken string of evidence bearing upon the favour, and veneration, accorded to the Church of England by Virginians of the first two generations. The earliest emigrants brought with them the Reverend Robert Hunt, a learned divine, and exemplary man, who had been specially selected as their spiritual guide by Archbishop Bancroft himself The Company voted for his support five hundred pounds, which was a very substantial sum of money in those days The Virginia Code of 1612 included a provision under which those who spoke, or acted, in disrespect of any minister were to be "openly whipt three times, and to ask public forgiveness in the assembly of the congregation on three several Saboth daies" If any person refused to repair to the Minister for examination in his faith as a Churchman, he was whipped daily until he complied. In 1623, a fine of five hundred pounds of tobacco was enacted as a penalty for speaking "disparagingly of any Minister without proof." During our Civil Wars, long after the cause of the Church was lost in England, Governor Berkeley, with the approval and sympathy of a large majority among the colonists, banished all Puritan Ministers from the confines of Virginia; and in 1649, when King Charles's head had already fallen, the colony contained twenty Church of England parishes in which the tithe was regularly and cheerfully paid, and the rector lived with his people in much "peace and love." After the Restoration, Statutes were passed at Williamsburg enacting that the whole Liturgy should be thoroughly read every Sunday, that no Catechism should be used other than that appointed by the Canons, and that no ministers "but such as were ordained by some Bishop in England" should be allowed in the colony. The children of marriages performed by clergymen of all other denominations were declared illegitimate, baptism was enforced by law; and Nonconformists were forbidden to teach, even in private, under pain of exile.

APPENDIX IV

See page 310

Among the extraordinarily accurate political prophecies which, amidst all his wild writing, were occasionally thrown out by Dean Tucker, was a forecast of the effect that would be produced on the question of American bishops by a separation between Great Britain and her colonies. The first of those bishops was appointed in 1787; and as far back as 1774 the Dean had written as follows about the grievance under which the Episcopalians in America then suffered.

"The Church of England alone doth not enjoy a Toleration in that full Extent which is granted to the Members of every other Denomination. What then can be the cause of putting so injurious a Distinction between the Church of England, and other Churches, in this respect? The Reason is plain. The Americans have taken it into their heads to believe that the Episcopate would operate as some further tie upon them, not to break loose from those Obligations which they owe to the

Mother-Country ; and that it is to be used as an Engine, under the Masque of Religion, to rivet those chains which they imagine we are forging for them.   Let therefore the Mother-Country herself resign up all Claim of Authority over them, as well Ecclesiastical as Civil ; let her declare North America to be independent of Great Britain in every respect whatever ; let her do this, I say, and then all their Fears will vanish away, and their Panics be at an end.   And then a Bishop, who has no more Connections with England, either in Church or State, than he has with Germany, Sweden, or any other Country, will be no longer looked upon in America as a Monster, but a Man." — *Dean Tucker's Fourth Tract;* 1774.

INDEX

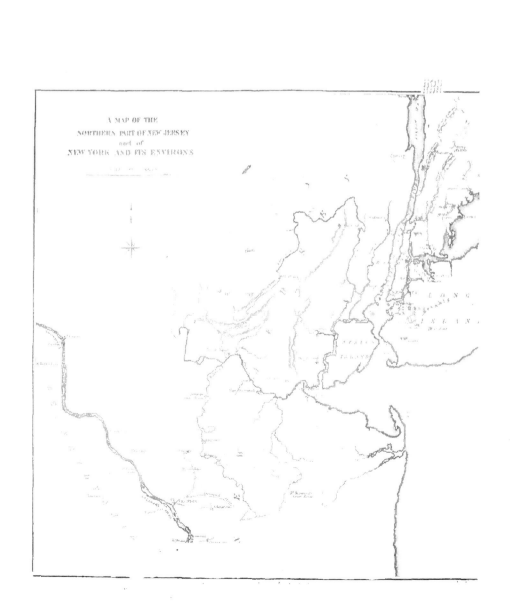

A MAP OF THE
NORTHERN PART OF NEW JERSEY
and of
NEW YORK AND ITS ENVIRONS

LaVergne, TN USA
03 February 2011
215151LV00003B/246/P